Children Learning at Home

Children Learning at Home

Julie Webb

 The Falmer Press

(A member of the Taylor & Francis Group)
London · New York · Philadelphia

| UK | The Falmer Press, Rankine Road, Basingstoke, Hampshire, RG24 0PR |
| USA | The Falmer Press, Taylor & Francis Inc., 1990 Frost Road, Suite 101, Bristol, PA 19007 |

First published in 1990

British Library Cataloguing in Publication Data
Webb, Julie
    Children learning at home.
    1. Children. Home-based education
    I. Title
    649.68

    ISBN 1-85000-811-6
    ISBN 1-85000-812-4 pbk

Library of Congress Cataloging-in-Publication Data
Available on Request

Jacket design by Caroline Archer

Typeset in 10.5/13 pt Caledonia
by Graphicraft Typesetters Ltd. Hong Kong.
Printed and bound in Great Britain by
Burgess Science Press
Basingstoke

Contents

Preface   vii

  1 Theoretical and Historical Background   1
  2 An Introduction to the Research   17
  3 Choice of Research Method   22
  4 Reasons for Change   33
  5 Making the Break   55
  6 Family Influence on the Choice of What to Learn   77
  7 Other Constraints on Choice of What to Learn: 99
     The LEA, and Resources
  8 The 'How' of Home-based Education   124
  9 Activities with Others   148
 10 Relationships Between Families and the LEA   165
 11 What Next?   182
 12 The Relationship Between Home-based Education and   195
     Society in General

References   199
Index   203

To Erlend

Preface

This book developed out of work for a PhD degree carried out through the Open University and completed in 1988. It is hoped that three types of reader will find it useful: parents interested in alternative forms of education for their children, teachers and student teachers, and academic or LEA education specialists.

There are two minor points to note. Firstly, all interviewees appear under pseudonyms, except the following (for reasons relating to the publication of their real names elsewhere): the Baker family, Hugh Boulter and the Heads. Secondly, I have used *EO News* and *EO Newsletter*, and 'Home education' and 'Home-based education' interchangeably, reflecting the ways they are commonly referred to in the home education movement.

I am deeply grateful to all those who gave up their time to take part in the study, whether by post or in person, and to all those contributors to *EO News* and *Growing Without Schooling* whom I have quoted anonymously. Heartfelt thanks are due to Roger Dale and Roland Meighan, without whose advice and encouragement during my PhD research this book would never have been realized; to Mimi and Ron Tupper and Rose and Gordon Webb for their moral support and babysitting; and to Erlend for putting up with a sometimes preoccupied Mum.

I am also grateful to Leila Berg for permission to use an extract from her article 'Reading and living (and loving)', and to Penguin Books for allowing me to quote extensively from David Head's *Free Way to Learning*.

Chapter 1

Theoretical and Historical Background

So, absorbed and happy, we would pore over the microscope. Filled with enthusiasm, we would tack from subject to subject, and if Theodore could not answer my ceaseless flow of questions himself, he had books that could. Gaps would appear in the bookcase as volume after volume was extracted to be consulted, and by our side would be an ever-growing pile of volumes. . . . Tea would arrive, the cakes squatting on cushions of cream, toast in a melting shawl of butter, cups agleam, and a faint wisp of steam rising from the teapot spout.

    '. . . but, on the other hand, it is impossible to say that there is *no* life on Mars. It is, in my opinion, quite possible that some form of life will be found . . . er . . . *discovered* there, should we ever succeed in *getting* there. But there is no reason to suppose that any form of life found there would be identical. . .'. Sitting there, neat and correct in his tweed suit, Theodore would chew his toast slowly and methodically, his beard bristling, his eyes kindling with enthusiasm at each new subject that swam into our conversation. To me his knowledge seemed inexhaustible. He was a rich vein of information, and I mined him assiduously. (Durrell, 1976, p. 82)

After her experience of attending classes, for a time Melanie refused her lessons. We watched with interest and permitted her to do what attracted her — mainly arts and crafts activities, and playing outdoors. Then at twelve, Melanie decided to start a school of her own, with her younger sister Felicity as pupil. . . . Felicity, then aged seven, responded with enthusiasm, and learned to read. This was something she firmly declined to do under the tuition of an enthusiastic mother and other temporary residents. . . . Melanie herself continued lessons all day. She asked me to teach her arithmetic, history and geography. Her mother took her in French (they used the BBC records), English grammar and composition. She went to an outside teacher for lessons on the guitar and has taught herself to play the recorder from a book. Now 16, Melanie has enrolled in a new free school in Montreal. (Steele, 1978)

Once her prepared environment had been achieved in the home on the hill, Maria embarked on a carefully prepared plan of activities, embracing rituals and learning games as well as specifically developed apparatus. . . . Maria watched over these experiments, taking the greatest care not to introduce new ones to Christian until he seemed to have absorbed the lessons of the previous ones: until, in fact, she judged the doors of perception were open once more and he was ready to receive new information. . . . One day, when Christian was still only two and a half, he saw a set of plastic capital letters in a shop window and immediately announced that he wanted them. He proved so determined that Maria emptied out her purse, scraped up the price and bought them then and there. Already at two and a half Christian could memorize photographically the actual characters composing the words of almost everything that was read to him, so that no sooner was he home with the plastic letters than he started making up complete words with them. Within an hour, to his parents' astonishment, he had made the words 'train' and 'engine'. (Deakin, 1973, p. 44)

The above excerpts, from Gerald Durrell's *My Family and Other Animals*, from an article entitled 'Educated at home' by John Steele, and from Michael Deakin's *The Children on the Hill*, illustrate three of the widely varied ways which have been found to educate children at home, and, I hope, give a flavour of the material on which my study has been based.

This chapter begins with an examination of the thoughts of the most influential deschoolers, and continues with a summary of the historical and contemporary background to home-based education in practice, ending with an explanation of the law relating to it and an introduction to the largest support group for British home educators, Education Otherwise.

The DeSchoolers and their Theories: Possible Functions of Home-based Education in Society

In using the term 'deschoolers', I am referring only to those who are concerned with education outside school on a wider basis than that of application to the circumstances of individual families. The most influential thinkers and writers in this field have probably been Jean-Jacques Rousseau and then, leaping forward chronologically to the 1960s and 1970s, Ivan Illich, Everett

Reimer and Paolo Freire. Also in this category comes some of the later writing of John Holt, who was himself heavily influenced by time spent with Illich and Reimer at Cuernavaca. The sudden interest in deschooling in the Western world was probably related both to the values which developed in the 'hippy' era and to the new appreciation of the future role of leisure in our lives. It took as a focus theories originally worked out by Freire and Illich in relation to their knowledge of the educational and political difficulties of peasants in the quite different social systems of South America. In giving an outline of the main ideas of these gurus of the early 1970s (Rousseau included, since he underwent a rediscovery during this period) I would like to emphasize that their influence on this study in limited, because I, and many of those whom I interviewed, would regard their position on the abolition of institutions as too extreme, preferring a more varied, pluralist, approach to the provision of educational alternatives.

A common thread running through the work of these writers is the position of education in relation to political power, and the social change which may result from it. Rousseau saw the 'natural education' he proposed for Emile as essential to the bringing about of the society described in *The Social Contract* (Rousseau, 1972). Freire suggested that the liberation of Brazilian peasants from the oppression of exploitative bosses could only come about through what he (or, rather, his translator) called cointentional education, a critical dialogue between teacher and pupil (Freire, 1972). Reimer saw the American schools of the 1960s as instruments of preparation for acceptance of the status quo in a technological society: as a way of ensuring that the powerful members of this society will be those who profit from its domination by technology and do not question this domination (Reimer, 1971). The latter point recalls the writing both of other deschoolers and of radical school reformers such as Postman and Weingartner (1971). It is repeated in the work of Illich, who also echoes Reimer's concern with the domination by technology, and Freire's belief that schools as presently constituted, in Latin America particularly, constitute an effective means of keeping those at the top in position:

> Curriculum has always been used to assign social rank. At times it could be pre-natal: karma ascribes to you a caste and lineage to the aristocracy. Curriculum could take the form of a ritual, of sequential sacred ordinations, or it could consist of a succession of feats in war or hunting, or further advancement could be made to depend on a series of previous princely favours. Universal schooling was meant to detach role assignment from personal life history: it was meant to give everybody an equal chance to any office. Even now many people wrongly believe that school ensures the dependence of public trust on relevant

learning achievements. However, instead of equalizing chances, the school system has monopolized their distribution. (Illich 1971, p. 19)

Two articles published in the journal *Prospects* (Blat-Gimeno, 1972 and Nassif, 1975) put the other side of the argument as it relates to education in the Third World: the authors believe strongly that structured education is needed there. Nassif, an Argentinian, responds to Illich's *Tools for Conviviality* (Illich, 1975):

> A tempting ideal, this fascinating, lofty goal of conviviality proposed by the 'chosen ones' of CIDOC, [Center for Intercultural Documentation]. The goal is attainable in the eternal spring that Cuernavaca breathes. It is unattainable in our Calchaqui valleys, in the dark forests of Peru or Brazil, in the colourful, though wretched, indigenous communities of Mexico and Central America, or of Peru, in the hard and forbidding region leaning against the volcanic ranges of the Pacific. There, teachers and schools are needed, for, at the present time, the distant descendants of the Mayas, the Aztecs and the Incas, the inhabitants of the villages, plains and mountains, and the socially excluded groups in the great towns of our vast Latin America have no other form of 'conviviality' than that of silence. (Nassif, 1975)

The practical compromise between the extremes of these views and those of the deschoolers appears to be the kind of initiative in the Third World which Ian Lister was exploring when he wrote 'Deschooling re-visited' (Lister, 1976): the Programme for Political Education, and the Project on Alternatives in Low-income Countries, whose workers were trying to find and examine examples of alternatives to schools all over the world, in order to identify those which might serve as models for the Third World. Studies of home-based education might be important here in showing how necessary resources, both material and human, could be adapted and shared, and in indicating the way in which support groups for alternatives, such as Education Otherwise, could function.

John Holt, whose passionate concern for the happiness of individual children had always operated against the larger background of the political preoccupations exemplified by his early work with the world government movement, was profoundly influenced in his attitude to deschooling by a two-week visit to Illich, Reimer and their colleagues in Cuernavaca. Prior to this, he had been an advocate of a school reform which would allow more and more people into and out of the schools, so that eventually it would be impossible to determine who was actually 'in school', and thus the school attendance laws would become pointless. Before his fortnight at CIDOC in Cuernavaca he began to feel that the programmes which were being put into action along these lines, such as Parkway in Philadelphia, were benefiting only the rich and already-privileged, and that this would be the pattern for any future programmes, leaving the poorer children as much victims of the old, inflexible system as they had ever been. After much discussion with Illich, Reimer and the rest, Holt became convinced that his view that schools had originally had the noble aim of promoting individual self-fulfilment was naively wrong:

> Man is for the state, and the function and business and duty of schools is to prepare him to fit into and serve the state as efficiently as his nature and talents will allow. And everything that was said in education about individual differences meant only that not all men would be the same parts, but that some would be gears, some nuts, some bolts, some bearings, some piston rods, some cotter pins etc. (Holt, 1974, p. 44)

He was also convinced that since the school's only use was to fit people for their place in Western technological society, it was redundant, as other institutions (by which I presume he meant such as the media and marketing specialists) could do the job better. (He still felt, nevertheless, that something along the lines of his previous proposals must be carried out to make the school system bearable for those trapped in it, until its eventual collapse.)

The other major issue of importance in the work of the deschoolers is the practical question of what means towards personal education should replace the present schooling system. There were some nudges among the writings of school reformers such as Goodman in the direction of deschooling on a tentative, experimental basis:

> Have 'no school at all' for a few classes. These children should be selected from tolerable, though not necessarily cultured, homes. They should be neighbours and numerous enough to be a society for one another and so that they do not feel merely 'different'. Will they learn the rudiments anyway? (Goodman, 1964, p. 40)

This suggestion resembles the ideal of home educators such as the Heads (Head, 1974), but it clearly doesn't go far enough for the deschoolers, influenced as they were by Rousseau's plans for an education that would involve everyone in learning by watching, doing and experiencing the natural consequences of various actions. Illich and Reimer incorporated this principle into their theory of network learning, whereby people in possession of skills would make themselves available as models to people who wanted to obtain them, and access would be provided to all the resources society could furnish. Where these differ from Rousseau is in seeing the autonomy of the student as paramount: he or she should be the one to determine what is learnt and at what stage in life (though there is a restriction on autonomy where the 'how' is concerned, since, according to some writers, the option of learning through school will not be open to them). Rousseau had predetermined the stages of education which Emile would go through and had appointed a tutor to ensure that these went as planned, thus rather negating the arbitrary effect of natural consequences on Emile's life. The tutor's other major task was to keep Emile away from his peers and the 'civilized world'. This is the antithesis of the system Illich, Freire, Reimer and Holt would like to see, since for them, all are to be involved in both giving and receiving education, on a peer-matched basis. It appears that there are among home educators some direct ideological descendants of Rousseau, at least as far as isolationism and careful management of the children's environment go: the family described in *The Children on the Hill* (Deakin, 1973) would be one example. More numerous, though, are those who have taken ideas from Illich and Reimer, often filtered through the medium of John Holt's writing (particularly *Instead of Education*, 1977, and *Teach Your Own*, 1981), without necessarily adopting a political view of the wider significance of these ideas.

Holt's combination of work towards making deschooling legally possible for those who wanted it and the provision of practical inspiration, leads us conveniently on to the next part of this chapter, which is devoted to home-based education in practice.

The Individual View: A History of Home-based Education in Practice

Pre-1880

It is impossible to know the extent of home-based education in Britain before the advent of the Acts imposing compulsory full-time elementary education for all in 1870–80, since, even if it were possible to develop statistics for school attendance over the centuries, this would shed no light on which of those children not at school were working, which were taught formally by tutors or governesses, and which were learning from their parents or haphazardly on their own. Information about the substance and method of learning must come mainly therefore from anecdotes in biography, autobiography and the writings of contemporary observers. It is interesting that the approach to education before it became compulsory was linked less to rigid ideas of what was appropriate for a person of a certain age to learn, and that the attitude taken was more akin to the 'lifelong learning' idea which features in modern thought on education:

> To the humanists of the Renaissance education spread over the whole span of human life, without giving special value to childhood. You

could start school at ten years old or at twenty. In the fifteenth century instruction was given in the same room to several hundred children of all different ages. Eton in 1517 had only one school room, and even in seventeenth century France you could find a twenty-four year old man in the same class as an eleven year old child. . . . Levels of education were not attached to different ages, so there are many examples of what we could consider precocity. (Hoyles, 1979, pp. 19–20)

I was interested to see whether there would be evidence of this precocity among any of my interviewees who had been allowed to work at home at their own pace. I was already aware of one rather startling modern exponent of this method: the father of Ruth Lawrence, who taught her mathematics at home to such a high standard that she passed an A level in it at nine. Among home educators of the last century the same attitude seems to have existed in certain families: this was definitely the case with the infant John Stuart Mill, one of several children all educated at home in the early 1800s by their father. He began Greek and arithmetic at three and Latin at eight and was very interested in ancient history, which he wrote about for his own pleasure:

> My father encouraged me in this useful amusement, though, as I think judiciously, he never asked to see what I wrote; so that I did not feel that in writing it I was accountable to any one, nor had the chilling sensation of being under a critical eye. (Mill, 1964, p. 33)

The importance of this lack of fear in learning is a point also made by William Cobbett in his description of his son's arithmetic teaching. His method was to explain why the learning of arithmetic was necessary:

> . . . in order for us to make out our accounts of the trees and seeds that we should have to sell in the winter, and the utter impossibility of our getting paid for our pains unless we were able to make out our accounts, (Cobbett, 1825, quoted in *Growing Without Schooling*, 1977)

and then, to mix arithmetic practice with pleasure (riding and hunting).

Like Cobbett, Mill had other insights into the problems and benefits of home education which are relevant to home educators today: the teacher/pupil relationship for example: 'I well know that the relation between teacher and taught is not a good moral discipline to either' (Mill, 1964, p. 30). I wondered whether the parents I interviewed would agree with this observation or whether they might feel, with John Holt and others, that the experience of having to explain something, or learn it for the first time, was valuable to the teacher, and that the example of a sensitive teacher/parent could be very valuable to the taught.

On the positive side Mill recognized the important part played by his father's high expectations: would modern home educators accept this, or would they see it as 'pushy' and feel that, as far as possible, expectations of any sort should be avoided, to leave the child free to follow his own pace and interests? Perhaps all would agree that lengthy discussion, of the sort Mill frequently had with his father, is a valuable way of learning and that even if, as was sometimes the case with Mill, it is in parts beyond the child's level of understanding, it may still be beneficial, as it was for him: it 'left seeds behind, which germinated in due course' (Mill, *ibid.*, p. 37).

The achievement of learning through his own efforts rather than by spoonfeeding was another feature of Mill's home education. About his father's course in political economy, he wrote: 'striving . . . to call forth the activity of my faculties, by making me find out everything for myself, he gave his explanations not before, but after, I had felt the full force of the difficulties' (Mill, *ibid.*, p. 42).

Mill's father was evidently home educating from principle rather than expedience. He was a man 'of a democratic radicalism then regarded as extreme' (Mill, *ibid.*, p. 39) and, as such, of the same cast of mind as those today who see home-based education as a way of equipping children to change society. Another category of home educators in the last century was that of parents doing it for religious reasons (a large group, now, in the United States). Anna Sewell's mother, Mary, for instance, saw home education as a Christian duty based on the biblical passage 'train up a child in the way he should go and he will not depart from it'. She based her educational principles on those of Rousseau, as interpreted by Richard and Maria Edgeworth in their book *Practical Education*:

> They did not go as far as Rousseau, who had suggested that his imaginary pupil, Emile, should invent a microscope before using one, but they considered that children ought to be allowed to discover the truths of the natural world for themselves. In moral education, also, they should experience the results of disobedience, even if these were painful to the point of being dangerous. . . . Mary was true to Richard Edgeworth's principle that 'the knowledge that cannot immediately be applied to use, has no interest for children', and she threw herself with enthusiasm into simple experiments in chemistry recommended by him. One suspects that she was as delighted (and surprised) as Anna and Philip when water coloured blue with radish skins turned red when lemon juice was added, thereby proving the presence of an acid. (Chitty, 1971, p. 58)

Those for whom home-based education was merely expedient, rather than a matter of principle, for example, parents of girls in an age when private schools were mainly provided for boys, or those who found themselves abroad, were perhaps more likely to employ governesses or tutors to teach their children. This was so in the case of Eleanor Farjeon's father, though he was concerned to tailor the education to the individual needs of his daughter:

> ... because of my headaches and almost sleepless nights, I was allowed to sit at the piano as long as I liked, muddling out Schubert and Mendelssohn accompaniments. . . . Lessons were set for me too, in history, geography, grammar and sums; but the first three I was already absorbing ignorantly and copiously from my reading, and as for the sums, I never really knew, and don't quite now, just what the two little brackets were for in Long Division. (Farjeon, 1960, p. 411)

Bertrand Russell's education until the age of 16, by governesses and tutors, was perhaps more stereotypically that which one would expect of an upper class, educated, family in the late 1800s (it is not made clear in his autobiography why he did not go to school), though there was, as in Eleanor Farjeon's family, concern lest the child should study too much. This concern was, in his case, counterproductive:

> My grandmother was always afraid that I should overwork, and kept my hours of lessons very short. The result was that I used to work in my bedroom on the sly with one candle, sitting at my desk in a nightshirt on cold evenings, ready to blow out the candle and pop into bed at the slightest sound. (Russell, 1967, p. 36)

Post-1880

Within ten years of the 1870 Act the country had enough schools to accommodate all those eligible to attend them; but their quality was not reckoned to be universally high and for this, and other reasons, attendance was also far from universal.

Nevertheless, the advent of the School Attendance Officer may have increased the amount of systematic education going on at home among truanting children who would previously have been left to pick up what they could. This is certainly the impression given by Flora Thompson's description of her own home education during the period in question:

> Their father brought home two copies of Mavor's First Reader and taught them the alphabet; but just as Laura was beginning on words of one syllable, he was sent away to work on a distant job, only coming home at weekends. Laura, left at the 'C-a-t s-i-t-s on the m-a-t' stage, had then to carry her book round after her mother as she went about

her housework, asking; 'Please, Mother, what does h-o-u-s-e spell?' or 'W-a-l-k, Mother, what is that?' . . . there came a day when, quite suddenly, as it seemed to her, the printed characters took on a meaning. There were still many words, even in the first pages of that simple primer, she could not decipher; but she could skip those and yet make sense of the whole. 'I'm reading!' she cried aloud. 'Oh Mother! Oh Edmund! I'm reading!' (Thompson, 1973, pp. 43–4)

The Elementary Education Acts of 1870 made it clear that children need not attend school if 'under efficient instruction in some other manner', the word 'efficient' being undefined then as now. The 1876/80 Act emphasized for the first time the *parents'* duty to ensure that their children were educated, education being instruction in the three Rs.

After this it appears that home education was restricted to children who were either aristocratic, ill or abroad, since the only evidence of its practice which I can find relates to one or other of these circumstances, for example, Gerald Durrell's account quoted at the beginning of this chapter. Yehudi Menuhin's unorthodox education (as described in his autobiography) was perhaps an exception to this, as his parents appear to have had ideological objections to school:

I went to school for precisely one day, at the age of six, by which time I could read quite well and write and calculate a little. Tremendous discussion preceded the experiment, whose brevity suggests that my parents thankfully accepted the first token of its unwisdom to return to basic convictions. . . . (Menuhin, 1977, pp. 42–3)

The picture composed by this historical review is one of home-based education based on learning at the child's own pace and according to individual needs and interests (with a firm emphasis on numeracy and literacy), without fear (though over-strict governesses and tutors were probably common) and often through the everyday life of the family. The major difference between the era described and the modern one appears to be the amount of formality in learning, though there were exceptions to this, such as the Cobbetts, who managed to impart the basics in an informal way.

Home-based Education Today: Personal Accounts

Few of the writers whose accounts I shall examine in this section had the benefit of a support group such as Education Otherwise (EO), which exists today, so that the background against which the events they describe took place is in most cases a very different one from that of today's home educators, but familiar to those of my interviewees who were teenagers before EO got off the ground. The situation was one of at best lack of knowledge, and at worst hostility, among Local Education Authorities (LEAs) who felt home education a threat to general confidence in the state system. There was little written on education at home when I began to prepare for the study: most were subjective accounts by the mother, as the mainly responsible parent, but one (*The Children on the Hill*, Deakin, 1973) was written by a TV producer who had 'discovered' and filmed the family in question, and one (*What Shall We Do With the Children?*, Kiddle, 1981) was written by one parent on behalf of the many who had been involved in a group home educating enterprise. I was able to obtain one of the much larger number of accounts written by American home educators, Nancy Wallace's *Better Than School* (Wallace, 1983) which provided an interesting contrast in terms of the legal and social setting of home education in the USA as well as a lot of compulsively fascinating detail about everyday home-schooling life.

The mothers' books are all written in a chatty, anecdotal style: only Joy Baker's *Children in Chancery* (Baker, 1964) took an obviously defensive tone, not surprisingly in view of the years of argument and court cases she had with Norfolk LEA over home education. One account, Jean Bendell's *School's Out* (Bendell, 1987) was published as this study was drawing to a close. It is part personal history, representing the new breed of home educators with young children and lots of support from EO, part solid advice to others, and part background information.

No easy and generalizable reasons for home educating emerge from these accounts: in each family the circumstances and catalysts were unique, though they shared some similarities. Two contrasting situations will illustrate this. The families described in *The Children on the Hill* (Deakin, 1973) and *Anything School Can Do, You Can Do Better* (Mullarney, 1983) shared a geographical isolation which made school initially unreachable (deliberately so in the case of Maria and Martin, fortuitously in the case of the Mullarneys), and an interest in the work of Montessori, with her quite structured early approach to formal academic tasks. However, they exemplify the distinction between ideological reasons for home education and those which are only expedient, though it is interesting to note that Maire Mullarney later became a convinced advocate of early education at home. The Harrisons, on the other hand (documented in Meighan, 1984b and 1984c, and Kitto, 1981), believed strongly in the importance of leaving children alone to develop as they would, and used their geographical isolation to provide lots of outdoor space, animals to look after, and unstructured opportunities for playing and learning.

There was no unifying feature among these families such as parents' background (a spiritualist, an Irish Catholic with eleven children, a plumber, a journalist, an ex-model, and a Jewish revolutionary would seem to have little in common), and no unity in their aims for their children or the age to which they educated them. The Mullarney children all went to school at eight (thus her book's title obscures the fact that her substitute for school covered only the first three primary years) so that they could learn Irish, which was needed for Higher Education, and which neither of their parents, one assumes, knew well enough to teach. Joy Baker, on the other hand, resolutely kept all her children out of school for the whole of the period of compulsory education.

Despite this variation between families in every conceivable area, certain common themes did emerge. Some, such as reasons for home educating, family background, and educational approach, have already been mentioned. Others which seemed interesting were the place of literacy and numeracy, formally taught by all but the Harrisons; the encouragement of creativity (the Wallaces, for instance, became accomplished musicians, and many of the Mullarneys produced prizewinning paintings while at home); the relationship between families and the local education authority; and the extent to which children appeared to suffer from social isolation.

The Contemporary Legal Situation

Interpretation of the law by the various LEAs involved with home educating families will be discussed in a later chapter, so for the moment I shall explain how the law stands on the issue of home education and related matters such as child benefit and part-time schooling.

The duty of parents to provide for their children's education, whether in school or not, is laid down in Section Thirty-Six of the 1944 Education Act (amended in 1981 to take account of provision for children with special needs):

> Duty of parents to secure the education of their children.

> It shall be the duty of the parent of every child of compulsory school age to cause him to receive efficient full-time education suitable to his age, ability and aptitude (and to any special educational needs he may have) either by regular attendance at school or otherwise.

'Efficient' is not defined and is therefore open to individual interpretation by LEAs, and 'suitable to age, ability and aptitude' is likely to be a highly subjective judgment. The courts are the final arbiters here in cases of dispute. Neither is it clear whether 'full-time' means full-time in one place of learning or whether alternatives such as part-time schooling are legally possible. An extra boost to the power of parents to educate 'otherwise' under this Act is given by its Section Seventy-Six:

> Pupils to be educated in accordance with the wishes of their parents.

In the exercise and performance of all powers and duties conferred and imposed on them by this Act (the Secretary of State for Education and Science) and local education authorities shall have regard to the general principle that, so far as is compatible with the provision of efficient instruction and training and the avoidance of unreasonable public expenditure, pupils are to be educated in accordance with the wishes of their parents.

David Deutsch and Kolya Wolf comment on the application of this section to home educating families:

It is hard to imagine any group who would satisfy the conditions of Section 76 better than parents who provide (efficient, etc.) home education for their children because they are opposed to schooling as a method of education. It might even be (though the legal position is unclear) that Section 76 would suffice to permit education otherwise than at school even if it were not mentioned explicitly elsewhere in the Act. (Deutsch and Wolf, 1986, p. 4)

The LEA's responsibility towards children is laid down in Sections Thirty-Seven and Thirty-Nine of the 1944 Act. Section Thirty-Nine deals with 'registered but not attending' children, whose parents can be taken to court forthwith — for this reason EO always suggests that parents request to have a child deregistered as soon as it is certain that the child will not be attending the school any more. Under Section Thirty-Seven, a parent failing to comply with Section Thirty-Six must satisfy the LEA, within fourteen days, of the efficiency and suitability of their home education or possibly find themselves served with a School Attendance Order, which they may be taken to court for ignoring.

The children themselves have no rights under any of these sections, though Education Otherwise would like to see some established, as the third of the organization's principal aims, printed on the cover of all their publications, makes clear: 'To establish the primary right of children to have full consideration given to their wishes and feelings regarding their education'.

The right of parents of children with special educational needs to educate otherwise is legally the same as any other parent's under Sections Thirty-Six and Thirty-Seven discussed above, but there may be two problems for them. The first is that where a child is to be withdrawn from a special school, deregistration may not take place without the permission of the LEA. The second is that parents of children who have had a 'Statement of Special Educational Needs' drawn up which does not incorporate the possibility of home education may find it very hard to get the statement changed.

One final legal issue which has recently been clarified is the law relating to child benefit. It is now established that parents of home educated children over 16 will receive benefit until the child is 19 (as do the parents of children attending school) provided that the education is approved by the LEA.

Education Otherwise

It was perhaps either because there was virtually no home education in ordinarily placed families in the first half of this century (as suggested in the section on the history of home-based education) or because any who did home educate kept exceedingly low profiles, that the case of the 'Baker infants' in the 1950s created such a lot of media publicity and encountered so much entrenched stubbornness on the part of the local education authority (though this was almost equalled some thirty years later by the Harrison family's LEA). Joy Baker, as may become apparent later in the study, was the ideological predecessor of many home educators today who want to allow children to direct their own learning at a pace appropriate to their individual development and interests. The fact that a group such as Education Otherwise did not emerge out of this cause célèbre was perhaps due to the climate of the times, the period before the hippy 1960s being rather a conventional one as people heaved a sigh of relief at getting back to normality after the traumas of war.

After the emergence of hippy culture and the beginnings of exploration into many different ways of life which this engendered, social opinion in some quarters was obviously ready for a group which would provide support for people looking at other ways of educating their children than the traditional ones. Education Otherwise was one of several offshoots of the Alternative Society, some of whose principles were outlined in *New Humanist*:

> There is a belief that education comes from schools and that health comes from the National Health Service. The difficulties are not solved by just 'dropping-out' — people who do this lose a good deal of cultural value. However, dropping out might to some extent be part of a strategy, e.g. home-based education. Parents have a responsibility for the education of their children, either at school or at home. By opting for home-based education, parents could be trying to achieve a responsibility shift rather than just a drop-out. We should use (or not use) the educational system in a responsible way so that it does not dominate — it should be the servant of the people, not a master. (West Glamorgan Humanist group, 1977, p. 212)

EO (now Education Otherwise Ltd., since it acquired charitable status in 1985) was founded by Dick Kitto, Stan Windass of the Alternative Society, and a handful of other interested people in 1977. The 'Operation Otherwise' discussed later in this study was a family-scale experiment which preceded the formation of EO by six years but did not have the success hoped for in spreading outwards to form a network of home educators. EO, on the other hand, which is the only indicator of the spread of home education in this country, has grown steadily since its inception. Numbers on the 1980 Contact List suggest that it had grown in three years from ten or so original families to at least 300 (though it must be remembered that not all members were necessarily also home educators, many were merely interested; and that not all members asked to appear on the Contact List, perhaps because they wanted to keep a low profile regarding the LEA).

At the time of the interviews, EO's membership had grown to over 700 and the Contact List had begun to incorporate a register of available skills and resources. Between then and 1988, when the list entries numbered around 1500, there was a gradual change in emphasis among the members from those who were characteristically the parents of older children unhappy in school to families with preschool age children, who were interested ideologically in an alternative to state education. The most recent comprehensive membership details are as reported in the minutes of a Core Group meeting held in September 1987:

> Membership stood at 1840 families and was escalating again. There are 1081 pre-school members, 1320 primary age members of whom 622 are listed as out of school and 599 secondary age members of whom 362 are listed as out of school. The steady loss of existing members accounts for the slow increase. (*EO Newsletter*, 56, 1987, p. 48)

What accounts for the loss of existing members is not known, but one could speculate that some people had joined in a state of desperation and then found a different solution to their problems; some people's children might have grown up; some might be disillusioned with home education or dissatisfied with EO as an organization. (Affording the subscription would not have been a problem, since people in straitened circumstances are given free or reduced rate membership.)

What do members gain by belonging to EO? I have already mentioned the Contact List with its register of skills and resources others are willing to share. Support of various kinds is available through, locally, a coordinator and whatever local meetings or visits are organized. These may be of an educational or merely social nature, and provide important opportunities for parents to chat and children to play. As there are, in some sparsely populated parts of the country, few local activities, EO holds national meetings for the whole family (one popular week-long one being held in a castle), and camps for older children. Specific advice and help is available in the first instance from the local coordinator, who may refer members to those with greater understanding and/or experience of the problem in hand: to the Legal Group or the Special Needs Group, for example. Booklets giving suggestions for home education during the *Early Years* and *Later Years* are also available, as is one on the legal situation, *School Is Not Compulsory* EO, 1985. What EO does not do, despite being asked regularly, is to provide a prescribed curriculum and materials for home education, since this would be anathema to the principle of education tailored to the individual child's needs.

Chapter 2

An Introduction to the Research

Its Origins

The impetus for this research came about with the birth of our son and consequent discussion about his upbringing. An initial interest in alternatives to orthodox schooling led to the discovery of Education Otherwise. Its newsletter and the other published accounts of home education which it steered me towards, while helpful on the practicalities of home-based education, failed to provide me with any information about a question which seemed of crucial concern: what sort of grown-up lives did home educated people lead? Did they get on well generally with other people? Were they able to form close relationships outside the home? Were they able to run the practical sides of their lives? Were they qualified for the kinds of jobs they wanted to do? What jobs did they do and how did they do them? Were they well equipped to make use of their leisure time? What was their attitude to involvement with the community in which they lived and to society as a whole?

A letter to me from the general secretary of EO at the time confirmed its relevance to the educational field: 'I have always thought that this information would be valuable to counteract the argument that "only schooling can fit you for work"'. Though I had expected no generalized answers to these questions, I had hoped to find enough individual evidence to give me an idea of whether home education might work for us. When I realized that my need for information in this area was shared by fellow prospective home educators, as well as by other interested parties, it seemed to me that it would be best to undertake a formal research project, with suitable guidance, after which the material would be available to anyone who wanted access to it. The Open University provided an appropriate means of achieving this on a part-time basis, which fitted in with looking after (and later home educating) my son, and supplied useful insight into the possible problems of learning at home.

A passage from an article by John Holt on the ways in which the home schooling movement in America could be of interest to conventional education led me to consider another use for the research I proposed to carry out: it could be seen as a report on a long-term experiment in effective learning which would not be possible in schools, but which might have many implications for school learning:

> Not in the foreseeable future can we imagine a school district saying to its students, 'You can read anything you like, and as much as you like, and we aren't going to grade you on it'. Or, 'You can study whatever you want, and we don't care what grade you're in'. Or, 'If you're working on some project, take as much time as you need to finish it'. If educational experiments such as these are ever to be undertaken on a large scale (as they should be), it is not likely to be in schools as we know them. . . . There is only one place where this kind of research is likely to be carried out on a large enough scale and for a long enough time to yield significant results. That place is in the homes of families who are teaching their own children. This is the main reason why the home-schooling movement is so important to schools. . . . Some people might argue that this family activity could not properly be called research, that it would not be significant because it would be haphazard and uncontrolled. Careful sampling and other matters of research protocol may indeed be necessary if we want to know what large numbers of people are doing, but these procedures are worthless if we want to learn what people might be capable of doing. It took only one person, Roger Bannister, to prove that the four-minute mile was possible. That no one else had done it was beside the point. Not only did he show that it could be done; he showed that, if you wanted to find out how to do it, he — not the average runner — was the one to ask. (Holt, 1983, p. 393)

Holt's observations suggested some possible features of research into home-based education which I decided to incorporate into my own study. The most important of these was the emphasis on exploration of the achievements of individual families rather than the gathering of statistical data, for the reason that Holt gave: more could be learned about the factors leading to fulfilling home-based education through a detailed qualitative analysis of approaches and progress than through the collection of information on the numbers of people taking arbitrarily defined courses of action (although this might have a place in certain circumstances: for instance, where the average cost of resources for home-based education needed to be ascertained in order to apply for grants or subsidies). This issue is developed more fully in Chapter 3.

Other Recent Research

Formal comparative or case-study research on home-based education is thin on the ground: Roland Meighan appears to be the only academic to have taken the subject seriously. He has published a number of articles and chapters in books which have influenced the direction of this study through their choice of themes for discussion. Because of his involvement in EO and his work as an educational witness for families involved in court cases (for example, the Harrisons) he was in a position to combine an insider's view with that of the professional sociologist of education. Meighan's original interest in home-based education developed out of his own and his wife's experience as teachers at both primary and secondary levels, in relationship to the education of their son. In 'Locations of learning and ideologies of education' (Meighan and Brown, 1980) he questioned the assumption that education needed necessarily to take place in the school and, through an examination of the varied ideologies of EO members, discovered that their only common feature was the use of the home as a learning base — thus formally establishing another resource in addition to those proposed by the deschoolers who had concentrated on learning in work places and communal areas.

Writing in 1981, Meighan took up a topic he had begun to examine in the 1980 article: the wider involvement in their children's education of parents generally, using Education Otherwise as the example of greatest possible involvement. He pointed out that some EO parents would opt for partnership with the schools where this was possible, with a contracted part-time schooling arrangement (a theme he later developed in 'Flexischooling' (Meighan, 1984a)). In the same article, Meighan discusses the contribution being made by new technology such as home computers, CEEFAX and PRESTEL, to the resources available for learning in the home, and comments: 'The likely picture that emerges is that of most homes gradually being equipped as sophisticated information retrieval centres whilst schools, under financial pressures caused by cuts in government expenditure, are forced to contemplate a return to slates and slate pencils!' (Meighan, 1981a). (Postscript from *Times Educational Supplement*, August 1988, *No Comment* column: '"We have run out of money for anything other than absolutely essential standard items such as paper and pens." From a City of Birmingham Education Department Memorandum — Stationery and Equipment'.)

Two articles in 1984 tackled political aspects of home-based education (Meighan, 1984b and 1984c). The first examined the way in which home educators become more confident in the exercise of their rights, less trustful of the LEA, and more independent and non-authoritarian in their practice of home education. The other article focused on the ways in which LEAs attempt to resist the threat to their perception of the 'correct' method of child education by the conscious or unconscious maintenance of myths: that school is compulsory; that home educating parents must be qualified teachers; that the LEA has a right to cooperation from home educating parents in carrying out assessment of the children; and so on.

Other research concerning home-based education has taken the form of short dissertations for BEd degrees (Kate Blinston's in 1982, for example), and three longer works for MEds. The first, by Christine Brown, was written when Education Otherwise was only eighteen months old (Brown, 1978). Its purpose was to ascertain, through a reading of EO's literature, and interviews with its members, the place of the organization within the tradition of radical education in this country. She concludes that, because of the (already noted) diversity of ideologies of members, there are overlaps between radical and non-radical positions, and that the location of learning in the home rather than the school is the only radical element common to all members, but that this in itself could have far-reaching implications: taken together with the development of the Open University, the growth of Education Otherwise might suggest that open learning was becoming available at every educational stage. Apart from this, the main thesis of her work, she throws up several interesting questions about smaller matters: the danger of the mass media as a controlling force (reminiscent of Holt's similar point); the parallels between the situation of the child at school and that of asylum patients as analyzed by Irving Goffman (Goffman, 1961); and the degree of freedom enjoyed by the home educated child in relation to the control of the learning process by his or her parents. A brief outline of some of the concerns of Brown's work appeared in the *Wolverhampton Polytechnic Faculty of Education Journal* (Brown, 1982).

Sandra Blacker's study (Blacker, 1981) was stimulated by curiosity about the relationships of teachers with their own children, of whom home educating parents are an interesting subgroup. Her intention was to show how parents unhappy about their children's schooling found happier solutions, and what the educational and social consequences were for the family. She used interviews to collect her information, both face-to-face and over the telephone, and had access to the eighty-four 1980 EO questionnaire returns. Her conclusion was that the parents she interviewed were not radical deschoolers but were doing very much what the schools did in terms of curriculum and method. She felt that their effectiveness in this indicated that parents of children in school could be made far more useful than they were at present, as Meighan also suggested (Meighan, 1981a). She took up the suggestion, made by Dick Kitto on a tape produced for the Open University, that parents could be characterized as belonging to one of three groups: competitors, compensators and rebels. This approach has been criticized elsewhere as being static and not allowing for a change in outlook over the course of the family's experience of home education (Meighan, 1984c).

The final MEd study I came across appeared the following year (Maiden, 1982) and was written by a fellow home educator. It took the form of a case-study of the EO movement, based on the intention of letting participants speak for themselves, and it incorporated extracts from, and comments on, a ten-minute film made by the BBC in cooperation with Maiden. The film was based on examples of his own version of Kitto's tripartite division: 'alternative life-style', 'school phobic' and 'rejection of falling school standards', and on an interview with a Chief Education Officer (CEO). A large part of the study dealt with detailed interviews with two LEA officers and a report of the visit of one such officer to a local family proposing to deregister their oldest child. John Maiden made the interesting point that individual biography is important in shaping the approach of LEA officers as well as home educating families. He also remarked on 'a tendency for there to be a period of apathy towards study when children are first withdrawn from school, and an increase in self-confidence as the effects of schooling wear off' (Maiden, 1982, p. 64). Other than these, he drew no general conclusions, preferring to wait for the response to his paper before making any.

A final piece of research, recently published in book form, concerns not the general area of home education so far discussed, but the specific group of children whom LEAs have labelled 'school phobic'. Patricia Knox's book *Troubled Children* (Knox, 1988) draws together parts of the writings of professionals from educational and psychiatric fields, and the case histories of EO members who have had difficulty in convincing the authorities of their view (which is also hers) that the school, rather than the 'phobic' child and his or her family, is the problem, and that therefore home education would be a happy solution all round. An article by Knox appeared with others on research into various aspects of the subject of home education in a special issue of *Educational Review* devoted to it (*Educational Review*, 1989).

Chapter 3

Choice of Research Method

Theoretical Approach to the Study

The ideas concerning research and analysis developed in Glaser and Strauss' book *The Discovery of Grounded Theory* (Glaser and Strauss, 1967) appeared to be highly relevant to the aims of this study. They approach research in a spirit of exploration and open-minded enquiry, rather than with the intention of testing already established theories. They aim to generate theory in the course of their research by analysis of qualitative data based on a method of constant comparison, whose possibilities can be extended by careful choice of new sample groups where these are seen as likely to shed fresh light on emerging themes.

Because this approach demands no prior knowledge of the important concepts of a research field, and is in fact directed towards identifying them as an integral part of the research process, it seemed an appropriate one to adopt in the present case, where lack of theories to be verified meant that description and tentative explanation of features were prime objectives.

Choice of Technique

Research techniques based on laboratory tests of learning progress or on the collection of large-scale survey results would clearly have been inappropriate to the goals of the research, which depended upon the analysis of qualitative data of a mainly biographical nature. The ethnographic approach of the anthropologist, with which I was familiar from my undergraduate studies, seemed likely to prove more fruitful, since it had been developed to further understanding of just the sort of little-explored social phenomena which the home-based education movement exemplified; and it focused on what seemed a useful combination of participant observation, observation of context, and informant interviewing.

These techniques needed adaptation to suit my purpose and to fit in with restrictions of time and money. As far as participant observation went, I was already a member of Education Otherwise and was aware that involvement in their activities, and access to their literature, were important factors in developing my sense of what might be interesting to investigate, and in getting an impression of some of its members' concerns. My original interest in the group had been a purely personal one, related to my own son's education, and this interest continued throughout the study, giving me on some occasions helpful insight into the behaviour of my interviewees, and doubtless misleading me on others. I could not go beyond this kind of observation (in a role which I made no attempt to disguise, having announced my study in the *EO Newsletter*). Observation of short periods of home education would not have been productive. Families would have been selfconscious and it would have been hard, in the informal atmosphere maintained by most homes, to judge what learning was taking place, without the detailed knowledge of each child's previous accomplishments which I could not hope to obtain in the course of this kind of research. I suspect, too, that families would have been most unwilling to take part in the study on this basis. Furthermore, the information obtained in this way would have been fairly meaningless, comprising at best a tiny fragment of the total and changing picture of that child's learning, and some data on phenomena such as the child's ability to concentrate, or the relationship between parent and child, both likely to be affected by the observer's presence.

Such observation as did take place was therefore in a natural setting: either in the form of noting the activities which happened to be in progress in the home at the time of my visit, or in the form of observation at national and local meetings. This technique, while valuable to the provision of contextual information, was clearly inadequate when it came to identifying important events in the history of a child's education and obtaining interpretations of the reasons, attitudes and approaches involved. At this point, therefore, I turned to the tradition of informant interviewing as a way of obtaining explanations of an ill-understood social system. There seemed, though, little point in searching out one or two 'insiders' who could be said to know more than anyone else about home education in Britain, since the phenomena I was interested in were not highly institutionalized ones where one or two knowledgable informants might have been adequate, but of a diverse and essentially subjective nature where there could be no substitute for obtaining information directly from the families concerned in the form of an educational biography. A method involving the collection of individual biographies also seemed more appropriate to a theoretical framework involving constant comparative analysis, since it provided for the kind of theoretical sampling (extending the data for comparison and therefore the possibilities of new categories) suggested by Glaser and Strauss (1967).

The next problem was how to obtain the required information. The first possibility I considered was to use postal self-completion questionnaires with open-ended questions (rather than the fixed-choice questions appropriate to a statistical survey) capable of qualitative analysis. However, my preliminary reading and attendance at EO meetings had suggested such diversity of experience among home educators that it would be difficult to construct a once-and-for-all questionnaire flexible enough to incorporate all the aspects I might be interested in. Furthermore, the limitations of my knowledge of the area, beyond the general impression of great diversity, produced a difficulty in the formulation of questions precise and relevant enough to be clearly answerable. This problem might have been overcome by the use of a pilot study, but limitations of time, money and likely numbers of volunteers made this impossible.

There was also the possibility that a distorted picture might be obtained because the particular formulation of the questions predisposed them to particular sorts of answer (a problem not unique to this method of data collection, but less easily controllable than in face-to-face situations for example). On the other hand, the absence of the researcher in person would eliminate sources of bias arising from lack of rapport, or too much of it, in interviews.

The most serious objection to this method lay in the information which would inevitably be omitted. Elements of doubt in a respondent's mind, changes in attitudes and in practice, would all tend to be disguised by the need to compose a written answer and are all crucial to an understanding of the process of home-based education. More importantly still, I would be unable to follow up at will those points which, on the basis of comparison with other data or on their own merits, struck me as needing deeper investigation. Though this could have been carried out through further correspondence with the family concerned, it seemed to me that there was no substitute for striking while the iron was hot, and that the successful development of hypotheses would depend on the opportunity to pursue emerging themes through a number of case studies.

A couple of practical points dissuaded me further: many people find it tedious to write at the kind of length which would be useful to me, and might be unwilling to participate in the study because of this; and I might obtain only the views of one member of the family, since the work of filling in the questionnaire would probably be delegated to the person deemed most adept at that sort of thing. Individual questionnaires could have been sent to each family member, but the perceived duplication of answers (particularly where factual information was concerned) might well have resulted in only one being filled in and returned in any case.

These considerations pointed me firmly in the direction of the method of data collection used by the three previous studies of home-based education (Blacker, 1981; Brown, 1978 and Maiden, 1982): the face-to-face interview. The advantages of the interview over a postal questionnaire seemed to be at least three. Greater rapport between researcher and subject might lead to greater interest on the part of the latter, a greater commitment to help and therefore more detailed and extensive information. Secondly, the possibility of taping the conversation between interviewer and interviewee would ensure that a recording of feelings and attitudes took place which was in the interviewee's own words and which would therefore be a more vivid and natural description of those feelings and attitudes than either the subject's written responses to a questionnaire or the interviewer's hurried notes made while interviewing. Thirdly, and most importantly, there was the question of the ability to follow up interesting points, to introduce new ones that occurred to the interviewer in the course of the interview, and generally to ensure that the data were both relevant to themes already emerging and continually opening up new avenues of exploration.

The possible disadvantages appeared to be mainly those of biases arising out of the relationship between interviewer and interviewee, or out of the interviewee's conscious or subconscious need to distort the information given in some way, though there seemed no compelling reason why families involved should deliberately dissemble. Further consideration of these problems is given later, but for now it is sufficient to note that they suggested another string to the methodological bow: the use of documentary sources, firstly, to provide a variety of perspectives on some features of the interview data, and secondly, to supply information not obtained in the interviews (for example, I could read about the experiences of home educating families too far away from me either spatially or temporally to be interviewed, but often interesting precisely for these reasons). The documents involved were mainly periodicals: the English and American national home-schooling newsletters (*EO Newsletter* and *Growing Without Schooling*), the *Times Educational Supplement* and *Where* — later *ACE Bulletin*. During the progress of the study, several books appeared employing an autobiographical approach to the telling of a home education story: these supplemented the articles in periodicals written by home educators and the few books already published. The writings of other researchers were another obviously useful source, as were relevant novels and biographies. One of the disadvantages of documents is the limited and partial picture of a whole educational career they may portray, often omitting a sense of process and of inconsistencies and indecisions (as already noted in the discussion of the pros and cons of postal questionnaires). It was sometimes difficult or impossible to counteract this with supplementary information. Also, the problems of bias and distortion, whether deliberate or not, apply here as much as anywhere, and these may include the particular political, social or philosophical bias of a periodical.

The Sample

The sample used in this study was self-selected, firstly from the home educating population in Britain as a whole, and then, as the study progressed, from the groups which were the targets of the theoretical sampling procedure suggested by Glaser and Strauss (1967). Representative sampling would have made no sense in this context, partly because of the huge number of variables to choose from as bases for this type of sampling but mainly because the very low response rate to a previous investigation of home education (Grant, 1983) suggested that it would be impossible to obtain satisfactory numbers of inter- viewees. It might be useful, however, to raise the question here of the relationship between the home educating population at large and the families interviewed.

In terms of sex and geographical distribution, the children were similar to the whole population. Three more males than females participated: a count of the children marked as 'out of school' in the 1984 Contact List revealed 177 girls, 171 boys and 11 whose sex could not be determined due to the propen- sity of many EO members to give their children unusual names. I visited families in most of the English regions and in one or two more remote places, such as the Scottish islands. People living in both urban and rural areas partici- pated, though not in equal numbers due to the financial need to combine interviewing trips with family holidays and a reluctance to spend these entirely in Hull or Stoke-on-Trent. No comparison in terms of age can be made, since I deliberately picked a lower age limit of 14 for the prospective interviewees: this ensured that those visited could be followed up over a couple of years into their post-compulsory education age period, providing information about higher education and employment (as well as giving a fairly complete picture of their compulsory education years). This emphasis contradicts that of the annual Contact Lists, where an increasing number of very young children (under 5 years old) is being recorded.

Regarding the psychological aspects of the relationship between the sample and home educators in general, one could perhaps say that the respon- dents were more self-confident and articulate than the majority of the home educating population. The degree to which this is true varies with the degree to which they were self-selected. Those who replied to published letters about the study on their own initiative could be said to be entirely self-selected, while those who responded only after some sort of direct personal invitation to participate were less so.

The decision to interview only adults, or families with older children, suggested that there would be a majority of children who had, at some time, been to school and who had parents who were, or who had started out, essentially pro-school. This is not so in the EO population as a whole: the literature and EO questionnaire answers (Grant, 1983) indicate that it is increasingly the families with very young, often preschool-age, children who are committed to home education as part of a philosophy of life.

As the study progressed, the process of comparative analysis provided another means of relating the experiences of the families in the study to those of other home educators, through the use of documents and through the directed sampling procedure. For example, a comparison of the evident differences in the category of how people are treated by LEAs led to the need to interview some LEA advisers to attempt an explanation of this: two authorities with markedly different general educational policies were chosen.

There were four other main areas where theoretical sampling was used to increase the possibilities of comparison. The first of these concerned the lack of perspectives on home education from people who were already adult and had pursued some kind of job or career for several years. Interviews with more people in this category provided useful data to compare with the views of those still in home education, or who had only recently left it. Secondly, I was interested in talking to more single parents, since discussion indicated that there were, in these families, possible problems of a financial and emotional nature which had not been adequately investigated in the basic interviews. The third area of theoretical sampling was that of commune dwellers. My interest in having further data for comparison here was engendered by one respondent's observation that very few commune dwellers do educate their children themselves, despite their frequent pride in many other forms of self-sufficiency. Fourthly, the development of various themes discussed by the first interviewees seemed likely to benefit from comparison with the views of various 'education people' other than the advisers mentioned above. These included a local authority educational psychologist, a retired teacher-trainer and teacher (herself home educated), and an FE lecturer who had been involved with the education of one of the interviewees.

Practicalities

Finding the Interviewees

Contacting of the original group of interviewees was carried out on the basis of one or more of the following:

1 Inclusion in the 1982 contact list of Education Otherwise, which notes ages of children;
2 Readership of *Times Educational Supplement, Where,* Journal of the World-Wide Education Service of the Parents' National Education Union (PNEU), or *EO Newsletter;*
3 Having contributed to *EO Newsletter;*
4 Being personally known to myself, my supervisors or other interviewees.

Since source 2, the first line of attack, yielded altogether only five replies to letters in the relevant journals asking for volunteers, a more personal approach was tried. Handwritten letters were sent to families in categories 1, 3 and 4, and a very small number, who had written books about their experiences, were contacted through their publishers.

In all, I was in touch at the beginning of the study with seventy-one families or individuals, and of these, thirty-six replied positively (many also expressing an interest in the research per se), four refused (for reasons to be explained), and thirty-one were never heard of again. Of those who agreed to be interviewed, apart from those mentioned above who were keen enough to take up paper and pen on their own initiative, the letters based on personal contact proved the best way to produce a positive response.

Attempts to track down various well-known home educated people, in the main child prodigies like *The Children on the Hill* (Deakin, 1973) and 'A-level wonder girl Ruth Lawrence', were largely unsuccessful, despite current addresses being obtained for them: too much publicity already, perhaps. I did, however, manage to get in touch with David Baker, the eldest of the famous Baker Infants (Baker, 1964 and 1987), and carried out an interesting transatlantic correspondence with him.

Reasons for non-participation were given by only four of the thirty-five who did not agree to be interviewed. One felt she had lost contact with the home education movement, and her son was, in any case, very unwilling to talk about his experiences because of bad publicity in the local press. One (a well-known lady traveller) lived in Ireland and sent her child to school there whenever they were not travelling together, so felt she did not qualify as a home educator. One, the astronomer Patrick Moore, did not refer to my request for an interview but briefly described his home education in a letter. The fourth letter came from a couple of classical musicians who were simply too busy to talk to me, but they, also, described what they were doing with their son in a letter. The first and last reasons (children unwilling to talk or parents too busy) could perhaps have been operative in the case of many who were never heard from again, as might innate suspicion of research, and the loss of letters in the post. A further clue appears in this reply to one of six requests to non-respondents to give their reasons for not answering the initial letter:

> My disinclination to join your study grew from a desire not to be treated as an unusual (potentially anti-social?) phenomenon to be studied, but rather as a normal person pursuing her private (and it was/is my *private*) life in a perfectly legitimate way.

Carrying out the Interviews

Interviews were conducted as much like a normal sociable conversation as possible, so that a relaxed atmosphere would prevail which would help interviewees to express themselves freely. It was expected that interviewing families in their own homes would contribute to this relaxation, as well as giving me some idea of the everyday context in which home education was taking place.

Ideally, I would have liked at each interview to have been able to talk to parents and children separately as well as together, in order to have independent views of the same events: some families suggested this themselves, and some seemed to think that I should talk to the children only — in fact in one case I arrived to find the parents actually away, and a very competent and friendly 15-year-old-boy in charge of a household of assorted siblings, animals and aunts. Where parents appeared determined to sit it out, I did not like to suggest separate interviews for fear of arousing hostility, so made the best of things as they were. There were only two occasions on which I felt the parents' presence was probably inhibiting the children from expressing their point of view, and this might well have been the case had the parents been physically absent.

The construction of the interview guide was based on the premise that its main use would be as a prompt, to encourage people to follow their own trains of thought, and as a checklist for myself, at the end of the interview, to ensure that no relevant points had been missed. I needed it to cover three main sorts of information: the factual details of a person's educational career, the way in which the various features of this career appeared to them and how they felt about them, and what relationship these things had to the wider social and educational worlds in which the events were situated. (It was anticipated that the latter would not always be made explicit by the interviewees themselves, but that it might be deduced from what they said and corroborated using documentary sources.) These three groups, and the detail of the questions which derived from them, were suggested by my preliminary reading and by discussion with others.

Interviewing took place mainly during an eighteen month period lasting from the middle of 1982 until the end of 1983. Each interview lasted on average two hours and usually ended with a welcome cup of tea and an informal chat. As I have already discussed, it seemed a good idea to tape record interviews where people were willing, in order to preserve the flavour of what they said and to prevent the omission in notetaking of things which seemed irrelevant or uninteresting at the time and on later consideration might have proved to be the reverse. A few family members appeared slightly nervous of the recorder at first, but far fewer than I expected, and even these very soon seemed to forget that it was there.

It was found that most interviewees were able to give very fluent, comprehensive and detailed pictures of their home education, once reassured that the questions were only there as a back-up, and that there was no need to stick to them. The atmosphere was, as I had hoped, usually that of a fairly relaxed discussion, to which I often contributed myself if I felt that my comments were unlikely to prejudice the rest of the interview. Further questions about something of particular interest came naturally as part of the conversation and generally I did not have the feeling that this curiosity was unwelcome, in fact rather the opposite: most people appeared thoroughly to enjoy talking about their experiences, and some have voluntarily kept in touch with me since. The presence of my small son at some of the interviews (people were always asked in advance if they minded about this) was a difficulty for me, in that I often had a conflict of attention, but it sometimes helped to break lingering ice and dispel any sense of formality: this was particularly so for some of the younger children, who found it easier to approach me to start with by talking to him.

As soon after each interview as possible, I made notes on the context of the interview, wrote down anything said after the recorder had been switched off (so long as the interviewee had agreed that the information could be used) and wrote to thank people who had been to a lot of trouble on our behalf. In the months following the interview I transcribed each into typescript. The intention was then to write to people annually in order to pursue anything in the interview that needed further exploration and to follow up those who were going from home education to work or Further/Higher Education. Only half of these letters received an answer, despite the inclusion of a stamp: again, there may be various reasons for this, for example, disillusionment with home education, or moving to a new address.

Twenty interviews were carried out on the basis of the original question guide, and these were followed by seven more which attempted to develop the themes already discovered.

Validity of Data

There are two points involved in the question of possible sources of bias which need to be borne in mind, and clearly stated, in any study based on open-ended interviewing. One, mentioned previously, is the problem of rapport, whether good or poor, between interviewer and interviewee. The other concerns the intentional or unintentional construction of 'accounts' by interviewees, which is an inevitable part of the interview process: a person's memory or subconscious thought may distort the retelling of events or their emotional impact. Relevant here is the point made by many ethnographers, that the subjective effect of an event on a person may be more important to the researcher than its objective reality (if such a thing could be defined), particularly where the consequences of the event are concerned. Another factor to be considered is that of the degree of articulacy of the interviewee and the amount of introspection he or she applies to the telling of a learning experience: some were able to provide only a kind of chronological catalogue of dire events, whereas others supplied me with a ready-made analysis of their entire intellectual and emotional response to home education. The construction work that went into such an account probably made the latter group of interviewees more vulnerable than the former to the problems affecting validity already discussed. Only one of the interviewees, Mary Parsons, appeared to have given these matters any thought. She said:

> I wish I could be a fly on the wall sometimes in other people's houses. You don't know from what they're saying. I mean, I think I've been fairly honest with you but often people aren't. People want to be proud of their children, which is very natural, but I think it's something one should resist.

Checks on validity, where these were appropriate, were three:

1 Checks for internal consistency, where flaws revealed by a re-reading of the interview transcript would lead to hypotheses concerning the subjective interpretation of the experiences involved, which could be developed in follow-up letters.

2 Checks for external consistency — often another view of an event, obtained mainly through documents, but sometimes through interviews with other family members. A further check here relates to the noting of the context of every interview: did the activities in progress in the house, the things revealed by the home itself (for example, the sorts of books around) tie in with the learning experiences described by the interviewees?

3 Checks on the validity of patterns in the data, relating mainly to the work of others interested in home education. For example, the interestingly high proportion of qualified teachers among my sample was discovered independently by at least one other researcher (Meighan, 1984c).

Data Analysis

The first step towards analysis was the grouping together of the few notes made whilst transcribing which appeared to relate to one category. This was done in loose-leaf form to enable changes to be made to the categories if detailed consideration of the transcripts and documentary sources made this necessary. When the twenty interviews were completed and transcribed, they were then examined in detail, and each element of the data was assigned to the existing or newly devised category it suggested. The same process was applied to all the available documentary sources. At this stage, comparison between and within the categories established the areas in which further interviewing was necessary, and the data from these interviews were treated in the same way. These investigations produced some hypotheses about the process of home education and its interrelated elements, and combination of related categories often led to the emergence of a particular theme. Discussion of this analysis, then, which forms the next part of the book, consisted of summarizing all the hypotheses relevant to each theme and illustrating them by reference to the original data.

Chapter 4

Reasons for Change

In this chapter, I shall investigate the reasons families gave for home educating their children for all or part of their educational careers. The analysis is based on a recognition of two types of cause: an already existing interest in educational alternatives and (the more common experience) problems at school. The following quotation illustrates the former point:

> Why, when I don't remotely believe in the revolutionary overthrow of our society, do I want to keep my children away from one of its most powerful institutions? Why, when I like the idea of my children being literate, numerate, curious, informed and cultured, do I want to keep them out of those special places where professional teachers are supposed to be able to do the job for me? And above all, why, when I want them to be disciplined, obedient, brave and sociable, do I want to run the risk of their being at least a little isolated, some of the time, from their conventionally schooled contemporaries?
>
> I want to do this peculiar thing . . . because I believe schools are bad places and cannot be reformed. . . . Professional teachers in special places (these are the defining characteristics of schools) are by nature bound to depend on, and train children for, the industrial world which is collapsing around them. . . . This is a divided society, but one of its greatest divisions is between those who accept and excel in a schooled world, and those who resist or resent it. . . . I believe that almost all the good that ever flowed from the human mind flowed from minds which either never were schooled, or managed to unlearn their schooling. And that is why — if I can't stop it for everyone — I would at least like to find a way of sparing my children from it. (North, 1982, p. 15)

Richard North's view of the desirability of deschooling is quoted as an example of the position often taken by parents of preschool children. It contrasts with those of the families interviewed in two respects: firstly, it relates the school system to factors in contemporary society for which it appears in various ways inappropriate, and secondly, as a consequence of this, it sees deschooling as nationally generally desirable rather than as an individual good in particular cases.

Those interviewed took a more personal view: their own deschooling had happened in response to the immediate needs of particular children. In only two cases did these needs have a single identifiable focus, one example being the medical requirements of Daniel Scheaffer's hypothermia and autism, and the other being the refusal of an English school to admit a boy of Scots parentage who wore the kilt.

For the majority it appeared that several factors (often widely differing in terms of attitude to school or qualifications, for example) were influential. Some were practical, as in the advantages of home-based education for the constantly travelling life of families in a touring theatre company. Some, like Richard North's, related to parents' theoretical thinking on education, developed by reading and/or their own experience as teachers or pupils in school, and the ways in which the ideals engendered in the parents' minds matched up to reality in the form of local schools. The individual child's own personality, and experience in school (if any), were modifying factors here, since theoretical considerations often did not become a conscious concern until the school was seen not to be serving the child well (truancy or psychosomatic illness being common triggers to this realization). A further element bearing on all these things appeared to be the way in which families viewed society and their place in it, how they felt about society's values and how this in turn affected the child's ability (potential or actual) to identify with, and conform to, school values, derived as these inevitably were from those of society. Alison Head describes the mixture of factors relevant to the decision to home educate in her case:

> It was a combination of things. It was partly that Father was very much into the theoretical side of education, Illich and Freire and people like that, and also the practical side of it. I don't know what school I would have gone to. I was very against unisex schools myself, and my brother had been to a school called —, it's a huge comprehensive school . . . they had huge classes . . . there was no positive learning at all, it was all getting away with as little as possible. And he was just getting more and more negative, and we just had no idea what school I could go to . . . so we thought we'd try it.

Three further points of interest, all interrelated, are raised by this: the influence of local or national policy on aspects of school management, the effect of types of management on pupils' interest in learning generally, and the child's own thoughts on the desirability of particular elements in his or her education. It was noticeable that children and parents appeared to enjoy a large measure of consensus on the latter issue, the only obvious exception being the rather autocratic 1930s household of Alison Hartfield.

It is interesting to note that the tendency for several factors to be involved in a decision to home educate is confirmed by the responses to the 1982 Education Otherwise questionnaire, and that the categories into which these factors fell are similar to those detailed earlier, with the exception of the 'religious' families and the group of families home educating as part of a total 'alternative' lifestyle (what that means is not explained, but perhaps it implies self-sufficiency) of whom the members of the Trunkles Top community were the only representatives among my interviewees. It must be noted, though, that the question asked of EO members was 'Reasons for joining EO' rather than 'Reasons for home educating' and that many of the respondents may have been merely sympathetic towards, rather than practising, home education. 173 people replied.

Responses . . . were as follows (most people placing themselves in more than one category):

(a)   Those who approve of or at least go along with the sort of education that schools aim to provide but feel that parents can do as well or better: total 63
(b)   Those who do not approve of the morals and social attitudes implanted by schools: total 129
(c)   Those whose motivation is religious: total 26
(d)   Those who have adopted, or are hoping to adopt, an 'alternative' lifestyle: total 59
(e)   Those who are driven to EO by problems arising in school:
                                                                              total 55

The particular problems specified under (e) included: bullying; a 'bright' child held back; boredom; withdrawal of the child; school refusal; an 'unacademic' child being neglected; child generally unhappy; concern on the part of the parents that the child was not being allowed to develop in a wholesome way; that 'practical' conditions at the school were far from ideal (too few teachers, too little equipment); that the attitudes pervading a particular school or schools in general were in various ways undesirable (competitive, sexist, materialistic, etc.). (Grant, 1983, p. 4)

The Experience of School:
Factors Affecting a Change in Attitude

An interesting starting point for this discussion is the thoughts of those parents who were still or had been teachers in some part of the established system, since they constituted a majority of those interviewed. More than half the families in the study (eleven out of the twenty) contained at least one parent who came into this category, and some, the Heads and Golds, for example, had two. Another study, by Roland Meighan, revealed that: 'at any given time, a quarter of the families in Education Otherwise have a parent who is a qualified teacher' (Meighan, 1984c, p. 273). The fact that they predominated in my study could simply be due to greater articulacy or willingness to talk about their home education programme, but the large number of teachers, compared to other occupations, in the general membership of EO indicates that there may be other factors involved.

Firstly, teachers may feel more confident in the face of a decision to home educate, despite the fact that 'EO is anxious to show parents that teaching qualifications are not necessary for home educating' (Newson, 1984, p. 20). This could imply that among the ranks of unknown home educators qualified teachers might figure even more predominantly, since of all occupations they would be the least likely to feel the need to join a support group such as EO. However, only one parent said that her teaching qualification had given her greater confidence, and that was for a reason unrelated to any feeling she might have had of possessing the appropriate expertise for the job: 'I thought "Well, I am qualified, that's something to combat the authorities." It helps a lot' (Marie Gordon).

A more evident reason for the high number of teachers, both in my study and in EO as a whole, seems to be disillusionment with a system they have experienced from the inside, often for a period of many years, which has changed they way they think about education (originally influenced, presumably, by the philosophies they were exposed to at teacher training college: in this way they differ from some non-teacher parents in that the latter may develop their theories of education directly out of the situations they are presented with through family experience). The EO enquiries secretary has stated: 'a number of enquiries are from teachers who "don't like what they see", some of whom have given it up because . . . "they're fed up with having to compromise".'

The teacher parent's view of the education system is shaped by his or her own area of experience, and this varied considerably among those interviewed from primary to secondary to further and adult education, with two or three representatives at each level.

At the primary level, too much academic pressure and too many expectations of conformity were mentioned by one ex-teacher as the principal causes
of her disillusionment with school for both herself as teacher and her children
as pupils (though she recognizes that her whole attitude to education has
changed alongside her experience of education):

> *Marie Gordon:* It's very hard to say how I felt then, and now, because
> I've changed. I didn't like the regime of school. I didn't like
> competition. I wanted them to have more choice, more time to do
> things when they wanted, how they wanted to and what they wanted
> to. Petty things involved in going to school, things you have to do at
> certain times . . .
>
> *J.W.:* And you found these were things you couldn't do anything
> about in your own teaching?
>
> *Marie:* Yes. I tried.
>
> *J.W.:* This was because of the Head or . . . ?
>
> *Marie:* No, no. Other members of staff. Unless the whole school
> feels like this — and then you need the parents to support, and half
> don't. And the ones who don't tend to be the middle-class pressure
> ones . . . get him onto that reading book, and, you know, putting
> pressures on them. I didn't like that. I find that too hard. I thought
> we could change it but it was so obvious it would take years and
> years I didn't want them to go through it. And the nearer it got to
> him coming from Infants, although it was beginning then, he was
> beginning to feel the pressures, the higher up they go the worse it
> gets. So I thought, 'Well, there's no need for it'.

Among those who were teaching, or had in the past taught, secondary age
children, the elements of dissatisfaction mentioned by those who had been in
the primary sector recurred: emphasis on competition on the one hand and
conformity on the other, the lack of choice in learning, and the arbitrary
distinction between 'work' and 'play' which Marie Gordon mentioned as another of her concerns. Roger Merriman, particularly, had some critical
reflections on his experience of secondary teaching, which had influenced
deeply his attitude to his youngest son's education. He felt that schools at this
level tended to destroy a child's self-esteem, very often through manipulation
of classroom relationships: 'most children, if not all children in secondary
schools, to some extent are put down . . . I would hold that the children do a
lot of the putting down, on behalf of the teachers'.

He also said that many secondary teachers had a poor regard for what
they considered the soft life of a primary pupil, seeing it as their duty to
prepare children for passive reception of the harsh realities of adulthood, as
opposed to the educational philosophy favoured by many home educators

expressing the wish to equip children actively to make adulthood enjoyable and fulfilling.

The destructive effects of increasing pressure to conform in the secondary schools and constant awareness of the penalties for stepping out of line, were some of the major worries mentioned by two FE college teachers, one of whom also worked with truants from the secondary system. She commented:

> They seem frightened always . . . they make, in these conventional schools for boys and girls, so much fear. . . . The fear is partly the regimentation — you know, your shoes aren't right or your jersey isn't right, or you're walking or you're running, or you're not on the left or you're not on the right, or you're late. (Rachel Williams)

> And it gets through to the kids unfortunately, and then they also pick on other ones, you see, just a little bit different. (Jenny Arthur)

Jenny felt that fear of authority dogged these children into the FE college, where many apparently sought sanctuary as soon as they were able:

> We've got so many young people enrolling at our college this year because they refused to go into the Sixth Form. And some of them, even when they're talking to me, and I'm the most unauthoritarian person, I can't get them to call me Jenny.

> *Piers* [Jenny's son]: They call you Sir!

Apart from the destruction of self-esteem and peace of mind resulting from this creation of fear, Rachel Williams expressed the commonly encountered view that it killed interest in learning: 'they'd been so battered and regimented and everything else . . . they'd just lost interest . . . I'm so appalled at what goes on round here in the name of education'.

These views of the system in one area had taken shape partly through their teaching experience and partly through the school experiences of their respective teenagers. Previous awareness of these possible pitfalls in local secondary education probably made the parents more easily able to appreciate the difficulties of the situation their children were in. This may be a common factor among teacher/home educators, and therefore another reason for their disproportionate representation among EO members and in this study.

The Influence of Alternative Education Writers

The non-teacher parents and the children who were interviewed reached some of the same conclusions as the teacher-parents and often went on to read the theoretical writers relevant to their point of view. The lack of choice in learning mentioned by Marie Gordon, for example, and the coercion it implies, were elaborated on by one of the teenagers interviewed. He had very strong views on the subject, coloured by his own experience at school and that of a father who had been sacked from his teaching job because of his refusal to comply with the school's policy of corporal punishment:

> . . . the progress that can be made just by leaving someone alone, just because they do it for its own sake, for the enjoyment, not because the sanction of fear is there, that is the only way to make progress in learning at all and that is what all these educationists and all the system fails to see. It's based on the fact of original sin, as you would say, that they regard the child as inherently lazy, thick, etcetera, etcetera and must be forced, beaten, coerced into learning something. Whereas the exact opposite is the case. (Jim Merriman)

John Holt, a powerful influence on the thinking of this family, set out the effects of coercion in terms of a hidden curriculum:

> He learns to dodge, bluff, fake, cheat. He learns to be lazy. Before he came to school he would work for hours on end, on his own, with no thought of reward, at the business of making sense of the world and gaining competence in it. In school, he learns . . . how not to work when the boss isn't looking, how to know when he is looking, how to make him think you are working when you know he is looking. He learns that in real life you don't do anything unless you are bribed, bullied or conned into doing it, that nothing is worth doing for its own sake, or that if it is, you can't do it in school. (Holt, 1971, p. 25)

The question which this raises of how people are, or can be, motivated to learn is one more properly discussed in detail in the section on how families set about their home education, but for the moment it is important to note that objections to the compulsory aspects of school education and awareness of its possible deadening effect on the will to learn are reflected in the interview data as in the theoretical writing on alternatives to the system of such as Holt, Goodman, Neill and Illich. Although all of these writers based their views on systems either geographically or temporally removed from that in question here, it is clear that their readers among those interviewed found parallels with present circumstances. The Head family describe in the book *Free Way to Learning*, the ways in which Illich and Freire influenced their 'otherwise' thinking (prompted partly by the lack of satisfactory local schools as described by Alison earlier):

> The work of Paolo Freire in adult literacy in Brazil and elsewhere had taken hold of our imagination, with its vision of 'education for liberation'

and its practical effect of raising the consciousness of peasant workers who had lived in the 'culture of silence'. In June 1971 David took the opportunity of attending a European university chaplains' conference at Eveux . . . to hear Freire speak for himself. With broken English but unbreakable assurance, he added to his scornful condemnation of the 'banking' concept of education (storing up information, often with the purpose of reproducing information) a fascinating glimpse of new possibilities of learning. We tried to think through what this might mean for our advanced industrial society.

Four months later, we were challenged by another prophetic voice from the third word: that of Ivan Illich. Speaking to an audience of eight hundred in London, he aroused bewilderment and no little antagonism, as he bombarded schooling with his uncompromising accusations, and gave some concreteness to the idea of a future society without schools. (Head, 1974, p. 123)

The experience of hearing Freire and Illich led the Heads finally to shape for themselves the concept of a 'community of learning'. However, as Dick Kitto points out, the influence of Illich on practisers of education otherwise has been less than that of Holt and (because of his ideas about children's needs rather than how to cater for them educationally) Neill:

It is evident that whatever the intentions of the founders of Education Otherwise, the movement has not become an ardent advocate of Illich and the earlier deschoolers. It derives its ideas much more from John Holt . . . and A.S. Neill . . . (though the writer of 'There are no problem children: only problem parents' and 'Most of my work seems to consist of correcting parental mistakes' would hardly have been a keen supporter of the spread of home education). (Kitto, 1984, p. 113)

The influence of John Holt has undoubtedly been the most pervasive: to judge by a casual reading of the newsletter, almost all home educating families have been inspired by the gentle conviction and extraordinary insight of his writing about children and learning. The specific practical advice on subjects such as how to enable a child to learn multiplication tables or how a single parent could combine work and home education, often given in personal letters to American home educators, was as influential and as valuable an aspect of his work as his public speaking role and his production of the *Growing Without Schooling* newsletter. Many British families heard him speak on his visit to Britain in Spring 1982 and expressed their reactions in the form of tributes to him on his death in 1985. These made it plain that home educators felt that they had lost a supportive friend rather than the charismatic leader of a social movement.

Having acknowledged the profound influence which Holt appears to have had on the modern generation of home educators, as exemplified for instance in the 'Aims' of EO, it remains to say that only a couple of those interviewed mentioned him at all, and these only in passing. In this respect I feel they are untypical of home educators generally, perhaps because their first experience of home education took place in some cases before John Holt had given up hope of reforming the schools and had fully committed himself to the cause of home education.

Another writer who has had a great influence on home educators is Rudolf Steiner, whose three stages of childhood with their emphasis on the spiritual aspect of human nature and the need to postpone academic study until much later than the age at which it is generally tackled, seem to appeal particularly to parents of very young children. Only one of the families interviewed was sympathetic to this rather arbitrary approach or had been at all influenced by it, and it had led her to send her child initially to a Steiner school (this seems often to be a first choice for home educated children who want to try school), but here she found a conflict between the ways in which her son's academic and on the other hand, spiritual and emotional, needs could be catered for:

> The Steiner theory is that until a child is about seven, or at least six, they haven't come down properly from where they were. And when Paul was a baby he was very much back up there. In fact he had homeopathic remedies to try to bring him down ... but the only effect that had was to make him walk in his sleep, and so they stopped it. He was, as a very small child, one of these extraordinarily bright children. He could do very agile mental arithmetic when he was two, he could play chess before he was six, he could read a Bradshaw, an old-fashioned Bradshaw, at five and he was reading quite a while before he was five and without any training ... so he really was a misfit. He used to say that he was afraid that when he woke up in the morning he'd belong to a different family. He could so clearly remember other lives obviously, but he was very frightened when he went to sleep because when he woke up he might not be with his own mother and father. (Lynne Simmons)

In contrast to those influenced by Holt, Illich, Neill and Steiner, one family, the McGills, seemed to feel that there was something to be said for a certain amount of coercion, and they displayed a concern for what they saw as declining academic standards which differed sharply from the majority of families' concern with what might be called 'humanitarian' standards (e.g. of caring, motivation or creativity). This shows clearly how home educating families starting from quite different places philosophically have arrived at the same destination in practice. It was surprising that the original reason for their removal of one child from school, the head teacher's refusal to let him wear the kilt, did not generate thoughts about regimentation or lack of humanity (though these developed later after contact with the LEA). Perhaps this confirms that at least to some extent an interest in, or previous awareness of, the 'alternative' thinkers' objections to school helped to shape people's attitudes to the events they experienced there. Roger Merriman, for example, is quite explicit about this:

> I would say the real reason we had trouble with him and not with the other two was because I was doing an Open University course, and reading Neill's books and I'd never read this stuff before, and once I read that . . . the whole family embraced Neill's ideas, including him. Because it was in the family, when he went to school he went to school with a different attitude to his older brother and sister, pre-Neill.

He seems to be implying that Jim went to school as an outsider from the point of view of his attitude to learning and school's role in it, and that the bullying he received from both teachers and pupils was somehow a result of their perception of his alien status. Whether or not this was the case, the family's awareness of the work of Neill certainly acted as an intellectual catalyst towards finding an alternative when problems did occur.

The Influence of Family Background and Concerns

Another influence on personal philosophy of what school should be like, and attitudes to actual events there, was apparently the parents' own education. Rachel Williams explained that her experience of a rather Quaker-like grammar school, with lots of emphasis on the arts, and lack of regimentation, had led her to want something similar for her artistic daughter.

At the other extreme, Joy Baker explained in her book *Children in Chancery* (Baker, 1964) how a personally traumatic experience of school education had made her determined never to send her own children. She seems not to have considered whether schools might have changed since she was young but in any case many parents reported that it was exceedingly difficult to find out what a school was like before the child was actually there and it was then too late. Corrine Dey changed to what was said to be a 'model' school but, she said, it turned out to be: 'just a harsh sort of place, it wasn't friendly or anything, it was cold'.

Some families had formed their views on the school system today in the light of a knowledge of its origins: 'I'm so hostile to conventional school education and its historical background, why it came into being and this social thing about it, you know, and how inappropriate it is nowadays' (Lynne Simmons). This view of things is extended into the contemporary political arena by the Merrimans: 'in this country the people in power have a vested interest in keeping the system as it is. They want people without any minds to pull the levers in their factories. . . . They don't want people to think for themselves'.

These last two quotes are interesting also for the emotion with which they were expressed, indicating how strongly held the family's philosophy had become and, perhaps, how traumatic the events which contributed to its formation had been. Other families, particularly the McGills, Williamses and Arthurs, were equally vehement in their condemnation of a system which apparently they had once accepted as a more or less tolerable status quo.

Some people had specific objections to the content of the school curriculum as it reflected attitudes in society they wanted to see changed. Frequently mentioned was sexism in the choice of subjects allowed: ' . . . the boys do metalwork, the girls do sewing and cookery. They weren't both allowed to do both things. The boys went swimming more than the girls did so that was unfair, because I like swimming' (Caroline Parker).

One mother was concerned that a school environment was not sufficiently challenging or interesting for the younger brother of her deschooled teenagers:

> I think the thing that worries me is if he gets stimulated enough, because he obviously now loves learning and you can see at this age. He enjoys the learning parts of living and it would be such a shame for that to be pressed down. (Margaret Gold)

Another mother felt that the school system took upon itself the role of removing children prematurely from the family home:

> There seems to be a conspiracy to take children out of their families — and then they're surprised that the parents haven't got any influence over them! With all their time and all their leisure increasingly carried out outside the family, how do they expect parents to keep control over them? (Amy Dey)

This aspect of moral influence was one of the main reasons for choosing an alternative mentioned by a classical musician who wrote to me about her son's education at home:

> . . . one of the great advantages of working at home is the influence one can quietly exert to counter the shocking anti-Christian, anti-culture, anti-home, anti-discipline attitude which has crept in, not only to our schools but to society as a whole. Unlike most other boys

of his age, Jeremy is growing up aware of and proud of his Christian/ European cultural heritage. (Ruth Petersen)

Finally, an antidote to these idealistic considerations from a parent who has a strong practical commitment to home-based education and plays a very active part in the Education Otherwise organization:

> *J.W.:* You, unlike a lot of other people I've spoken to, haven't said anything about the philosophy of home education . . .
>
> *Mary Parsons:* Well, I blow a raspberry at that. It gets on my nerves. . . . People go on about freedom and so on in the newsletter, I think they know damn all about it, I certainly know damn all about it. I don't think they do. I think it's a lot of talk.

Conflict between Home and School Values

The discussion so far has related to families who had ideals of education, derived from a reading of relevant literature and/or from school experience, which were at variance with some aspects of day-to-day life in their local schools.

Even if parents did not have a philosophy directly related to education which made available schooling unacceptable, they often had a family lifestyle which presented the children with a conflict of values between those of the school and those of the home (hinted at in Roger Merriman's point about Neill, and in the comments on moral influence). This often contributed to many of the difficulties they experienced in fitting into a very alien way of life, and could best be described in the case of most of those interviewed as a conflict between humanistic, democratic, open values at home and, as we have already seen, a frequently authoritarian, regimented and rather dehumanized atmosphere at school. Conflict of this sort is identified elsewhere in the literature on the sociology of education (Woods, 1977) suggesting that children other than those with parents willing and able to opt for home education may be susceptible to it. Wood's perspective is, however, at variance with some of those interviewed, in that he sees society's values as changing faster than those of the school, which ought to be trying to adjust to this change, whereas some families have felt that school mirrors modern society and that the values of both are undesirable influences on children.

One of the manifestations of this conflict is the classification of pupils who don't fit in with the school way of doing things as 'maladjusted', with all the pejorative connotations such a label carries. The possibility that the school is being too rigid in its expectations of the individual was not entertained by the head of the school attended by one of those interviewed:

... that sort of authoritarian school atmosphere was quite OK for some kids, but it was totally inappropriate for Piers, and then they threw at me: in that case he must be maladjusted. You know, like if he can't conform to our system there is something the matter with him. (Jenny Arthur)

One family's local GP expressed a different view of this conflict:

And the doctor said, 'I always think, when you get a child that really hates school', and I was quite prepared, I thought he was going to say it must be something the parents are doing, he said, 'there's something wrong with the school'. And I was quite taken aback. (Pat Maxwell)

Other families were conscious of conflicts similar to that experienced by the Arthurs:

J.W.: What do you attribute this difficulty with being able to fit in to? Is it that the schools generally hold different values from you as a family, or what do you think creates that difficulty?
Malcolm Gold: Certainly different values, different ways of behaviour.
Margaret Gold: The big thing for us is, we've always said to them, we've stressed the importance of not saying 'You do this because I tell you to do it. Because I am — you will do it.' We've always spent time talking it out with them, giving reasons, and we've always moaned at impoliteness, more or less 'We're polite to you, you should be polite to us.' They get teachers who say this, which is quite common, and teachers obviously 'You'll do this because I say so.' They just couldn't cope with that.

These conflicts were sometimes related directly to the family's theoretical thinking on education as discussed above:

... the values and attitudes of the school about homework and passing your exams, I think this probably caused our children some problems in a number of ways. There was conflict between the attitudes at home and the conventional attitudes at school. (Brian Budd)

In the case of the families living at Trunkles Top, the consensus values of their community, many of whose members were ex-teachers dedicated to exploring various facets of the 'alternative society', were clearly at odds with a philosophy which encouraged loss of independence and initiative.

Some families had gone to great lengths, short of removal from school altogether, to try to reduce the areas of conflict for their children, for example, by withdrawing them for RE lessons or even by changing schools in the hope of finding a more sympathetic atmosphere. The lack of suitable and congenial schools seems to have played a part in promoting conflicts of values and subsequent unhappiness, since some children recalled rather wistfully one particular school which they liked but which they had had to leave due to age or moving house. Three of the children had changed schools more often than is usual: this could in itself have been a factor contributing to inability to settle at the school from which they were eventually withdrawn.

Specific Difficulties

Bullying

Apart from difficulties due to objections of one kind or another to the theory of school education, or its working out in practice, and other sorts of conflict between family values and those of the school, individual children interviewed had often experienced specific personal unhappiness or plain practical problems relating to school attendance which could be traced to various sources, by far the commonest being bullying, by both teachers and pupils. Perhaps the authoritarian ethos of the schools concerned promoted an atmosphere in which bullying thrived, explaining why the children having the home-school conflict already described tended also to be those who suffered from bullying, coming from families with 'outsider' status, as discussed in the case of Jim Merriman, by virtue of their different lifestyle or educational philosophy.

There were, however, cases where a child from a perfectly conventional family, committed to making school work (and with other children who continued to attend school even when their sibling was out) was victimized for some other reason. Martin Maxwell's mother described how the fact that Martin was 'different' (he was very shy and rather slow to learn certain things due to cross-dominance) had led to him being appallingly treated by a junior school teacher:

> . . . there was a specific teacher who was very, very bad . . . I didn't find out at the time what was going on, he didn't tell me, but apparently he did eventually go to the headmaster and she was pulling hair, smacking kids' faces, pushing them off their seat; partly Martin and also this little West Indian boy, who also had problems, he had a very strict family and a stutter. And when she took over his stutter came back. She picked on two kids that had already got problems obviously, she was that sort of teacher. (Pat Maxwell)

Mrs. Maxwell was one of several parents who felt that certain teachers always bullied the sensitive pupils.

There were many among those interviewed who had suffered from this kind of teacher bullying at some stage in their educational careers and Jim

Merriman was quick to point out what a devastating effect it could have on the will and ability to learn. Though he could not absorb the mathematics he was taught at school because of the state of fear the teacher kept him in, once away from this source of tension he discovered what must really be called a vocation for the subject, though his tendency to rely heavily on textbooks, even when at college, showed how unwilling he was to entrust his learning to a teacher again.

Jim being, as he put it, 'smaller and brighter' than the rest of the class, also had to contend with bullying from the other children, as did Corinne Dey: 'they were awful. I think me and my sister were the only coloured children in the whole school and we were really badly picked on for this', while Phil Minchin said of his little sister: ' . . . she'd had a complete mental breakdown. The boys used to break milk bottles and chase her around with cut glass'. The disillusionment with school which this experience triggered off for the Minchin parents resulted in all four children being educated at home, a vivid example of the way, already discussed, in which specific events alter an entire family's attitude to a system previously taken for granted.

Another set of parents, the Budds, pointed to the way in which bullying early on at school could destroy a sense of security and happiness there which even a change of school might not restore:

> She had the most unfortunate experience there which I think actually relates to everything that subsequently happened . . . it was really quite appalling . . . she was being picked on as a middle-class kid in a working-class school, she wasn't being allowed to do things because she was a middle-class kid and we didn't know until this friend told us, so we went to see the head and he really couldn't deny it. Oh, and she ran away once or twice, jumped the gate and disappeared but didn't come home.

The desperation which led her to do this at the age of seven set up a pattern of truanting and inability to settle at school which continued to affect her learning until her parents began to educate her at home when she was fourteen.

Organization and Regimentation

There were other aspects of school life, mainly related to organization of classes and curriculum or to regimentation, for instance in dress, which put difficulties in the paths of individual school careers irrespective of parents' educational philosophy. Class separation from friends was a factor in two cases:

> . . . it so happened that all of Emma's close friends were all doing
> sciences so that separated her out from the sciences, and it also meant
> that in her form there were none of her close friends, not her best
> friend, none, nothing, although that could have been arranged. (Rachel
> Williams)

It seems surprising that the total separation from school friends during school
hours which home education implies should have appeared to be the answer
but the explanation probably lies in the fact that it was the best solution to the
other difficulties the children were encountering at school.

Lack of appropriateness or interest in the curriculum was a problem for
Dickie Tansley: 'some of the lessons were quite enjoyable, like woodwork,
practical lessons; I enjoyed art; but I didn't like sitting down in front of a
blackboard writing. It bored me to death. So I started not going in'.

Discrimination in the curriculum which prevented children from studying the subjects they were interested in (as Caroline Parker described in the
section on philosophical reasons for home education (p. 43)) was a practical
problem for three of the children interviewed. That this was a matter of policy
at the time in certain areas and therefore not susceptible to change to suit the
individual is revealed by the following comments in the year of the interviews
from the Chairman of Devon Education Committee. He is talking about a
suggestion that girls should do woodwork and boys home economics: 'we don't
want our sons growing up as fairies and our daughters turning into butch
young maids' (quoted in *EO Newsletter*, 21, 1982).

The sheer size, and constant moving about, to cope with in some secondary schools was another policy-type factor mentioned as contributing to
children's unhappiness:

> It's a big school and confusing and walking round all the corridors I
> think she just got fed up with the whole thing . . . instead of getting
> used to a teacher, she had forty minute, eighty minute lessons and
> switching classrooms. (Malcolm Gold)

The wasting of time by both other pupils and the teachers was also mentioned
as lowering morale and interest in learning in those who had initially been well
motivated:

> The master, one thing they used to get fed up about, if the masters
> came in late, they never, ever, apologized, and it would be a waste of
> a forty minute lesson, they'd come in ten minutes late, they'd have a
> thirty minute lesson. In the meantime, because Piers had been put in
> the lowest stream, all the rest of the kids were messing around. (Jenny
> Arthur)

The wearing of uniform is another aspect of school organization about which there is frequent controversy between children who want to express their personality and parents and teachers who have to spend time enforcing the school regulations. The *Little Red School Book* sums up part of the pupil's side of the argument while exposing the weaknesses in the school's stated reasons for having a uniform:

> Headmasters and other teachers who support the wearing of school uniforms claim that they help to disguise differences in parental income and encourage a sense of belonging to the school. But in almost any school it will be obvious whose parents haven't been able to afford a spare uniform or regular drycleaning bills. For parents with very little money, buying a uniform (often from a rather expensive shop which is the only one that has the uniforms) can mean not buying some other clothes. They can get a grant from the LEA — if they can 'prove' that they're poor — but this has to be spent on the school uniform, not on other clothes which might be both cheaper and more hard-wearing.
>
> As for making pupils feel they 'belong' to the school, there are surely more subtle and less superficial ways of doing this than making everyone wear a uniform. In any case, schools should be trying to make themselves more a part of the community they are meant to serve, not less. (Hansen and Jensen, 1971, p. 176)

However, this does not get to what some consider the heart of the matter, the 'hidden' reasons for schools insisting on pupils wearing a uniform: the way in which control over conformity and uniformity in all aspects of school life, the fixing of the pupil in the desired role, is expressed through control over what in normal life is a potent means of asserting individuality. The in-between system of 'anything you like so long as it's grey' negates the expressed wish to disguise poverty, since chain stores compete every year with the latest fashions in school uniform colours. The fact that teachers do not wear uniforms goes some way towards dispelling the argument that it promotes a feeling of identity and corporateness: in the Woodcraft Folk movement, for example, adult leaders and children alike wear the same green shirt as a symbol of unity.

The lengths to which headteachers will go to protect their regulations are exemplified by the experience of Ian McGill who, after happily wearing the kilt from toddlerhood right through to secondary stage, and despite being equipped with the important bits of uniform connected with identity, was refused admission to his new school unless he wore trousers: 'he never did wear anything else and that was it. It was just impressed within him, instinct sort of thing. And this man jumped on him, and he was going to stop him, see' (Andrew McGill).

The unbending attitude of the school authorities in this case reminded me of a similar situation regarding Sikhs' turbans, though in a private school (*The Guardian*, 1983), and illustrates how a desire for uniformity can become an obsession leaving no room for tolerance of cultural characteristics which could make no practical difference to the running of the school (even if the school's attitude prevented it from considering variety the spice of life). The Sikhs' appeal was accepted in the Lords on the grounds that Sikhs were primarily an ethnic, rather than religious, group, and therefore covered by the Race Relations Act of 1976. Had Andrew McGill chosen to use his knowledge of Scottish history to press the point, he might possibly have shown that the headmaster's action was illegal discrimination. A puzzling irony in this situation is that this particular LEA had taken a strong line with other heads on the matter of uniform:

> The authority sent out a circular saying that no child should be debarred from participating in school activities because its parents were unable to provide uniform. In February 1976 the *TES* reported that — shire education department overruled a headteacher who twice sent home fifteen-year-old twin girls because they wore trousers in school during cold weather. (Stone and Taylor, 1976, pp. 232–3)

A final note on the question of uniform from the home educated boy quoted in *The School That I'd Like*, who mentions freedom from it as a benefit of home education: 'we dress in comfortable, sensible clothes and do not have to wear some ridiculous uniform' (Blishen, 1969, p. 38).

Special Needs

Children with learning difficulties, including children likely to be statemented under the 1981 Act, are a large enough group among EO members to have warranted a newsletter devoted to their interests. Since, in general, discussion of these problems and their solution is technically rather involved I shall concentrate on describing the difficulties of just one child for whom the answer had to be home education. Daniel Scheaffer was born hypothermic and continued so throughout childhood. The implications of this as regards school attendance were explained by his mother:

> If you go to school you then fill his life with 'You can't sit by the window, you can't play games, you mustn't go into the cloakroom, it's too cold, you can't change classrooms, you mustn't sit in that desk' and his whole life is 'not'. . . . 'What are you going to do while they play football, you can't do that' and it goes on and on and on 'The paper's too cold, you can't put your hands on the paper.' (Penelope Scheaffer)

She emphasized that he could have a far more positive life at home than if he were at school; rather a different situation from that of children with a learning disability such as dyslexia whose practical needs do not exclude the possibility of school so firmly. Hypothermia appears to have been complicated by infant autism (hard to imagine now when chatting to a confident, outgoing and articulate teenager) which resulted in late talking, clumsiness and social with-drawal, though not slowness in learning: it was evident from Daniel's attempts at participation in his older siblings' activities that he was of at least average intelligence.

The need for flexibility due to the emotional problems of autism and the sleepiness in winter cause by hypothermia, combined with the need constantly to control his exposure to changes in temperature, made home education virtually inevitable in Daniel's case, though his parents were not at all prepared for it or in favour of it from an ideological point of view, and both his brother and his sister had been right through the private school system.

In smaller ways, other children found their needs inadequately catered for at school, though, except in the case of Martin Maxwell's cross-dominance, this was either because school subjects failed to coincide with their interests or because the level of work was inappropriate (pitched too high or too low) resulting in the children expressing boredom in both cases:

> *Glenn Banks:* . . . I was never particularly keen on the lessons.
> *J.W.:* Why was that?
> *Glenn:* Well, I think they seemed rather dull and boring. I could
> have got on better on my own.

There were two specific cases where children received early discouragement, instead of help, in the 'basics' because of learning difficulties in these areas (one in reading, one in mathematics):

> Because I'm no good at maths they said I was useless and they just
> packed me in on maths at Birchester. I fell right back, so I had to
> virtually go back to the beginning. I've pulled up now and I'm fairly
> good. (Phil Minchin)

One wonders whether Phil would have got the mathematics O level he later obtained had he completed his education in school: this reflection suggests that in some cases the teacher's inability, due perhaps to class size, to estimate a child's potential correctly is the cause of the child coming to underestimate himself and lose self-esteem and self-confidence in learning.

In some families the perceived shortcomings of school education were being compensated for by parents at home long before the question of leaving became imperative:

He didn't learn to read at school. I taught him. . . . Somebody gave me the Peter and Jane books, just as I was discovering that he seemed to be floundering when he was about seven. And we went right through from 1a to 12a in about six months, but I had to teach him phonetically, he couldn't do look-and-say, that's basically the problem. He couldn't learn the alphabet on his own. I had to actually set to and teach him the alphabet. . . . The days of the week I had to actually teach him and the names of the months, all that sort of thing he couldn't learn, not in the ordinary school situation. (Pat Maxwell)

In the majority of cases, then, it appears that several factors were operating in the decision to educate at home, of which the inappropriateness of what was being taught or how it was being taught was just one.

'The Open Road'

Like the severe medical problems of Daniel, discussed earlier, an itinerant lifestyle presents a practical bar to regular school attendance, as people involved with gypsy and circus families' education have long recognized. Like illness, it forces the issue for the authorities of recognizing as legitimate locations of learning other than the school.

People sent to work abroad for a period often opt for education in the local British school, but if this is not available or does not appeal for any of the reasons already discussed, home-based education may be an attractive option. The courses run by the World-Wide Education Service (WES) are tailor-made for this situation, from which they find 90 per cent of their customers (five or six hundred families in 1983). Others manage to intersperse trips with longish periods at school, reckoning that the educational value of travel more than makes up for lost time:

When we got back from Baltistan Hannah, aged six and a half, went to the local primary school for three years, then when she was nine and a half she was off for a year in Mexico and Peru (camping and riding, no teaching). Then back at ten and a half to primary school and a year later off to secondary school where she is eighteen months younger than the average form age and gets honours in all subjects which at least proves that it doesn't matter missing years at primary school. Personally I have no great faith in formal education, but one can't — I feel — opt out completely on behalf of a small child; so really I've compromised by taking her off whenever it suited me but when at home she's had conventional schooling. (Cathy Brannigan)

The potential for learning from the environment while travelling, implied by Cathy Brannigan and emphasized in the WES courses, was one of the features which drew the members of 'The State' touring theatre company towards home education as a solution to the problem which forms the title of the book describing their experiences: *What Shall We Do With the Children?* (Kiddle, 1981). Its author, Catherine Kiddle, emphasizes that the environment, like that of gypsy families, need not be exotic for life in it to be educationally worthwhile and for families to take from it for education purposes whatever suits their aims for their children. This feature combined with some of those already discussed, particularly the changing educational philosophy of disillusioned teachers which focused itself on the ways in which children could acquire the basic skills necessary in society and develop creativity and imagination through participation in the everyday life of the company, as they had been doing before the age of compulsory education.

All these aspects, consciously considered by members of 'The State', can be seen to apply to the situation of travellers in general. Catherine Kiddle's experience of teaching gypsy children enabled her to draw comparisons between the two types of education, whose main similarity lay in the inability of families to take advantage of one-school formal state education. She points to the self-reliance which this necessarily engenders in each case, and the way in which it has become a tradition among gypsies, as it may become in time among other home-based educators:

> The traveller's child's family must itself provide for the children. This is a heavy responsibility, but the parents themselves have been brought up to understand and accept it. They are not qualified to have these responsibilities except as parents and people already experienced in the kind of life that their children will have to lead in their turn. In this they are the same as any of us. How they respond to their circumstances has been part of their education and could be an education to all of us. (Kiddle, 1981, p. 82)

The differences between Traveller education (including that of hippy groups such as the Peace Convoy) and the education provided by 'The State' lie in two directions: the concern to have their system officially sanctioned; and the greater amount of formality and structure involved, particularly in the areas of literacy and numeracy.

The conclusion of this chapter must be that, unlike many ideologically committed home educators today, those I interviewed had generally been forced to look for an alternative by the inflexibility or other unsuitability of available schools, in particular, usually, the one their child attended. This was so even where the parents had a predisposition to consider alternative education by reason of their personal background.

The large number of parents who were qualified teachers (over half) provided insights into the extent to which other home educators' concerns about schooling were indicative of a general situation: unnecessary regimentation, bullying and inappropriate academic pressure were chief among these.

Chapter 5

Making the Break

This chapter examines factors affecting a decision to home educate, and discusses the process of making the decision in the context of the lack of public awareness of, and support for, the right to home educate. The chapter ends with some observations on the transition between school- and home-based education.

Alternatives

Many of those interviewed came to home-based education as a last resort. Their decision was not based on wholehearted belief in a positive alternative: for most, the option to home educate became a possibility worth considering only because other alternatives, on examination, seemed in one way or another unsatisfactory:

> I'd enjoyed my own school, and we did our very, very best to make the Grammar School work because she wanted to make it work; she didn't want to go anywhere else. And my idea would have been rather to send her to boarding school, that would have been one of the Quaker ones like I'd been to. We wondered about the Rudolf Steiner and things like that, but none round here. So I'm not a typical person, I was driven to education otherwise. I had no high-falutin' ideas at the beginning. (Rachel Williams)

Alternative types of education considered by the families interviewed were in the main either other schools within the state system (apart from Paul Simmons, who went to a Steiner school, all those interviewed had been at state schools prior to leaving) or independent progressives of some sort, such as Dartington. The Williamses tried first to make suitable changes at the school Emma already attended, but the school, though keen to retain her as a pupil, was inflexible: 'they would have liked her to go to school but they wouldn't have part-time school, only full-time, you see. The only thing I could have got her back to was part-time'. They also tried a counselling course with an independent psychologist to try to help Emma make the best of things at school, but this was not a success either.

Other state schools appear not to have been looked at with a great deal of enthusiasm by those who did consider them, presumably because of the insights into the system their previous experience had given them. They seem to have been visited almost as a formality (perhaps just for the sake of being able to tell the LEA they had looked at them) where families got as far as visiting them at all. In some cases there was total disillusionment with school per se:

> *J.W.:* What alternatives did you consider apart from EO?
> *Dickie Tansley:* Thought of changing schools.
> *J.W.:* What, to another sort of school? Or one of the same type?
> *Dickie:* No, another style.
> *J.W.:* Did you look at any others?
> *Dickie:* No, we didn't get round to that.
> *J.W.:* What, because you came across EO before that?
> *Dickie:* I was more interested in getting out altogether.

In some case places at other state schools were actually volunteered by the LEA (see Chapter 10 on relationships with the LEA):

> He did have an alternative in Manchester which was to go to a school for disruptive kids but most of them had been, most of the kids who went to that school, were kicked out for things like stealing, violence, you can imagine. (Malcolm Gold)

In no case was the proffered place taken up except in that of the McGills, who sent Ian to a middle school where all went well, and then on to a secondary school where they encountered the original problem with the kilt. It appears that complying with the authority's wishes regarding a child's education does not necessarily guarantee cooperation on their side in ensuring that changes will be made smoothly.

Several families considered schools in the private sector, mostly those with a reputation for the importance they attach to humane values, for example, Steiner and Quaker schools. Kilquhanity in Scotland and Dartington in Devon were two other schools, both within the progressive tradition, mentioned as possibilities by families interviewed. The reasons why these were finally rejected as inappropriate were various, mainly financial and/or related to the necessity for boarding:

We went and visited a few of the Quaker boarding schools, but there was nowhere local, there wasn't a local Quaker school. We would have been awful hard up actually, but we did, yes. There was one in Yorkshire. . . . But at the time Pip had been so cheesed off with being pushed together with all these boys, he'd had awful nightmares. And I think that the thought then of being all day and all night as well; it was too late. (Jenny Arthur)

On the question of finance for alternatives to state education, the one single parent interviewed said that the Assisted Places scheme would have been valuable, had it existed at the appropriate time, in providing her son with the very academically orientated education she felt he needed. Another child was prevented from attending the progressive school her mother and sister had been to by lack of necessary finance at a time when it might have solved her school problems:

We found the way to send her sister to Dartington and Gerry very much wanted to go too, and it would have been if we could have afforded it — I mean, we really couldn't afford it for her sister. The fees were terrific and all the other things that go with it. So Gerry had this terrific desire to go to Dartington and I think in the end they were almost suggesting we got her there quick, she wasn't going to last out at Lord Tom's in their opinion. . . . I thought, well, really it was very unfair in a way to do this to Gerry, and in a way she might have got much more out of Dartington. (Veronica Budd)

Home education, it is worth noting, is really the only practical alternative education for families who can't afford independent school fees unless they're lucky enough to receive scholarships, or reduced-fee places at Steiner schools. The only exceptions to this observation are the very few Free Schools, the best known of which, Kirkdale, is in London and therefore inaccessible to anyone not living in the capital.

The Campaign for Human Scale Education (which replaced the Campaign for State-Supported Alternative Schools) and the Leicester collective Lib Ed are both active in trying to create support for alternatives within the state system: in the first case through lobbying for local authority money for small parent-run schools on the Danish model; and in the second case largely through trying to bring about changes in the way existing schools, particularly at the secondary level, are run, to incorporate greater pupil participation in school management and choice of their own curriculum. In both cases, the aim is to give consumers greater control over more aspects of their school careers. Neither organization appears to have achieved much popular support: this is particularly obvious in comparison with the higher profile of Education

Otherwise. As Marie Gordon said, to change the schools would take too long: parents are concerned with the here and now of their own children's education.

How Families Discovered Home Education as a Legal and Practical Option

In talking to a random social and occupational collection of friends, family and acquaintances about my research or my son's education, I became aware that there is very widespread public ignorance about the legality of educating otherwise. This observation is confirmed by Roland Meighan's comments on the EO questionnaire returns:

> The questionnaire returns of the members demonstrate the existence of a . . . myth — that schooling is compulsory. This illusion was encountered by members first in the case of friends and relatives, and then by a whole range of misinformed full-time educationalists ranging from education welfare officers, headteachers, schoolteachers, school inspectors to chief education officers. (Meighan, 1984c, p. 273)

In reply to my question: 'I'm interested in people who are being taught by their parents at home, rather than by the home tuition service. Do you come across people in that category?', a careers officer for one of the new towns answered: 'We come across people in the category that they're not being taught primarily by the local authority. Technically they should be, by law; parents aren't supposed to teach, by law'.

He was willing to withdraw this statement when I gently attempted to put him right, but the exchange provides a specific illustration of the general situation reported above, one in which it can be convenient for the authority's officers to remain in ignorance of the law until faced with a family who know their rights and are determined to claim them. (This is not universally the case — there are some authorities, and some officers, who are fully informed about education otherwise than at school and may even recommend it when they feel it is appropriate, to be discussed in Chapter 10.)

Since there is such general ignorance about the provisions of Section 36, how did those who were interviewed come to realize that school was not compulsory? For the majority, the media in one form or another had brought both the legality and the practicality of home education to the family's attention at a time when it was at least receptive to the possibility of alternatives, if not actively looking for them. In some cases the idea lay dormant for some years before being investigated when the need arose. Many had seen an *Open Door* television programme, made by some of the original members of EO (and which generated 1000 enquiries and eighty new members). The McGills saw the television film *The Harrisons Don't Go to School* and rang the Harrisons for further information. Two people had been influenced by newspaper articles, one in *The Guardian* and one in *The Daily Telegraph* (an interesting example of the way in which home education may appeal to people of very different political persuasions).

Media programmes and articles generally focus on the lives of two or three families to explain what home education is about, since Britain has no spokesperson with the high profile of a John Holt, who used to publicize the concept of home education in the USA and elsewhere through personal appearances. The media apparently find home education an attractive subject to feature on several counts: it is unconventional, controversial ('What about their social life? How will they get on when they have to settle down to the routine of a nine-to-five job? Will they be able to get a job at all?'), often has elements of the romantic, back-to-nature lifestyle associated with it, and recently has been linked to the more or less acknowledged disasters in the state education system. From EO's point of view, it is an ideal way to reach people who might like, or need, to know about their rights concerning education at home. Some of those interviewed, grateful for the way in which media publicity helped them solve their educational problems at a crucial time, have in turn agreed to be interviewed by the press and television, or have spoken at public meetings.

Personal contact was the route by which one of those interviewed, Rachel Williams, became familiar with the idea. She had a friend (Jenny Arthur) who had a son out of school. The Gold family encountered home education through a brush with alternative educational theory: they heard Ivan Illich speak in Manchester. Jenny Arthur discovered her right, or, as she saw it, duty, to home educate, through reading the 1944 Education Act. Her interpretation of it was that since Piers, in his grammar school, was not being educated 'according to age, ability and aptitude' it was her responsibility to see that he was suitably educated 'otherwise'. This is a view which might surprise a majority of the general public, media, political opposition and so on, who take it for granted that it is the LEA's statutory duty to see that their school provision is 'suitable to age, ability and aptitude' in each case.

In two families, the suggestion that home education was both a legal and a practical option had developed partly from the rather erratic schooling of the mothers involved. Both had had lengthy periods out of school due to illness, and were aware that their education had not suffered:

> I had a lot of time away from school myself . . . and I think probably
> my attitude towards somebody who was to be educated at home was
> possibly broader. I wasn't in the least bit disturbed by the idea or

wasn't put off. I didn't care if other people thought it was odd or peculiar or whatever, and I knew that when I had come through the in the end rather small amount of school that I had, because I didn't go to school, two years was the longest time, I did actually come out with the school certificate and whatever at the end of it. (Penelope Scheaffer)

Clearly, an unconventional personal education makes the acceptance of alternatives such as home-based education easier for parents in the way that particular experience of school education influenced parents' expectations of children's schooling, as discussed in Chapter 1. This has implications for future generations; in fact, Jim Merriman said, 'I can't see any Education Otherwise person who had been at home sending their children to school if they really understand what it did for them'.

Another way in which home-based education might come to the notice of those who could benefit from it was suggested by two discussions with interested professionals, one a county primary school headmistress, Jean Mortimer, and one an LEA psychologist, both of whom said they might recommend home education if they felt it appropriate to the situation. This could be, in the psychologist's words:

> . . . when parent and child are quite convinced that unhappiness caused is a result of conflict between value systems and interest of the child against those the school, and that the school isn't going to shift, there are no suitable alternative schools, and the parents show a positive interest in the idea.

He also offered them continuing support in the form of return visits, which could be important in enabling them to make the decision, since they would feel they had an ally in the Establishment.

Jean Mortimer gave a similar emphasis to conflicts between home and school leading to circumstances in which she might recommend home-based education:

> If you meet with a very inflexible system where there's not going to be any give for the individual at all: 'unless you go through that particular gate you're out', it is really like grading peas in fact, then I think the answer is take them out.

These two were also interesting in that both were representatives of a local authority noted for its conservatism towards unconventional ideas in education, showing, as Chapter 10 will discuss in more detail, how greatly individual personalities affect the way in which the LEA's policies, if any, are put into action.

A comparison with the EO questionnaire returns shows that the large number of families finding out about home-based education through the media is reflected in the wider membership — this was how the majority of respondents had first encountered EO. More of them, proportionately, had found out about it through friends or other members than had those in my sample, probably because home educators were much thinner on the ground in the days when most of the families I talked to were thinking about alternatives (mid-late 1970s, as opposed to 1982). Support for them from EO members came at a later stage, when the idea was being investigated, and was often a great help to families in finally making the decision to home educate.

How the Decision to Home Educate was Made

The first point to be made is that a decision of this kind can be quite traumatic for a family that likes to conform to society's expectations, for example, the Maxwells: 'We're actually quite a conventional family and to take a child out of school was something that took an awful lot of thinking about' (Pat Maxwell). Its unorthodox nature makes the family vulnerable to crises of confidence of several kinds, for example, fear of relatives' disapproval or despair at the responsibility and commitment involved.

There were several other considerations mentioned by families as playing a part in the process of making a decision. One was a lack of confidence in their ability to home educate either to their own standards or, more frequently, to those of the LEA, about which they had little or no knowledge at this stage. One mother writes in *EO Newsletter* 23 about 'our personal misgivings of being able to cope and meet LEA requirements . . . in short, being good enough to do the job well'. Marie Gordon, herself an ex-teacher, recommends families not to attempt it unless they are confident:

J.W.: Would you advocate it for everyone?
Marie: Only if you're confident. If you're under pressure I'd say it's a nightmare.
J.W.: What, pressure from the authorities?
Marie: Any pressure at all, because you'd make the children feel that way too. I started under a bit but I think you can feel it the other way, perhaps those who give up, they start and then they lose confidence but I think it's entirely a thing of different personalities. It probably is something most people could do, it's lack of confidence.

Since few of those interviewed started out confident (except perhaps Mr. Hartfield and Sally Banks) this is obviously a counsel of perfection: the growth of confidence and the discovery of unsuspected abilities and interests were great spin-offs for many of the families. Another difficulty in making a decision to home educate occurs where only one of the parents sees it as an appropriate solution to the child's dilemma in school. Many couples have emphasized in the *EO Newsletter* that home education can only be a happy experience for the family if both parents are equally behind it, because of the support needed and the conflict generated by disagreement over such an important feature of family life. In the case of the Budds, there was a difference of views, but this was eventually resolved because it appeared there was no other course open to them:

> *Veronica:* We did it because it was expedient. I was more unhappy about doing it than Brian, much more unhappy.
> *J.W.:* Why was that?
> *Veronica:* Because I think that school is so important for the social contact that it provides and having a lot of peers of the same age . . .
> *Brian:* I think there is an underlying problem in that I have a kind of scepticism about the attitude to education in schools. I, in fact, in a sense fortunately, missed out on being educated, I was a choirboy, we only had schooling four hours a day, but had a very good general education.

(Here is another parent whose own unconventional education made him more open to alternatives and so perhaps less worried about the decision he found himself making — though Veronica Budd, who went to Dartington herself, appears to have a comparatively orthodox view of the school system.)

The question of parents being jointly committed to home education even if, as in most families interviewed, the mother was most involved in the day-to-day practice of it, made me wonder whether a decision to home educate is generally harder to make for a single parent, as might be expected because of considerations of lack of emotional support (though, on the other hand, the potential for conflict may also be absent). Surprisingly, this does not seem to be the case:

> *J.W.:* How have you found it, being on your own . . . ? Did you find the responsibility for making the decision very difficult or — or just the same as all the other decisions you made?
> *Sally Banks:* I think initially I felt it was what I wanted to do, I did wonder, not whether I *could* do it but whether I *should* do it, but then when it got to such a state his health was really being affected, I did. And when I'd made up my mind to do it, well, that was it, you know, I just got into it, but I never regretted it.

This positive thinking is echoed by several of the contributors to the EO one-parent families' supplement (April, 1986). It appears that a more important factor in the decision than that of emotional support is that of finance, or rather lack of it, as this writer to *EO Newsletter* 46 comments: 'I think most of us are terrified of the almost inevitable financial insecurity'.

Another worry that parents had, influenced perhaps by adverse media publicity of the Joy Baker variety, was the possible threat of their children ending up in care. Two mothers, Pat Maxwell and Amy Dey, mentioned this as a serious consideration, a reflection perhaps of their lack of knowledge at that stage of their rights under the 1944 Act.

In the Deys' case, the worry seems to have originated in the comments of an LEA adviser:

> I got terribly wary about him. He made oblique references to children being 'taken away', that sort of thing. I then got quite worried about it and I knew some people who, one of them said, 'Oh yes, I knew a woman in Essex, her child got taken into care' and so I went down to the Community Relations office in Becksham, as I knew a chap who worked there, and explained it all to him, and he said 'Oh well, we'll fight for you, if it comes to that'. (Amy Dey)

This introduces the subject of the part played by EO and similar groups, such as that referred to by Amy, in giving families enough information and support, where they feel the need for it, to enable them to make the decision to home educate. As a writer to *EO Newsletter* 23 put it:

> In the end I suspect that the most important decisions in life are made more from personal inclination than from a rational weighing up of the arguments: all I need is a few enthusiastic people to tell me it's the best thing they ever did, and I'll do it too.

Contact with other members was also sought for reasons other than the reassurance this writer wanted that the approach could be successful. It was sought as a means of reinforcing families' awareness of their rights, and as a means of finding out what they could expect from the LEA (local EO contacts were particularly valuable here) and how to deal with it. There is a detailed discussion of the families' contacts with other home educators in Chapter 9 — for the moment, the importance of such contacts and the knowledge that support existed did play a part in the ability of some families to come to terms with the decision they eventually took. In the McGills' case the support and information given was of a straightforward and practical nature: 'we wanted to go it alone now. And of course we realized it was our right to go it alone, and you don't have to be a teacher either, we didn't know that either until Education Otherwise told us' (Andrew McGill).

For some, such as Joy Baker, and David and Pauline Head (who set up the original 'Operation Otherwise') no such help was available, since the machinery and experience were not yet there to provide it. The children of these two are the only representatives in my sample of what might be called the pioneers of modern home-based education (I do not include Alison Hartfield here, since her home education was, in terms of approach and philosophy, more a hangover from the days of governesses than an experiment ushering in a new era). As in the case of media publicity, many of those who benefited from EO's advice have now taken on the role of extending this advice to others, as is characteristic of many similar self-help groups.

Another question relevant to the outcome of the decision-making process is that of who is involved in it: how much control does the child have over what happens to his or her education at this stage? Where a nuclear family is concerned, this may simply be a question of whether to involve the children; where home-based education in a community is projected, it may be a more complex situation in that consensus as to the right course of action may have to be reached by all the adult members and probably the children too. When a consensus decision is made, the support of the group is instantly available to encourage individual doubters, whereas the nuclear family may find itself isolated from such support when it needs it most. But, if the make-up of the community changes, so may its ideals regarding education and its ability to carry them out, leading sometimes to a reversal of the original decision:

> There came a point when some of these people (obviously in a company of our size there was always a through-put of people), some of those people weren't there any more, and at one particular point a lot of the responsibility was falling onto my own shoulders and mainly the children involved were my own children . . . it was necessary to have a reassessment, think about the whole thing. (Kate Haward)

Similar break-ups of home education arrangements, often coinciding, as in this case, with a change of lifestyle (i.e. to a different community or a private house), occurred at Trunkles Top and at Kimber Hall. The nuclear families interviewed, by contrast, seem to have grown increasingly committed to home education as experience strengthened confidence in their original decision. Among most of the nuclear families interviewed, and at Trunkles Top, there was consultation and agreement between parents and children on the desirability of home education, and often strong support by children of the parents' educational philosophy. In some cases, the children almost forced a decision to home educate on their parents by their own outright refusal to go to school. Nevertheless, the decision was still ultimately in the hands of the parents in that they could have treated the child as a truant, with the consequences this would imply. That they did not must be considered the first step in giving the child some power over his own future education. To what extent was this power made absolute in the families interviewed?

In two cases, that of Alison Hartfield, home educated in the thirties, and that of the McGill girls, the impression given by those interviewed was that the parents did not consult the children about their wishes regarding education (to do so would have been, one imagines, a more unusual thing in the 1930s than in the 1970s). It seems that the children, had they had the opportunity, would have chosen school:

> *Alison Hartfield:* I would much rather have gone to school. I was very aware of this.
>
> *J.W.:* You didn't get an actual choice? It was decided?
>
> *Alison:* Oh no. You didn't get a choice in our family. And looking back I think we were not, sort of, gutless children by any manner of means, but we were fairly biddable and we didn't expect to be brought in on those sort of decisions.

Andrew McGill recognized that the children were not, to start with, keen to be educated at home: 'I got out of the school rut, and what's more I took with me at the time, perhaps very much against their wishes in the early stages, three kids out of it'.

I found it impossible, because of the danger of appearing rude to the parents, to question the children about their thoughts on the issue then and now, so have no evidence as to whether they felt, as Andrew seems to imply, that it had after all been worthwhile. One could possibly conclude from the evident success of their education, judged in academic terms only, that a certain amount of motivation was present, though in both this family and that of Alison Hartfield, it might be fair to suppose that the very strong personality of the father had a great deal to do with ensuring that the work required was done, and to the required standard.

Joy Baker is another parent who seems to have decided on the children's educational future without consulting them, but in the case of the eldest, David, at any rate, his mother's course of action had his wholehearted agreement. Mrs. Baker took a less formal approach to learning, relating it more to everyday life and the children's interests at the time, than did either the Hartfields or the McGills, and this may have had something to do with the children's support for a method of education they apparently had no say in choosing.

The question of how much it should be the child's own choice to be home educated is one which is often worked over by members of EO, and which hinges on two things: the child's age, and whether it is reasonable to expect a child to make such a decision if s/he has never had experience of school. In the case of families interviewed, all but three of the children had had experience of school, if only for a year or two, and several were in their teens, and therefore by many people's reckoning capable of judgment as to where their best interests lay.

Some of the older children (for example, Emma, Piers and Dickie, who had begun home education only a year or two before the age at which their compulsory education would have finished) were given a fair amount of autonomy regarding their educational future. A decision about whether to be educated at home was more or less theirs, the parent's part being to express their willingness to supervise, and to advise on the course they thought wisest:

> It was totally up to me what I wanted to do. If I'd wanted to stay I could have stayed. I didn't want to stay so I left. It was totally up to me what I wanted to do. He advised me . . . He said, 'You're always playing truant so you're not going to learn much anyway, so you might as well get out. Do something you enjoy even if you're not writing on a bit of paper or something'. (Dickie Tansley)

Where younger children were concerned the decision was either a shared one, as in the Cotton and Dey families, and at Trunkles Top, or one made mainly by the parents but to which the children did not object, as in the case of the Minchins and the Gordons, and Joy Baker, mentioned earlier. Some of the younger children with older, already home educated, siblings, such as William Parsons, were given the option of learning at home and accepted it: it must have seemed a natural choice to make under these circumstances.

These parents appeared to have a democratic style of family life in which it would be natural for children to have their wishes regarding education consulted (this was also reflected in the way in which parents made sure children had the opportunity to express their views in the interview) and respected if it were practicable; the larger measure of autonomy apparently given to older children being an acknowledgment of their greater experience of the world. This democratic approach to decision making is the basis for many alternative education projects akin to home-based education, such as those within the Free School movement, and has the same implications for child-centred curricula, self-motivation and cooperation amongst the group's members as it does in the home educating families who employ it.

Where the children were the major decision-makers, their considerations regarding whether or not to be home educated differed from the parents'. Emma and Tim, for instance, felt it would take them away from school friendships which they valued (even though they would have been separated from these friends in the course of a year or two anyway). Tim was finally asked by the head to accept home education or be expelled, as the school found him too disruptive:

> *Margaret Gold:* You wouldn't have left, would you?
> *Tim:* No. Loneliness mostly.

J.W.: What, because you'd be away from your friends?

Tim: Yes, I had fun with them.

It is possible that at this age, the mid-teens, when peer group pressure is purported to be at its strongest, existing friendships are of greater importance than among those confronted with a decision at an earlier age, for whom the social aspect did not appear to have been a significant issue (unless from a negative point of view). The confidence in their ability to make friends out of school, commonly observed in those out of school for a long period, would perhaps also have been missing.

Corinne Dey describes the things she thought about when deciding whether to start at secondary school after a year of home education (she was eleven at the time):

> I just enjoyed it at home. I didn't really feel I'd get on at school. I don't know whether I'd have enjoyed it: I don't think I would've. And to go back would have been permanent. I mean, to come out again at that stage, it would have been difficult, to go back in and say 'Oh, I want to come out'.

(Corinne was, at the time of the interview, attending the school in question part-time, also by her own choice.)

Many of the children interviewed, such as Simon, Jim, Glenn and Piers were, like Dickie above, unequivocal in their decision to be educated at home, having forced the issue by refusing to go to school. Their view of the matter was essentially the same as their parents', in that concern for their educational and emotional welfare was of ultimate importance (though parents may have had the additional worries already mentioned to take into account). In the next section I shall discuss the physical expression of their refusal and the ways in which the other families interviewed finally cut the ties with school.

Leaving School

How, then, did the leaving of school take place? In some cases, as already discussed, it had happened before the decision to home educate was made, being the factor which initiated the decision. Piers, for instance, made a thoroughly dramatic exit:

> He looked around and said to himself, 'What am I doing here?' They were all throwing ink bombs at each other and things. So he just picked up his briefcase and walked all the way home, which is about five miles. (Jenny Arthur)

This was not a typical way of leaving among those interviewed. For most, the experience was similar to that of Jim Merriman: 'he didn't have a sort of cut-off time, he didn't suddenly come out, he was starting to come out. The year before he didn't go much'. (Roger Merriman).

Such unofficial leaving, before deregistration had been granted, took two other forms among those interviewed: deliberate absence from school on a fairly regular basis (sometimes as truancy — defined by Maurice Tyerman as 'absence on the child's own initiative without his parents' permission' (Tyerman, 1968, p. 9)), and absence due to apparently school-induced illness, also occurring regularly.

Unauthorized Absence

David Galloway, writing about the results of his Sheffield studies of persistent unauthorized absence, including truancy, for which he adopts Tyerman's definition, suggests:

> Conflicting explanations can be put forward for the sharp increases in unauthorized absenteeism throughout the secondary school years. One possibility is that the pupils concerned feel that the school curriculum is irrelevant to their needs. They may also resent aspects of the school's regime. (Galloway, 1985, p. 17)

The parent of one of those interviewed reflected this when he said, 'Tim was out'because of that. He was just bored' (Malcolm Gold).

Galloway goes on to discuss family responsibilities and the influence of friends who have already left school, factors which, he finds, play a larger part in unauthorized absence than those already mentioned. Malcolm Gold gives an example of the economic considerations which may operate, from the experience of his family on one of the Scottish islands:

> *Malcolm Gold:* There are lots of things, on an island like this especially, truanting occurs because there's a harvest, the hayfields need emptying or whatever.
> *Margaret Gold:* Peats.
> *Malcolm:* The peats need cutting. It's accepted as normal truanting.

Two children in my study had, like the islanders, regular time off school with the concurrence of their parents, but this was directly related to unhappiness at school, rather than to external social or economic factors. In one case this was specifically to avoid the possibility of truanting:

> He was getting progressively more and more unhappy and in fact I'd reached the point I'd said to him, 'If you get a day you really can't go

in, I'll cover you with a note.' I didn't want him just playing truant so any day that he really felt he couldn't, he had a day off, and I used to cover him with a note. (Pat Maxwell)

The condoning of absence by the parents was hard to accept for at least one school; perhaps because it did not fit comfortably into either of the roles, regular attender or out-and-out truant, that the teachers were used to:

He started just refusing to go. And the school were very peculiar about it, it's hard to describe in what way they were peculiar. They couldn't understand, I think, why we didn't hit him over the head and make him go back to school. (Mary Parsons)

Truanting
Among those interviewed, the children who truanted were in a minority of three: Gerry, Dickie and Tim, and the reasons they gave, or their parents surmised, for their doing so have already been discussed in Chapter 4: conflict between home and school values and boredom being the major ones. Of Galloway's other relevant concerns, the influence of peers already over school-leaving age played no part in their truancy, neither were they from a social or cultural background where school might be considered of peripheral concern to the real business of life, as his main thesis relating to truancy and other forms of unauthorized absence suggests, since all three had well-educated, professional parents, three of whom were involved in education (which in itself may have caused rebellion: no-one admitted this, however). So, in relation to his findings, they are representatives of the apparently small number of unauthorized absentees for whom the school situation, rather than that of the family, directly provoked the decision to truant.

It is interesting that Reid, in a later study in South Wales where pupils themselves, rather than parents or teachers as in Galloway's sample, were questioned, found that a majority stayed away for 'institutional reasons' such as inappropriate curriculum, examination pressure, transfer to a new school, bullying, the school regime, the attitude of the teachers, and a feeling that they had outgrown school and were ready for work (Reid, 1985). Another study, by Reynolds *et al.*, came to a similar conclusion:

Large and consistent variation between schools in their levels of attendance — and, we believe, truancy — do not appear to be explicable by variation in the characteristics of their pupil intakes, whereas much more of the variation is explicable by using only a limited range of factors that describe the nature and process of the pupils' schools. (Reynolds, *et al.* 1980, p. 105)

Two out of the three teenagers interviewed appeared to have spent some time in the activities typically conjured up by the mention of truancy: aimlessly wandering around the neighbourhood, in the company of several others in Tim's case (who, because of his sociability, might not have played truant had others not been involved), and one other, her boyfriend Ben, in Gerry's case: 'they just used to go and sit on the rec' (Veronica Budd); 'they went off, got on the school bus and just got off and went round to somebody's house to watch telly instead of going to school' (Malcolm Gold).

Neither Tim nor Gerry had been in trouble with the police, but Dickie had had 'hassle' from them. Of the three, he was the only one who felt he had made a deliberate decision to use the time rather than merely spend it (although Gerry Budd's version of events might have shed a different light on this topic from her parents'). He describes his activities:

> Dickie: Whenever I played truant I never used to just sit on the streets. I always used to do something enjoyable, practise or something. . . . I used to go down the music shops and just play the guitar. I went to work a couple of times.
>
> J.W.: What did you do?
>
> Dickie: Building, because my brother was working with his friend doing up somebody's house, so I'd go round there.

Constructive use of truanting time may be easier if the child has access to his or her home, since the use of community facilities may provoke questioning and police involvement. This in turn depends on parents being out during the school day or being willing to condone the child's absence. The physicist Fred Hoyle described the education he provided for himself while truanting from primary school, where he was usually bored. He taught himself to read from the subtitles at the cinema (he could not cope with the small print of school texts), did experiments with chemicals his father left around at home, and went up the road to an astronomer friend to pursue his interest in the stars:

> I used to go and watch the looms at work and the boats coming through the locks on the local canal. I think I learnt quite a lot about hydrostatics from watching that performance. . . . I don't regret it in any way at all. I did pretty well out of my truancy. I profited enormously from not allowing the education system to educate me. (Radio 4 programme Desert Island Discs, 12.10.1986)

The originality and versatility which made it hard for him to fit into the system until much later may have been significantly enhanced by this unconventional early education, very much along the lines of many Holt- and Neill-influenced modern home educators who encourage their young children to pursue whatever interests them at a particular time to as great a depth as they wish; the difference being that the child has no feeling of going against authority in doing so, as the infant Hoyle and other truants presumably had, perhaps making future relations with authority in various guises less of a problem.

The lengths schools will go to, to ensure that pupils occupy the roles assigned to them, remind me of the old joke about hospital nurses waking up the patients to give them their sleeping tablets, as this article from the *Mail on Sunday*, (11 March 1984) shows:

Darren, the Truant with a £12,000 Job

A schoolboy who swopped log tables for log fires has been told to stop making money and get back to the classroom.

Darren Murfet, 15, stopped going to school so he could concentrate on the £12,000-a-year business he had built up, recycling industrial waste wood for domestic use.

He told teachers he couldn't return to the John O'Gaunt Comprehensive in Hungerford, Berks, because he has orders piling up from his 350 customers.

Last week his parents were fined £300 for failing to ensure that he attend school. His father, David, now drives him to school from nearby Lambourn but the youngster then hitchhikes 40 miles to his workshop near Oxford.

There he saws up wooden pallets for fire kindling. Darren, a remedial pupil who is legally entitled to leave school in May, said: 'I worked hard to get the business going. I don't want to end on the dole'.

But his headmaster, Mr. David Lee, said yesterday he deplored the example Darren had set other pupils.

This brings us round to the question of the school's reaction to truancy. In the case of Gerry and Tim, their truancy was the direct cause of deregistration from school, after several attempts at defusing the situation: both heads came to see home education as an alternative to expulsion. Gerry's mother describes how her school-leaving came about and how the school had an unsuccessful go at legitimizing her truancy, following a logic which is hard to fathom:

She and Ben had decided they were going to live outside in the garden shed, and they weren't going to school any more and the school were getting very worried. Ben's parents were getting very, very worried and at that time the School Attendance Officer descended on me in school, which was terribly embarrassing, to discuss the problem of Gerry. It really went from bad to worse and she started being suspended. The first time she got it for two days, just a short period of time, and it was really just a licensed holiday as far as she was concerned. I mean, she hated school anyway and she thought, 'I've got three days when I really don't have to go to school and nobody expects me to go to school'. (Veronica Budd)

Tim Gold was in a similar situation in that the head was anxious not to have him on the premises because of his truancy and disruption of classes in the past. One senses a feeling among the heads that this kind of attitude to school could be catching — 'truancy is not a problem: it is a contagious disease' (letter from three education welfare officers, quoted in Stone and Taylor, 1976, p. 230) — as well as the obvious worries they have about the abilities of teachers to cope. In fact, Tim was asked, before things came to a head, to take a couple of fortnights off during termtime in order to give the staff a break. Perhaps this was also the reasoning behind Gerry's suspension. Dickie's school's only action was to write to his parents to tell them about his truancy, and in doing so unwittingly to alert them to the fact that he was bored there and would be better off with an alternative.

Since truanting pupils are, on the evidence of at least two of these three interviewees, a nuisance to schools in their efforts to keep the others in line, it would seem that the negotiation of alternative ways of using school time, self-chosen for their personal relevance, would be in the school's interest as well as that of the disenchanted truants. This has been accomplished in some places through a form of 'education otherwise' provision which involves children remaining technically on the register of their school but allows the centre they attend to claim capitation for them. The Bridge Centre in Birmingham operated like this. The Bayswater Centre in Bristol also offers a model for a different sort of education: less authoritarian, more self-directed. It began as an independent unit which finally won state support. Roger White, writing about the Bayswater Centre, begins with the premise that the school failure and maladjustment which led to truancy in the case of the students who later attended it, are socially constructed definitions which can be successfully challenged by a different approach to the curriculum: 'our three Rs would be listed as Responsibility, aRticulation and Relevant education' (White, 1980, p. 36).

The key to this appears to be the student's involvement in the selection and structuring of appropriate activities, which, as Roger White makes clear 'would require a fundamental reappraisal of form and content within schools' (White, *ibid.*, p. 235).

There is an obvious parallel here with the possibilities offered by home-based education to children in as desperate a personal situation as those described in *Absent With Cause* (White, *ibid.*) but who have parents who are aware that a family solution exists and feel able to take this on. There are many similarities in terms of the 'how' and 'why' which White feels are so much more important than the 'what' of education — for example, features such as responsible involvement in the day-to-day running of the unit or family, the use of as many outside resources as possible, and an approach to self-discipline based on discussion. There is also more opportunity for individual attention in both situations than in an orthodox state school. They differ in that the family takes a long-term approach to education and often begins earlier in the child's career, normally planning it to cover several years, whereas the Bayswater Centre is concerned with doing as much for its fifteen year olds as possible during the one year the teenagers are at the Centre. Furthermore, the family has the advantage of knowing the child well, whereas Centre staff must get to know new children afresh every year, perhaps making the achievement of education relevant to the child a harder task.

Time off due to school-induced illness
Frequent absences due to illness were also a common way in which those interviewed found themselves gradually coming to a parting of the ways with the school which they felt had caused it. Often the illness was of a psychosomatic nature, leading the schools concerned to suggest that it was the child rather than the school which was the problem (a similar attitude to that of the schools who tried to brand nonconforming pupils as maladjusted). Christine Merriman described how school affected Jim during his year of sporadic attendance, and the school's reaction to her complaints:

> He was ill, I felt he was getting ill with it . . . nightmares and didn't eat properly, didn't sleep properly, he used to be in tears all the time . . . in the end I got a letter from the headmaster saying he thought James needed a psychiatrist. So that was when I'd had enough.

Emma's asthma, and the failure of the school to take this into consideration at times (such as games lessons), led to a bad attack which landed her in hospital and persuaded both her and her mother that she should not return to school, though they were unable to get medical support for their decision:

> We had this famous asthma attack and the doctor wasn't prepared to back me up; he wasn't prepared to say 'Oh well, the child is not well enough to be at school' or anything else like that, and it was quite clear that she wasn't, nor would the consultant at the hospital. They were all backing up authority. . . . They wouldn't accept that it was psychological stresses and strains that were at the bottom of it. And I found this very difficult to cope with. And I went to see the headmistress and I said I was taking her away and she wasn't coming back. (Rachel Williams)

There are many such anecdotes in the literature telling a tale of mental or emotional stress finding expression in physical illness. The impression that one gets from reading *EO News* is that home educators feel strongly that the labels 'school phobia' and 'school refusal' often given to these types of illness obscure the role of the school in promoting the symptoms, as the point of view of the two mothers quoted makes clear. As in Galloway's investigation of truancy, the situation of the family is seen by many psychologists to be most important: over-protectiveness on the parents' part or some psychological disturbance which results in the child being unwilling to leave home are two of the reasons given by, for instance, Kahn and Nursten (1975) and Ian Berg, (1981) to explain why it is that the 'normal' children in a class do not react to school by becoming ill. The emphasis on the irrationality of the child's reaction makes it plain that there is nothing of a concrete nature, in these writers' view, to be afraid of. Indeed, they do not entertain the idea seriously at all.

However, the home educators' view has some support from the shop floor; for instance, this writer to *EO News* 45, who is a teacher in a Birmingham comprehensive: 'children who fear school fear it for real and honourable reasons and their physical reactions are not a sort of pseudo-disease needing treatment but the response of a normal human being who feels threatened'. David Head, also involved in education, recognized the truth of this fifteen years ago:

> We might recognize rational and irrational fears of school, and what it can do to you, as a breath of sanity. School, after all, requires a very special sort of adjustment — and it is just that adjustment which worries some of us. (Head, 1974, p. 8)

Apart from these two rather gradual types of transition, there was a more orderly mode of leaving among those interviewed for whom the situation was less urgent. In some families, leaving school coincided with moving to a different part of the country, and deregistration was therefore granted with no questions asked. (This is sometimes a useful last resort for those who discover that their LEA is hostile to their intention to home educate.) In other cases, families waited until the end of term, then wrote requesting deregistration. They were not always told that this had been effected: 'it was a headmaster and I don't think he was overly keen on the idea. He didn't acknowledge the letter that my parents sent saying that I was going to be educated at home' (Maureen Cotton). Only in Piers' case did a head absolutely refuse to deregister, a formality as far as leaving school went since Piers had, as we have seen, already left, but it did affect his freedom to take up the offered place at a local college of further education.

Adjustment

Whether they left gradually over a period of months or attended regularly until their last day, some of the children found they needed a period of recovery from the strains of school life. This was particularly so if they had been ill, of course:

> For the first few weeks after leaving school, Jim behaved much as a fugitive might, but gradually he regained his former appetite and vigour although sleeplessness remained a problem because school nightmares still punctuated his sleep. However, as the actual fear of school hostilities had been removed the improvement in his general health was soon noticeable. (Christine Merriman in *EO News* 29)

One of the LEA advisers interviewed recognized that recovery periods could be crucial to children's development and that being pushed into a different way of doing things before they had had time to adjust could be fatal to the encouragement of learning: 'school just wasn't working out for him and a break seemed to be needed . . . it was really important to have that year to sort it out, the fact that he was unable to cope with secondary school'. Perhaps sabbaticals for schoolchildren at some point would enable more of them to approach their work with interest and motivation, and lead to a lessening of the problems due to continuous peer-group pressure.

Other children took a while to adjust to their freedom from school pressures (as did Neill's pupils from over-repressive schools when first at Summerhill — many, he reports, avoided lessons altogether for a term or more). In Piers' case, this took the form of a period of depression and inactivity. In most situations it was more a matter of the whole family having to adjust to a new way of life and a new approach to education. Parents often recognized this and attempted to help children over emotional blocks which had developed: 'he was so unhappy with things I made everything as different as I could' (Marie Gordon). Phil Minchin said, 'it took us quite a time to get over the shock but we got going in the end'.

This chapter has illustrated the lack of confidence with which many families made the decision to home educate, and the importance in these cases of support from a national body such as EO which was not available to most of them. The democratic nature of the decision to home educate, established by consensus between parents and children, was a feature (usually) of their new educational career which contrasted with the way in which educational decisions affecting children had been made at school.

Most children, having made the transition from school to home gradually, through time off due to illness in some cases, and truancy in others, needed a period of adjustment and recovery from school. Further aspects of this theme, the process by which children and their parents began to develop methods of working appropriate to the aims of their new educational plans, are discussed in the chapters which follow.

Chapter 6

Family Influence on the Choice of What to Learn

I shall discuss here the way in which the content of children's home-based curricula was affected by various, sometimes interacting, factors: the family's aims in undertaking home-based education (not necessarily static), previous school experience, and the child's own interests.

The Family's Aims in Home Educating

In considering how the family's aims in home educating affect the content of that education, a distinction must be made between aims already present in the school situation, where one existed (and perhaps not being satisfied, thus leading to home education), which will be discussed later, and those which developed as part of a re-think due to change of educational career or as part of the continuing process of home education. In this connection it can be pointed out that flexibility in content of education directed to achieving a particular goal is very much greater at home than in school, where both the limitation of subjects for study and the difficulty of 'disembarking' from a course once embarked on, could make changes of mind, due perhaps to the continuing process of adolescent self-discovery, very difficult.

In school, the available content is laid down partly by law and partly by the LEA, the local examining boards and the staff of the school concerned. Choice is therefore limited, in a way in which it is not in the larger world in which home educated children move, even before considerations of timetable clashes and estimations of intellectual suitability of children for particular courses of study place further restrictions on what is available to the individual at any stage. Children's interests may have to take second place to their ability in this situation, reflecting the pressure on teachers from their political masters and from some parents, to produce 'good results'.

At home, the aim is sometimes a deliberate recognition of the worth of allowing children to explore their interest, whatever their apparent ability (and, as most people know from their own or others' experience, assessment of ability at school may be wrong). The potential for personal growth afforded by this freedom to learn about the world as the individual's own developing interests dictate is seen by some as the most valuable aspect of home education, and is discussed further below.

Qualifications

These may be formal examination results such as GCE/GCSE appropriate to the obtaining of a wide range of jobs and to university or various types of college entrance, or they may be related to the skills needed for a particular job and in this case take the form of work experience (such as that found on Youth Training Schemes (YTS) as well as in the informal situation of practical activities based at home). Both types of qualification were found to be goals influencing content among families interviewed. A third type of qualification, the compilation of profiles such as those pioneered in some schools, had not been considered by any of the families I spoke to but one would expect that the potential for producing a fascinating history of one's home education, complete with examples of work, was great and might have considerable interest for employers looking for a way of distinguishing children with character and originality. Perhaps the best use of a portfolio approach would be in conjunction with formal qualifications, since there is evidence that these are used as a preliminary weeding out device by employers:

> Getting to the interview is qualifications, qualifications are used as a paper sift, right? Once you've got to the interview, forget about the qualifications, once you get to the interview it's on personality: interest, motivation. The factors there are personality, motivation, are you a motivated person generally, are you basically lazy or basically active, and the third thing is attitude, very much applies with young people, they're looking at attitudes: do they have a chip on the shoulder, are they keen to learn, are they pleasant, have they got the right sort of manner with them, and what are their attitudes to society, to different things, you know? (Careers Officer for a new city)

These questions could be partly answered by the inclusion in the profile of self-written descriptions of projects undertaken in the community or the home, and the thoughts of adults, parents and others, involved with the child's home education.

Academic qualifications

No-one in the study had aimed for anything other than GCE as an academic qualification while at home. The International Baccalaureate, which one might have expected to appeal to parents who felt English education to specialize too early was not considered, nor have I been able to find any reports of its use by home educating families outside the study, though there have been recommendations regarding its scope in the *EO Newsletter*. CSEs appeared also not to have been discussed as a possible goal. The element of teacher assessment which was a well-known feature of Mode 3 CSE perhaps led people to expect that this was a general requirement and therefore difficult to do at home (the GCSEs now being taken by home educated children are mostly of the external non-coursework variety), or perhaps families felt that where they were opting for academic qualifications they might as well go for GCEs, as being of more help in the job market. (Emma Williams, however, who had started them at school, did continue with CSE courses.)

What did families have in mind when choosing to base their curriculum content on formal academic goals (and often it was only a base, since many other interests were pursued in parallel with them)? For some, the acquisition of examination results may, like the concept of the value of exploring interests irrespective of where they lead in practical terms, be part of an existing family ethos relating to a general idea of a worthwhile education. In the case of the Scheaffers, for instance, there was no doubt that the aim of Daniel's education, once it was clear that he *could* learn, was university entrance and then a job, since these were the accepted goals for all the children of the family:

> What you're trying to achieve is an educated person at the end of this and you're trying to achieve, because this is the world we happen to live in, the requisite number of O levels and A levels producing a spread. (Penelope Scheaffer)

Daniel himself appears never to have questioned this; neither did Alison Hartfield when her father decided that she and her sisters should sit matriculation in preparation for teacher training, though this was not what she originally wanted to do:

> The goal was that we should sit for London matric., which you took then at about sixteen, as external candidates, and that would qualify us for entry to teachers' training college and in fact that is what we all did. . . . We were never consulted. I went through a phase at which I was going to be a nurse, or thought I was going to be a nurse, but even that was very much — I can remember my father saying to somebody

over my head one day, 'We thought at one time she might have been a nurse, but we've decided on teaching'. The 'we' did not include me.

In other families interviewed, children's own aims in terms of jobs and/or university entrance had determined their choice of a curriculum based on O level examination requirements. In Jim Merriman's case his own goals coincided happily with those of the LEA who insisted that he took courses leading to O levels: his leanings towards the sciences dictated the inclusion of physics, biology, chemistry, mathematics, and initially astronomy, which was one of his hobbies. Corinne Dey's choice of O level subjects was dictated by early ambition: 'at the time, I was a couple of years younger, I wanted to be a vet and so I thought I'd have to have sciences but I know I wouldn't do that now, it's very difficult'.

Some of the other children interviewed chose to do some or all O levels at FE college, seeing it as a specialized examination factory, but their choice of subjects and the reasons for it often stemmed, interestingly, from elements in their home education. George and Grace Gordon, as an instance of a point made earlier, both became interested in areas which they would have been unlikely to encounter in a traditional school curriculum:

> *J.W.:* So why did you decide to do O levels?
>
> *George:* Because I want to do forestry as a job, and to do that you need a degree, to get the degree you need the A levels and to get the A levels you need the O levels . . .
>
> *J.W.:* So when and why and how did you decide you wanted to do forestry?
>
> *George:* That was so long ago that I cannot tell exactly how it happened but what I do know is I like everything that's involved in doing it.
>
> *J.W.:* This is a super place to live for someone who's interested in forestry.
>
> *Marie:* Yes, he's got a job with them in a couple of weeks.
>
> *Grace:* He did grow trees in the bottom of his garden.
>
> *Marie:* Yes. We used to go walking in the Lake District a lot. I think it was kind of environment, just fascination with what was going on around. He found out what forestry was, and it's just everything he's always been interested in . . .
>
> *J.W.:* And have you got any plans, or not yet?
>
> *Grace:* Yes. I've got to do Os and As as well because I want to go to university to read psychology.
>
> *J.W.:* How did you get interested in that, then?
>
> *Grace:* Oh, I've always been interested in part of that but not sure how they joined together and Marie was reading the —

autobiography to us, which mentioned it in it and it kind of all linked together.

Subjects covered at O level included, and were mainly restricted to, the traditional school ones, though only Daniel took a modern language (French) O level, and he felt unsatisfied with the course involved because of the difficulty, unable as he was to get out of the house, in acquiring models for an authentic accent. This focusing on traditional subjects by families such as the Gordons whose previous learning approach had been very much integrated and based on children's personal interests, reflects the way in which the examinations and courses leading to them were often regarded not as valuable learning experiences in themselves but as necessary evils to be overcome before real and much-desired learning, at university in most cases, could be undertaken.

So far I have not mentioned the position of those families who continued with O level courses already begun at school: this will be discussed later in the chapter along with other influences on the home education curriculum related to school experience.

Skills for jobs

In Simon Parsons' case, a deliberate decision not to do formal examinations was thought likely by his parents to present problems for his future choice of career. In the event, the college of catering which accepted him for chef training was prepared to waive the usual three O levels requirement on the basis of his performance in an English and mathematics test. His mother shows how other aspects of home education may compensate for lack of academic qualifications:

> My general feeling about all this is that Simon knows what he wants and is able to organize himself to get it. That is his main asset. I was honestly a bit worried about not doing exams at home, but it wouldn't have been suitable for us, which is why we didn't. Events have shown us to be right. If you can show will and enthusiasm, then it can be possible to bypass some of the conventional exam system.

Simon's success on the course must have reassured the college authorities that examinations need not be the be-all and end-all, and made it perhaps easier for the next person, home educated or not, to be admitted on the basis of factors other than academic success. This was also the case with Stephanie Steele's applications for two sorts of vocational training, the first of which, drama, depended on talent rather than qualifications:

> Shortly before her sixteenth birthday, Stephanie auditioned for, and was accepted by, a nationally approved drama school. The director of

one drama school, on hearing she had no formal schooling said, 'Splendid, that gives us less to undo'. She decided she would require a skill for making a living between acting jobs and so applied to the local technical college for admission to its secretarial and business course. An admission test replaced her missing O levels. (Steele, 1978, p. 153)

The example of the Open University and various other institutions admitting unqualified mature students is perhaps making this idea more palatable generally.

The book *Unqualified Success* (Gabriel, 1984) lists 117 jobs, many of them very stimulating, for which no academic qualifications are needed. Their variety indicates that perhaps school orientation towards academic success may lead unqualified children to feel that they cannot find interesting and satisfying work when in fact this may be quite untrue. The home educated child's option to disregard academic criteria and set his own standards in terms of the attainment of skills is a valuable alternative, and the home educating family, with its flexibility and its potential access to the whole world of work, seems to be well placed to help its children obtain the skills relevant to their choice of future job. This extract from an adviser's report about a teenage boy whose parents decided to complete his education at home illustrates the variety of job-orientated skills that may be obtained in this way:

> Schools cannot always provide ideal conditions for all learning and certainly cannot provide the context in which Peter is operating. He is looking after a sizeable vegetable garden single-handed and has plans to extend considerably on to other land owned by the family. He has numerous animals to care for, he is playing the organ in the next-door church and the piano at home, and he also does some composing. He reads a lot, both for pleasure and factual books about farming and natural studies, and is following a correspondence course in gardening for adults with comparative ease.

As with academic qualifications, it is easier to keep options open at home regarding jobs, as Peter in the passage above is doing, particularly where the school-leaving age is not necessarily regarded as the cut-off point for education, the point at which the individual is expected to go out and earn a living. Fifteen-year-old Dickie Tansley was hoping to build up a job for himself playing with his rock band (they had made a demonstration tape to send to the record companies and had been booked for one or two unpaid gigs), but he felt he would like to have another means of earning a living so was making the most of his remaining period of education:

I'm trying to get some skills while I'm up here, so I've done a lot of things and I know quite a lot about farming, bricklaying, building, that's just from working on our land. . . . We bought a building about a mile away and took the whole thing down, put it over there . . . a massive great barn . . . that was tractor driving, backwards and forwards, bringing the timbers back. Then I started working putting it back up, concreting, then bricklaying on top of concrete and just generally getting the thing up. Then I decided to go in for joinery so that's what I've been working on the rest of the time, and gardening, ploughing, just put potatoes in and just put the barley in, bit of muck-spreading . . . they do woodwork . . . I'm going on a wood-turning course so I should get into that. I'm going next Wednesday, down to Bristol for the training.

The extent of Dickie's self-chosen curriculum means that a wide range of practical jobs will be open to him in comparison with some 'schooled' children whose job choices are more narrowly specialized through the conventions of the society that guides them: skills for one job rather than several alternatives is still the unquestioned aim of some careers staff for their pupils. In each of the cases where one of the interviewed children had decided on a job, the family in question had been able to tailor the curriculum to suit its requirements, though deliberately not to the exclusion of all other interests or academic pursuits, as the passage about Peter shows. Phil Minchin wanted to be a farmer and, at fifteen, was working with a lot of responsibility on the family's smallholding and attending Young Farmers where he was learning sheep judging and tractor driving, as well as, presumably, making useful local farming contacts. He was also keeping up academic subjects such as English, mathematics and geography as he hoped to study agriculture formally at college. Martin Maxwell's aim was to own a kennels and he had planned quite carefully the stages he considered necessary before this would be possible: a period working for someone else in a kennels, a period as an RSPCA inspector and then the setting up of his own kennels when his parents' plan to retire and buy some land came to fruition. Accordingly, he took correspondence courses in several O levels (the important one for an RSPCA inspector being English language, for writing court reports) and his mother managed to arrange some work experience in a kennels:

I'd rung one or two local kennels and this particular one sounded quite — she said they hadn't ever employed anybody but she did like boys and perhaps in the summer. And then they rang me and said that they would set up a YOP scheme specially for him. An individual one, if I could find a kennel to take him. So of course I rang her back. He went there for six months and never left. She can't manage without him. (Pat Maxwell)

Karen and Tim Gold also opted for a YTS method of acquiring skills they had not already picked up through life on the smallholding, though this appears to have been more a matter of having nothing firmly in mind to do and no academic qualifications. Karen decided to do childcare, which appealed to her, but lacked the application to stick at the scheme and was told to leave it. Tim had a similar experience with a more mixed scheme: 'he started on the local YTS. It covers assorted skills — he's tried woodwork, cooking, car mending and others, not sticking at anything for more than three weeks . . . ' (Malcolm Gold). Malcolm felt quite strongly that Tim had artistic talents which he was wasting but did not want to pressurize him into using them (an example of teenagers following their own bent irrespective of parental guidance, though Tim did, eventually, study fashion and design at college).

One family, writing in *EO News* 47, describes how a list of useful skills for work they came across in a book influenced their choice of curriculum content, and how they came to establish a logically planned, but flexible, curriculum which incorporated many of the traditional school subjects into a wider view of the world, and gave the children a basis from which to specialize if they developed an interest in a particular job:

> *You should be able to use:* a pair of scissors, a hand-held saw, a spanner, a hammer, a screwdriver, a file or emery-cloth, a paintbrush, a hand-held drill, a spade, a vice, a typewriter (two fingers);

> *You should be able to:* work in a team, work alone occasionally, ask people for help, listen carefully to others, offer help to strangers, follow spoken instructions, ask questions, answer questions confidently, add, multiply, subtract, divide, work with decimals and fractions, work out percentages, work simple figures in your head, use an electric calculator, measure in metric and imperial, use a stop watch, tell time accurately, read a bus/train timetable, find way with map, spell reasonably well, write messages clearly, write instructions accurately, complete forms carefully, use a dictionary, file things alphabetically, use a telephone directory, follow written instructions. (Crowley, no date, as quoted in *EO News* 47)

The Influence of School Experience

This may be in one of two forms: it may result in activities being chosen to give continuity to programmes of study already begun at school, abandoning the school career only in terms of location and perhaps method of teaching and learning; or it may result in activities which contrast with elements of school learning which were seen as not meeting the child's needs.

A School-like Approach

Where families have chosen the former course, it is for one of three reasons. The first, pressure from LEAs to follow particular subjects, has been touched on briefly earlier and will be discussed again in the next chapter, so I will not elaborate on it here. The second is related to examination courses the child has embarked upon: the family, including the child, considers it undesirable to waste work already put in and so includes the finishing of these courses at home, and the taking of the relevant examinations, as part of its curriculum. The Williamses would have liked to follow the mathematics and biology CSEs and art O level which Emma took, in cooperation with the school, perhaps on a part-time basis, but: 'they washed their hands of it. They said, "Well, you can do the exams", but you see it was too late to enrol anywhere else' (Rachel Williams).

The third reason for continuing work begun at school seems to be a common one: a psychological need on the part of parents and/or children to have a known base to a largely unpredictable experience. Parents may feel completely at sea when planning a curriculum, particularly where this has been asked for by the LEA and they feel a certain pressure of time, and so they may look to the school for a safe model. This is, of course, only likely to be the case where factors other than the curriculum have led to the child's leaving school:

> *J.W.:* So did you attempt to cover all the subjects that she would have been doing at school?
>
> *Amy Dey:* Yes. Well, we were quite ambitious at the beginning and we spent a long time drawing up timetables and also she watched a lot of programmes on TV . . . actual schools' programmes.

These subjects originally included mathematics and English, domestic science, history, physics, biology and chemistry, French and geography but the list had to be modified in the light of experience (temporarily as it turned out, since Corinne picked up chemistry again later on — illustrating once more the flexibility inherent in home education):

> *Amy:* Where it fell down rather was, my husband was supposed to be doing chemistry with her because he's got a science degree but it turned out that he wasn't very good at teaching, and then he had to

go away on his job quite a bit. And he was always having arguments with her.

There is evidence in the *EO Newsletters* that families starting off with a curriculum based on traditional school subjects as a confidence-booster in an unfamiliar situation are apt to abandon it gradually as they learn more about their children's needs and how to satisfy them more fully and naturally, perhaps in a more integrated form. One writer to *EO News* 45 describes how this happened in her family (partly a question of the 'how' as well as the 'what' of home education under discussion here):

> I remember the first year of home education as being extremely trying as I battled with a child who had no interest in any formal work. I soon came to find out that most of what children are expected to do is quite meaningless to them and indeed is a great imposition on them. Very little is learnt from within and no sense of self is developed or indeed encouraged. After four years of schooling we found Patricia unable to concentrate on anything or do anything for herself because she wanted to. Things have changed since then, since we dropped the compulsive need to learn things, to be endlessly doing, and she has found herself beautifully and has become an articulate, mature, sociable thirteen-year-old.

Another mother writes in *School Is Not Compulsory* (Education Otherwise, 1985) on the same issue:

> Our timetable is not rigid; enthusiasm is encouraged in any area of learning or interest and we continually seek to extend our awareness and knowledge. Whereas we had initially tended to clockwatch and were anxious if we found we had diverted from World Geography to Current Affairs and Politics or from Angles and Tangents to Aerial Navigation, we now are excited by our sons' inquisitive minds and ability to encompass a vast range of topics.

A Contrast with School

Another type of reaction to school expresses itself in the search for a curriculum quite different from that studied in school, as Marie Gordon tried to put together for her son when he left at seven, very disillusioned with school work:

> You didn't like the books you'd been reading so they all went by the board and I gave him a little book of stories. Writing, I taught him to do joined-up writing, just because it wasn't a bit like he'd been doing.

Maths. we did different base work, starting from a base of five and three, just to make it completely different, because he was a bit off. And you enjoyed it, didn't you, no end?

Another aspect of the opportunity to create a unique curriculum lies in the way it can be used to combat particularly disliked features of the school curriculum, such as the sexism mentioned by Caroline Parker in Chapter 4. This is a striking element of the education of most of the boys interviewed. They were quite at home cooking and pursuing other stereotypically female interests alongside traditionally male activities; Phil Minchin for instance: 'I do work on knitting machines, we've got another knitting machine and I knit garments on that. And knit by hand, I can crochet, I can cook. That's very useful'.

To repeat a point made in a different context, the curriculum can be designed to present wider opportunities than those the child would have encountered at school (for any of the reasons mentioned earlier):

He's doing things at home he wouldn't be doing at school, like geology and microscopes. He certainly wouldn't get a chance to do German in the sort of streaming system that they have because he'd be down in the bottom stream. (Mary Parsons)

There is also some evidence of a tendency for people to look for kinds of learning which are not a traditional part of the teacher's preserve or are easily self-taught: self-sufficiency skills and computer studies are two areas which come immediately to mind. Since these are both fashionable growth areas, they may indicate a generally increasing popularity of individually learnable forms of knowledge. Where children find it hard to accept instruction from a teacher, perhaps because of the involvement of early emotional blocks, the inclusion of such subjects in the curriculum may help to restore confidence. This was certainly the case with the Harrison children, who suffered from dyslexia and feelings of failure because of this, but whose gradual mastery of many different skills on their smallholding enabled them to face the world with a greater variety of means to earn their living than the majority of their schooled counterparts, and with a greatly increased sense of self-esteem (they also, eventually, had the courage to tackle reading on their own). The 'how' of this kind of approach is discussed in detail in Chapter 8 — for the moment, a quote from the judge's verdict in the court proceedings brought by Hereford LEA against the Harrison parents in its efforts to enforce a school attendance order shows how different from the traditional school curriculum, in both substance and effect, their self-directed programme was:

They are mature, confident, well-mannered, at ease in all sorts of company. They are lively minded, have good general knowledge and are intellectually athletic. They have a wide range of practical skills — plumbing, building, mechanics, husbandry — and are commercially and financially competent. Any individual gift — such as A.J.'s violin playing — is encouraged and given specialist tuition. (Meighan, 1984c, p. 276)

Paul Simmons, who also had difficulty accepting school instruction, found a great personal fulfilment in developing work with computers and the creation of educational programmes for young children. This led him both to make some good friends, which previously he seems to have lacked, and to pursue his adult learning in various forms:

Somehow, slowly, I got into computers. I did an evening class on programming, machine-code programming, about the time we bought all these bits . . . that interest has developed. Shortly after we moved here I made contact with a lady called Sheila . . . who was a teacher and had just had a year off to do an M Phil concerned with computers in primary schools . . . so I've been using her system . . . I've been developing educational applications in conjunction with her really, to her ideas, one of which the three of us, her and me and my friend the electronic engineer have patented or are in the process of patenting — it's a sort of electronic toy.

All the above element of home education programmes chosen because they differed from the traditional school curriculum in some way, resembled each other in being grounded in the child's immediate interests and it is this aspect of assembling a programme that I went to discuss next, with an examination of how much these may be affected by parents' expectations of eventual literacy or numeracy, and concepts of balance in the curriculum.

The Place of the Child's Current Interests

Two categories of activity present themselves here: one that exists where educational activity based on the child's interests is secondary to, or at any rate combined with, a curriculum chosen for other reasons (for example, the long-term aims already discussed) and the other where the whole of a child's education is built round his or her current interests, perhaps based on an A.S. Neill or John Holt type of philosophy which expects that children will naturally learn, or try to learn, what is appropriate to their needs at a particular time and therefore that they and their interests are the best guide to a suitable curriculum.

In the first case, the importance attached by the family to literacy and numeracy, and the ways in which these may be achieved can affect how much a child's own interests dominate his learning. In some families, such as Maureen Cotton's, definite encouragement by the parents to do formal work in English and mathematics resulted in this becoming a regular, though unscheduled, part of the curriculum. For her cousin George Gordon, daily diary-writing was the only activity his parents insisted on, and this is indicative of a general feeling on the part of those interviewed that a reasonable standard of literacy and numeracy was important, both as a pathway to examinations and jobs and as needed in everyday living. This seems particularly to be the case with literacy (which is still seen as the key to Western culture despite the increasing number of jobs in technological fields) and a family style which allows it to be picked up naturally does not necessarily mean that it is seen to be of less importance than in those families where it is formally taught. Dianne Cox, one of the earliest members of EO, describes the place of literacy in her family life in an article in *Woman's World*:

> 'Whenever Tom sees me writing — it might just be the shopping list — he wants to join in and that way he is learning to write. Eleanor and Madeleine picked it up in exactly the same way.' Reading and writing are the only compulsory subjects on the Cox curriculum. For the rest, the children do what they want when they want. Says Bruce: 'There are lots of things we would like them to learn, but we're prepared to leave it to them. I don't believe in making a list and forcing them to doggedly follow it'. (Lantin, 1983, p. 55)

The use of the word 'compulsory' here brings up the question of how literacy would be attained were it not picked up naturally: since the situation had not arisen for this family, the question had perhaps never been addressed. Two other examples, from an article on alternative education in *Living* magazine, indicate that emphasizing literacy and numeracy, but leaving the rest to the children, is a very common approach. First, the Fullwood family: 'Although they have a large say in what they do, subjects like maths. and spelling, for which they have a weekly test, are structured' (Baker, 1983, p. 47). And the Wilkins family: 'The children usually choose what they do, though Sally encourages regular practice in the three Rs' (Baker, *ibid.*, p. 50).

In one family, the Bakers, however, a child who showed no interest in reading and writing early on was able to abandon it until he felt ready:

> I recall my mother trying to teach me to read when I was about five. It was hopeless — I just was not interested. I could have been bored by it to the point when it would have made it harder to learn later. Fortunately she did not persist; she dropped it completely. Then when I was about eight years old I suddenly wanted to know how to read — I was fascinated by the printed word. At this point I would

probably have been considered backward, even retarded, in a regular school. But then I started learning to read. On my own. No formal 'lessons', no wishing I didn't have to do it. If there was a word I just couldn't understand I would either look it up in a dictionary, or ask my mother. But mostly it was on my own that I learned . . . by the time I was twelve I had reached a level of reading that even the education authorities agreed was that of an adult. (David Baker)

This is very much the approach to reading motivation that writers such as John Holt and Leila Berg advocate. Leila Berg reports how her grandchild came to choose to learn to read:

> She is surrounded by real-life 'educational materials', supplied by the whole of our society from birth; and her 'motivation' is to become more and more competent in her real-life affairs, which are interlinked with the real-life affairs of other people, of all ages and competences, who are important to her. Reading helps her living in a practical way, and enriches it in an artistic sensual way . . . entirely on her own terms. (Berg, 1984, p. 30)

Neither of these writers deals with the question of dyslexic children, who seem to need all the help they can get, as early as possible, if they are to read and spell normally — indeed, John Holt does not accept the existence of dyslexia.

In families where a basic standard had already been obtained, regular exercise of the skills they had often took place in an integrated way through the pursuance of the children's own special interest, as I shall show in a later chapter, and in these cases there was more opportunity for interests to become paramount and for the children to be increasingly self-determining in their learning. Caroline Parker describes how this worked in her situation:

> I choose a subject, say in history, I choose one country I'd like to do and I get loads of books on it and write things about it . . . natural history as well. I choose subjects like the badger, then I'd find out as much as I could about it and write it down. It was like that mostly. We used to sometimes go on walks trying to spot them, in the very early morning before it got light.

Many families, including the Parkers, emphasized the large amount of reading the children did, both for pleasure and information:

> I've always read quite a lot. Historical books I like . . . and I like the classics, you know, Jane Austen. I don't really like children's fiction. I mean some of them are all right — Hester Burton and Geoffrey Trease and that kind of thing . . . Elizabeth Gaskell's portrayal of the Brontes, of Charlotte Bronte, is very good. (Corinne Dey)

Andrew McGill said of his children:

> I think perhaps they read too much for other parents who want their
> kids to be reading. They do read a tremendous amount. A tremendous
> amount.

> *Tiffany:* What books do you read? *Little Women*, yes, she's read it
> once but she's had it out again. But they're never without a book.

A Tempering Factor: Balance in the Curriculum

Where the parents have a well-thought out theory of the kinds of knowledge
they would like their children to study, perhaps in connection with the aims
previously discussed, one might expect balance in the curriculum to be a factor
affecting the extent of a child's choice of learning activity. There is only a little
explicit evidence from those interviewed that this is so, although the range of
subjects studied in some cases perhaps suggests it was taken for granted. Phil
Minchin explains how in his family children had a fair amount of scope for
indulging particular current interests but a balance of subjects in the long
term, which his parents evidently considered important, was still ensured:

> *J.W.:* You say you do an hour of maths. and an hour of English. And
> the other subject, does that vary from time to time or — ?
> *Phil:* Yes. You've got to change it. You can't do that one subject for
> weeks and weeks and weeks on end. It's history, geography, science,
> art, craft, things like that.

Another way of ensuring more or less equal attention to all areas is the keeping
of some kind of record of work done, as in the Wilkins family: 'the children
keep a daily diary of their work and Sally corrects the balance if on occasions
she feels something is being neglected' (Baker, 1983, p. 50).

That there was sometimes a lack of traditional balance is accepted by one
interviewee, Alison Head, as a consequence of the curriculum being self-
chosen:

> It was really then following up interests and some things got left out.
> Now I wish I had done a bit more chemistry and stuff because I didn't
> do any of that really. But on the other hand if I'd done it at school it
> probably wouldn't have sunk in and I'd probably have dropped it
> before O levels. A lot of schools it's a choice between sciences and arts
> and I'd have wanted to keep my music up. At the time I really had no
> motivation to learn that sort of thing because I wasn't really interested
> in it. Now I might very well do a short chemistry course or something.
> There's never enough time to do everything you want to do.

Where a child's own particular interests are subordinate to what he or his parents see as relevant to future job or career requirements, they may still form a greater part of his learning than they would in school, due partly to the greater speed with which work on the other subjects can be dispatched and partly to the already mentioned greater availability of options. In the McGill family, for example, although what one might call a core curriculum was firmly established by the parents, the children had the time and opportunity to develop many different talents and interests outside it, calligraphy and dress-making, for example, as well as astronomy which provoked this opening comment:

> *Tiffany:*   I don't understand that but I just let her do it if she wants to. She gets an idea, like that writing and she did it and that was it. And then when pedal-pushers came in she wanted to make a pair of pedal-pushers so of course we got some stuff and we made them and they were really nice ones . . . We have a typewriter and Annie types quite well, doesn't she, she types not badly.
>
> *Andrew:*   Sylvia's interested in butterflies as well.
>
> *Tiffany:*   She traces each one you know, and puts it into a book, and does a page of that, and then just because one isn't just right she discards the book, throws it away. Every one has to be just right you see.

Where the children's interests dominated completely the choice of learning activities, this was sometimes due to parental humility: how, in such a rapidly changing world, could one person presume to decide what another needed to learn? What knowledge would be useful in ten years' time and what obsolete? Were there skills which positively ought to be learnt or was the school curriculum a relic retained to impose limitations on too wide and bewildering a range of possibilities? Mary Parsons expressed her thoughts on this in a letter to me about the education of her younger son William:

> I've been reading Marshall McLuhan just lately, *Understanding Media*, *The Mechanical Bride* and *The Gutenberg Galaxy*, which are all about how we are influenced by technology and tools. His books have really made me think about our assumptions about culture, and I have honestly no idea what I should teach William so at the moment I'm not doing anything. Our culture and rationality is really very simple minded and one-dimensional in its traditional spheres.

William was therefore pursuing his own interests and had become a fluent reader and comic artist of some talent through his devotion to a set of old *Eagles*. That this lack of parental control over the curriculum need not be the disaster some authoritarian educationalists might predict is given credence by the success of William's older brother Simon in obtaining training in the course of his choice (catering) following a very unorthodox combination of educational activities: he divided his time between playing snooker (first and foremost), learning Nuffield mathematics., making complicated Lego models, and, as already mentioned, studying geology and microscopy, and learning German — this activity arose from a deep interest in the Second World War. (William himself later decided he wanted to do civil engineering, and enrolled at a tertiary college to obtain the necessary GCSEs.) The original Operation Otherwise of the Head family took as its starting point progress outwards from particular interests of the children: 'investigation of our life together in society would be central. We should be working from particular problems or interests to wider analysis and possibilities of active involvement' (Head, 1974, p. 128). He gives an example of how this worked practically in the form of a specimen week's activities for both Alison and Martin and adds:

> Martin was spending a lot of time with Street Aid in Covent Garden, working with young adults and other children to make fifteen-feet models of 'rock' celebrities, which were later shown in the foyer of a cinema. . . . There was also screen printing. . . . We all visited the Tutankhamen exhibition. (Head, 1974, p. 134)

The Place of Parents' Background and Interests

There are four aspects to what the parents of home educated children have to offer in terms of personal resources which might affect choice of curriculum: their own educational background, their job or career, their interests, and their philosophy of life (discussed from another angle in Chapter 4).

As mentioned in Chapter 3, very little information was obtained on parents' own educational background and what there was seemed to have more bearing on the choice of an alternative type of education than on the content of that education, though where a parent had missed out on particular subjects for which they now found they had an interest, they were likely to set to and learn alongside the children; for example, Amy and Corinne Dey chose to learn French together, and Sally Banks found that Glenn was interested in much of her Open University material:

Sally: I always try to take an interest in everything, and although I wasn't very knowledgeable at science subjects I was interested in them.

J.W.: So you felt you learnt quite a lot with Glenn?

Sally: Yes, I did. And for the arts side, strangely enough we used to use quite a lot of the Open University units . . . I was doing all the arts degree . . . I did A291, the early Roman empire and he was very interested in the Romans and he worked his way through huge chunks of that. And 'Man's religious quest' I did, and he worked all the way through Islam. He's always been interested in that.

From the evidence of occupational backgrounds as well as the way in which parents talked about their children's learning, showing their own previous knowledge of subjects involved, it was obvious that all the families involved in the study had at least an average, and in most cases much higher than average, standard of general education so that there was no opportunity to investigate the problems of less well educated parents in educating their own children, sometimes posited as an objection to the home education movement. John Holt, however, refutes objections of this sort vehemently:

> I don't expect many illiterate parents to ask me how they can take their children out of school and teach them at home. But if any do, I will say 'I don't think that just because you have not yet learned to read and write means that you can't do a better job of helping your children learn about the world than the schools. But one of the things you are going to have to do in order to help them is *learn* to read and write. It is easy, if you really want to do it, and once you get out of your head the idea that you *can't* do it. If any of your children can read and write, they can help you learn. If none of them can read and write, you can learn together'. (Holt, 1981, p. 58)

There will be further discussion of this learning side by side in the section on the parent's role in the process of home education. For the moment, it is necessary only to note that the main influence of the parent's own education on the content of the curriculum seems to have taken this very positive form, rather than causing either the inclusion or the omission of particular areas because of a parent's expertise or lack of it in the area concerned.

What influence does the occupational background of parents have on the choice of curriculum content? Since over half the parents involved were teachers, we could examine an assumption such as that of Sandra Blacker that these parents might set themselves up as 'competitors' with the school system, trying to cover the same range of subjects in the same sort of formal exam-orientated way, only better. In fact, there is almost no evidence from my study to support this supposition: the teachers, with the exception of the McGills and Hartfields, were amongst those most concerned to give children a fairly free rein as to choice of curriculum without a backward glance at what the schools were doing. Where parents were specialist teachers, this also seemed to have little bearing on their children's choice of areas of learning: 'history and rural studies were my subjects and he didn't study either of them, so I couldn't help him at all' (Roger Merriman).

Other parental occupations appear sometimes to have decided children to opt for areas in which appropriate help would be available: Corinne Dey's choice of science was partly influenced by the willingness of her engineer father to teach her, and Maureen Cotton chose shorthand, which her father could teach her. They might still have chosen these if the only available help or teaching had been outside the family, of course: when Corinne's learning with her father did not work out, she continued with her chemistry through a part-time schooling arrangement, as we have seen.

Occupations which somehow involve the whole environment of the children are perhaps more likely to influence their choice of learning areas. Examples of this are the children of parents who earn their living through self-sufficiency or those such as Ben Haward, whose parents were travelling actors/artists. Ben constantly had the opportunity to take part in various aspects of his parents' shows and this led to further study in several areas (but not those in which his parents specialized), in one of which he eventually decided to make his career. His letter to me three years after the interview shows that this early interest, originating out-of-school, had persisted:

> At the end of the sixth form, I am going to try and get on a trainee course to be a sound technician, with either the BBC or ITV, but preferably ITV because the wages are higher. I am still working with 'The State' and we did a touring show in the summer that I was involved with. . . . I mainly play music in the shows, although I do perform, but quite often on stilts or unicycle. I also help to set up sound equipment and lights.

A primary school head, perhaps rather surprisingly, puts the case for the choice of learning farming skills before those of literacy and numeracy in a farming community, with reference to the Harrison family on their smallholding:

> I know children don't work on farms as much as they did in my day, but they're still going back to an environment where in fact if they're to survive at all they must learn to earn their living before they actually learn to read and write if you like . . . if you aren't taught farming and farming methods quite young — it's a different skill from working in a school. . . . The skill of farming really needs to be embedded, as the Harrisons wanted to, and I had great sympathy.

Parental hobbies might also be expected to influence choice of learning activities, since it is natural to want to enthuse others about your own interests and since those with the most powerful enthusiasm about their subject often make the best teachers. Caroline Parker gave an example of this, referring not only to her own education but to that of the other children in the Trunkles Top

community: 'my mum likes art a lot so the taught a lot of art to the children.
I've always enjoyed doing it as well'.

Other parents passed on a love of natural history to their children, so that
work in this area was almost a continuous part of family life, hardly a choice at
all:

> There's this interest in birdlife which I've had way back because my
> parents were interested in it, as I say. We began this as well, going out,
> not only for walks in the country but in the months of May and June
> we go up in the cornfields and when you arrive at the longest day you
> can go up there, sleep out for maybe an hour or two, get up with the
> dawn chorus and come home, practically falling to sleep, at eight
> o'clock in the morning. (Andrew McGill)

On the other hand there seems in some families to have been a two-way
flow in which children's interests appear to have influenced their *parent's*
curriculum:

> *J.W.:*   How much have your own interests and your husband's interests
> affected the things the children have done?
> *Marie Gordon:*   They did walking because we've always gone walking;
> they've always liked outdoor things like geography. I've always liked
> painting, sewing, knitting so I suppose they've picked those up, do-
> it-yourself, that kind of thing, gardening. . . . They've just kind of
> copied things we've done, which was the idea.
> *George:*   You can almost reverse that question though: how have *our*
> interests affected you?
> *Marie:*   Yes, yes, they have. I'm in their drama group now and Walter
> does the stage managing. Because they were in drama group, we've
> got involved with them.

The final aspect of the influence of parents on choice of learning-at-home
activities involves a contentious issue, which can be expressed as an attempt by
some to parallel the concept of 'hidden curriculum' in schools: do parents with
particular religious, social or political axes to grind enshrine these somehow in
the children's curriculum, hoping to indoctrinate them with the desire to
change the world in a particular way or to adopt a particular worldview? The
argument runs that the hidden curriculum of home education could be more
dangerous than that of the school, since opposing views may never be encountered. This disregards the writing of some educationalists (for example, Lister,
1974 and Meighan, 1981b) who see the school's hidden curriculum as a
subliminal influence presented by consensus among school authorities of all
sorts (though not necessarily by deliberate conspiracy).

A home-grown hidden curriculum is hard to separate from the attitudes that caring parents want to help their children to acquire. Perhaps it differs from the school in being in fact less hidden and therefore more open to questioning because more consciously encountered. Certainly assumptions about education tended to have been well discussed, because of their unortho-dox nature, both within the family and with ever-curious friends and relations. As far as the issue we are concerned with here goes, there was no evidence that choice of curriculum subjects was directly influenced by parental philosophy in any sense except the most general: for example, a number of parents felt that both boys and girls should be able to cook, sew and generally look after themselves, as we have already seen. Several parents were members of the peace movement but none had encouraged their children to take up peace studies, though some of the children had become involved in peace-group activities, as often happens in like-minded schooled families. Only one of the parents expressed an overt political standpoint and this had not influenced his son's choice of curriculum or materials at all (nor his political views, which were quite different from his father's although they had developed partly through family discussion).

Where parents had a particular view of the social system and how they would like it to change — for example, parents living in a community — there was evidence in one case, that of Caroline Parker, that the curriculum was influenced by considerations of community life:

> The schoolwork sort of gradually drained away and more and more practical work was being learnt by them because the schoolwork wasn't really helping the community very much but the other work, getting children involved in the community was, it seemed, better so we've gone more and more towards that sort of thing. And the children seem to enjoy it more as well. We've got our own time as well

in which she went to weaving, horse-riding, woodworking, astrology and watercolour painting classes, and rode around the countryside on her racing bike, all activities which she chose and which were unconnected with community life.

There was very little evidence of the home education curriculum being used as a vehicle for the inculcation of parental ideals, though many were strongly held and frequently the subject of open discussion. The situation today is perhaps a little different, in that the American fundamentalist-style parent, home educating for religious reasons, is becoming evident in the UK.

Another way to look at the hidden curriculum of home-based education would be to consider whether the home education movement as a whole encourages the acceptance of certain assumptions which parallel those of the schools. Lister (Lister, 1974) suggests that the latter include competitive rather than cooperative values, the necessity of being taught if one is to learn, and the importance of the school as opposed to the world outside as the site of such teaching. When EO as a group affirms the opposite of these assumptions, it does so in a thoroughly open way (on the cover of its bi-monthly newsletter) so that no hidden element can be identified here. Various factions of the group, however, appear to have their own areas of unspoken shared assumptions, regarding attitudes to self-discipline or to academic work, for example, which may constitute a local hidden curriculum to the extent that they may assume them to be held by other members when, in fact, this is not the case. In general, the members of EO are too various in ideological and practical approaches to home-based education for any proper parallel to Lister's hidden curriculum to exist.

Plans for particular careers involving the acquisition of qualifications; academic ability per se; examination courses already begun at school; and children's interests and hobbies were all apparent as determinants of curricular content. Competence in the fields of literacy and numeracy was almost universally desired and worked for. There was no evidence that a dangerously indoctrinating hidden curriculum was present in the choice of learning activities, although it must be noted that many religious home educators, particularly in the States, but increasingly in the UK, use materials such as those of the Christian correspondence schools with the intention of presenting one philosophy of life at the expense of consideration of any others.

Chapter 7

Other Constraints on Choice of What to Learn: The LEA, and Resources

Having discussed the choice of learning activities and influences on them from the point of view of families' own background and attitudes, I shall now examine the way in which this choice may be expanded or limited by external factors such as availability of resources of all sorts, and local authority expectations.

Local Authority Expectations

The latter can be dealt with briefly in this context, since there is an outline in Chapter 1 of the position of LEAs regarding home-based education and further discussion of relationships with the local authority in Chapter 10. There is plenty of evidence in the *EO Newsletters* that families' ideas about what LEAs might require in the way of curriculum have an influence on their choice; for example, the following two quotes, from *EO News* 38 and 21 respectively:

> We explained that we did not believe in formal methods for children under seven or even eight and that we had only encouraged the eldest two to read as a compromise between what we really wanted to do and what we knew the LEA would want us to do.

and:

> We had talked at length over the past year about what we would do and how, though in truth when we set out to plan our boys' education our practices started immediately to reflect what we presumed would be official requirements.

The extent to which advisers affect curriculum choice depends partly on authority policy, partly on the individual adviser's views and partly on the status (if any) assigned to the child by the authority, for example, 'GCE material', 'maladjusted', or 'school phobic'. One LEA Chief Education Officer (CEO) was adamant that 'we're an authority without policies really . . . our policy is not to have policies', while an adviser in a neighbouring county explained that its policy was to ask for a balanced curriculum from each family, about whose contents he was not, however, specific. My notes on his remarks read:

> He may point out to parents that certain areas are significantly lacking — again, would not be specific about what he regards as important but felt that particularly for the older child being at home puts undesirable limits on the curriculum.

It is obvious from these contrasting quotes that authorities' influence on the curriculum of home educated children can vary from an approach which looks at each child as an individual with its unique learning needs to an approach which seeks to have everybody adopt the same traditional range of subjects. In authorities at one end of the spectrum, families have full autonomy to work out their programme with advice from advisers — at the other they may feel almost threatened unless they comply with the expected norm. One child, Phil Minchin, felt under pressure from the adviser to do more writing:

> He looks at my books: 'Oh, there's not much in there' and that's it. Not what I know, not what I've done — it's quantity, just because there's not reams and reams of written work. I bet if I got a book and copied out every word, word for word, he'd be happy.

As an illustration of the wide variation in approach, it is interesting that the interviewed adviser quoted previously said in contrast that he:

> . . . expects to see some written work but has no preconceptions about the form it should take and regards evidence that, for example, the child is gaining some understanding of sequencing ideas as more important than reams of laborious written work.

Another adviser, from the same authority, but about ten years earlier, went for a compromise between the official interpretation of the law (erroneous, but accepted unquestioningly by the teacher trainer mother) and what the child involved, Gerry, wanted to do with her time:

> They were absolutely marvellous, they came round, they said what under the law they required as far as they could see it. . . . That she'd have to do I think it was about five hours' equivalent at home but it didn't have to . . . in fact, the man we had, who was a very nice man, who came to visit us, he said she could even do a job, because that's

another thing she desperately wanted to do, was to go out and earn her living, so she could work and do her work in the evening so it was a very flexible arrangement, and that she should do the basic maths., a science and English language and she would choose art obviously because art I could supervise her and Brian could help, but she would have a basic curriculum. (Veronica Budd)

Where the choice of curriculum depends from the authority's point of view on the label it places on a child, it may become a bargaining tool: you may only home educate this child if you ensure that it learns what we consider suitable. In Jim Merriman's case, as already discussed, this was definitely so. Christine Merriman said:

I wasn't going to confront them over anything and they were quite reasonable. And the area officer said, 'Well, you're well within your rights, there's nothing much I can do about it.' But what we had to agree with was to continue with O levels, according to his age, aptitude and ability.

Happily, as we have seen, the authority's estimation of aptitude and ability coincided with the Merrimans' own in this case, so that the curriculum choice could be made harmoniously. However, other situations may not be so straightforward, for example, where the labelling of a child may either be a bone of contention between family and LEA, as in the case of Piers Arthur, who was said to be maladjusted, or where the label has different implications for family and authority, as in the case of the Harrisons whose dyslexia was uncontested but whose parents saw a different educational solution to the problem of how to tackle it (by making the children competent and self-confident in other areas) from the authority (who wanted them to attend a special unit for dyslexics or at least accept LEA home tuition). The Harrisons were strong-minded enough to pursue the choice of learning activities that they and their children regarded as appropriate and interesting, but not without a great deal of worry and several court appearances. The question of statementing of children with special needs, under the 1981 Act, becomes relevant to families in this position nowadays, though none of those interviewed were young enough for it to have applied to them. The person with responsibility for advice to parents of children with special needs within EO writes in *EO News* 51:

Most disturbing of all is the number of parents I have spoken to who have been told that their child has been 'Statemented' but have not even received a copy or any details of the Statement. . . . When you consider that even where parents *are* given all the proper information, there is a likelihood of disagreement over any or all of the statutory (medical, psychological and educational) or other assessments, or of dispute over the determination of the child's 'needs', opposition to the 'Special Educational Provision' deemed suitable to meet those needs, and refusal to accept the suitability of the 'Appropriate school or other arrangements' . . . I won't go into the possibility of problems concerning the 'Additional non-educational Provision' specified. Is it surprising that we advise 'Avoid statementing if possible'?

Resources

We no longer have to force-feed education to children: they live in a world in which they are surrounded by educative resources.

There are around 500 hours each of the schools' television and radio every year in this country. There are several million books in public libraries. There are museums in every town. There is a constant stream of cheap or free information from a dozen media. There are home computers, which will soon be easily connected to phones and thus other computers.

There are thousands of workplaces which are, or could be made, convenient for children, where they could learn about the reality of working lives and join in them. There are, as there have always been, the old, the disabled, the very young, all in need of children in their lives, all in need of the kind of help caring and careful youngsters can give, and all of them rich sources of information about the world, and freely available to any child who isn't locked away in school. (North, 1982, p. 15)

For families whose children have been to school, the finding of resources appropriate to their needs may pose an intimidating problem. The adjustment from passive receipt of textbooks, laboratory equipment etc. (together with advice on how to use them), to active seeking out of the necessary facilities is an educational experience in itself for parents and children and often, by chance, introduces them to resources they had not previously been aware of and learning activities they had not previously considered. This may entail an opening out of their lives in new ways and result in a quite different vision of education from the one they had originally.

In the rest of this chapter I shall show how families overcame the problem of finding resources for existing interests and illustrate the effects of discovery of various resources on the things they chose to investigate, using one area of learning, science, as my principal example, but discussing other areas where relevant to the point being made.

Many of the objections to home education as a practical proposition relate to a supposed lack of resources: an Educational Welfare Officer I interviewed observed that no parent could satisfactorily cover the secondary curriculum because of inadequate facilities and apparatus; and this seems to be a generally held idea outside home educating families, to judge by comments offered to me in the context of my son's home education. Those who put this point of view, whether in relation to science, physical education, music or drama (the most frequently mentioned areas) have perhaps come to this conclusion by classifying home education to themselves in two stereotyped and largely erroneous ways: firstly, as being exclusively in the home and secondly, as being an attempt to ape the school in both content and method. In only one of the families interviewed (and that one, the Scheaffers, a special case because of illness) could both these features be said to apply. In all other families, outside resources were used regularly in addition to those of the home, and in most, education at home was never intended to be a carbon copy of the school situation.

The falseness of these objections can be illustrated by an investigation of how individuals with an interest in branches of science (since this is the subject most often suggested as a problem) found the resources to pursue them. Science, in one form or another, was studied at home, sometimes up to O level, by most of those interviewed, and gave some a good enough grounding and sufficient enthusiasm to pursue it to A level and then to university.

Outside the Home: Opportunities for Formal Learning

Flexischooling
Opportunities for learning outside the home were taken up by some of those interested in pursuing a formal science course for examination purposes, often after two or three years of informal study at home. These families managed to make use of facilities available in a way that suggests the possibilities of a future education system located neither essentially at home nor at school (dubbed 'flexischooling'):

It is possible to envisage a range of possible arrangements between schools and homes between these two poles, with part-time, school-based work and home-based work, working to programmes, agreed among teachers, parents and pupils, for either short or longer periods of time. . . . The administrative skills, systems and procedures already exist. The organization of the Open University, the administration of evening institutes in a multitude of study situations, and the operation of correspondence colleges and of technical colleges with large part-time populations of students are all working models that can be adopted. (Meighan, 1981b, p. 343)

One of the children in question was able, as we have seen, to pursue her interest in chemistry through part-time schooling, arranged virtually by accident (as so many resources do seem to present themselves to home educating families with open minds) with the headmistress of her sister's school:

> They had an Open Evening so I took Corinne there because I liked to show her now and again what she was missing really, and of course the headmistress was very surprised and said, 'Why isn't she at school?' and well, I think I told her. And later on I said to her, 'Corinne said if only she could come here for a lesson or two and choose her subjects she'd be quite happy.' And she said, 'Oh, well she *can*. We've had school refusers before'. But I think what she was thinking at that time, we weren't quite thinking in accord, at the time she thought Corinne was going to come and be gently weaned back into the school system. I sort of took her at her word and Corinne went along there to do maths. and chemistry. (Amy Dey)

Present possibilities for this sort of arrangement vary greatly between, and even within, local education authorities, depending partly on the status assigned to the child concerned by the authority (as in Corinne's case). One adviser I spoke to saw the child in part-time schooling as an administrative problem: it would be difficult, he said, for teachers to keep track of who they were responsible for, and the hard work of making a group 'gel' would be made even harder by the intrusion of a part-time pupil. A headmistress in the same authority saw the pupil more as an individual with unique educational needs and a right to have them met, and so had a completely different attitude. She talked about someone she knew who had taken an unhappy teenager out of school:

> The science bit was the only bit I was worried about because I knew science and maths. tend to be in line. . . . I said I'd heard this lady was sympathetic, a secondary modern school. And in fact the child now goes once a week into school for science lessons with the rest of the children. She's the right age and living in the right catchment area and everything — it was lucky. Well, not lucky — I mean, this seems to me to be the answer. . . . You could do this for all sorts of children. Because they're entitled to state education anyway, so why can they not have the bit they want? (Jean Mortimer)

A writer to *EO Newsletter* 19 reveals in the following cautionary tale the extent to which informal arrangements for part-time schooling are dependent on the goodwill of the head:

> John, at six and a half, had been home educated for eighteen months when we were approached by the headmaster of a nearby school. He suggested that John could attend class one morning a week, play games, and have swimming lessons at the school. He mentioned that he wanted to boost the number of pupils he had in the school. We immediately contacted the LEA, pointing out that we wished to be fully responsible for John's education, and also asking them to be sure that there was sufficient provision for insurance. They agreed, by letter, to both our points.
>
> There was no doubt that John enjoyed the next twelve months attending the school part-time — however, he showed no inclination to want to attend on a full-time basis. Then suddenly, we received a curt note from the headmaster saying that he could no longer accept John at his school because it was now full.

It seems that part-time schooling is an issue on which no clear guidelines exist, which is what led the advisers I spoke to in one authority to examine its legal status, since they felt rather favourably towards it as a possibility for certain individuals:

> *Chief Education Officer (CEO):* What do the words of the Act actually mean? Because they are open to more than one interpretation, I believe, though they've always been interpreted to be either full . . . time or not at all.
>
> *Primary Education Officer:* We suspect that this is because cases, 1927, you know, way back, I think have always come up in the context where an authority wanted to resist this and the magistrates have upheld that view. But, you know, is it polar opposites or could it cover quite a wide bit of ground? I don't think, we haven't been able to find any testing of this . . .
>
> *Secondary adviser:* If any of the few families I've been visiting had wanted that sort of arrangement, I certainly would have tried to arrange it.

FE colleges and adult education

A much more common source of formal science lessons, and exam-orientated courses in general, was the FE college, which those interviewed saw as a specialist institution from which they could take what they needed in the way of help towards obtaining qualifications. Marie Gordon explained why George was taking his O and A levels in this way:

It's an exam factory, full stop. Some of their teachers are also examiners so they can get them through an exam, that's the reason. . . . You can be pretty good at a subject but if you're not doing the right answer in the right way, you're not doing yourself enough credit.

Some of those who attended FE college had sufficient confidence to manipulate the system so that it bent (rather unwillingly) to accommodate them. Glenn Banks managed to get onto the FE college courses at fifteen, a year before he reached the official age of entry (as did Piers Arthur and Maureen Cotton) and once there he was very determined that he, and not the college, would choose what he was going to study:

Glenn: Practically as soon as I walked in the door, this head of department at college gave me a full timetable, which I tore up.

Sally: He wanted him to do sociology and economics and things like that.

J.W.: He didn't consult you about what you wanted to do?

Glenn: They had an impressive range of titles for the courses, which gave no indication of what exactly they were, and told me to go and think about it.

Sally: By the time Glenn went back and told him, he'd dropped half of them. But he did English language, drama, English literature was an evening course, and maths., maths. and computer studies . . . And all three of the English subjects were all modern, and a lot of them seemed to be repeating themselves and he didn't like that idea, and when we took it up with the head of general studies, he didn't like the attitude. You know: 'At fifteen you can't know what you want to do' but Glenn kept calm, he just sat there, he was trying to force the issue, and then went promptly off to the head of the English department and got onto the A level course instead.

Adult education classes were another source of teaching in subjects which parents felt unable to tackle at home — the definition of 'adult' appears to have encompassed thirteen-year-olds in Corinne Dey's case (she and her mother went to a French class where they were able to benefit from the conversation practice which, for example, Daniel Scheaffer found lacking in his tape/correspondence course). It appears that these classes are often happy to enrol youngsters to keep their numbers up.

After-hours use of institutional facilities
Use of schools or other institutional facilities after hours and under suitable supervision is another possibility which has been investigated by EO mem-

bers, particularly for science, though the adviser who was concerned about the administrative problems of part-time schooling saw this as a bureaucratic headache as well. Who, he asked, would be responsible for putting equipment back in its cupboard, or ensuring breakages were replaced? No such considerations apply in some other LEAs, however, as this writer to *EO News* 19 explains:

> We had decided on a scientific bias, and Nuffield Science, together with my own agricultural background, satisfied the adviser with regard to expertise, but it was equipment which presented the problem. I had previously asked the chief adviser for the division if there was any chance of laboratory time in a school — his reply was that labs were in full timetable demand but technically they could be available for hire as could any school facility, if not being used by the school, on payment of a hire fee, and with the agreement of the head of a school. It turned out that on school lab facilities the hire fee was very high and the availability (according to local heads) was inconvenient. It was the science adviser who came to the rescue with the suggestion that we approach the local Polytechnic, who not only had a lab but the full Nuffield kits which could be utilized by local schools on a loan basis. They also had greater autonomy to make their own decisions re. hiring etc.
>
> We negotiated and after checking my familiarity with the apparatus, we now have access to the lab and they lend us modules of equipment for use at home, on a hire and rental basis.

Sports facilities are another example of an under-used resource which is sometimes available to home educating families as part of their local community. None of those interviewed had in fact made use of school sports facilities (though one adviser did say that home educated children might be able to participate in an after-school gym club, on the basis of an approach to individual heads).

Youth and community centres

Youth clubs and community centres not under the aegis of the education department (perhaps funded by charitable trusts) sometimes offer courses, in crafts, drama, music and the arts, particularly. The Gordons discovered a Quaker institute which ran all sorts of courses, with no lower age limit: they studied Esperanto, attended a peace group and Grace was intending to do O level English there. Corinne Dey was able to attend a modern dance workshop locally and Alison Head a music class, where she was able to follow a formal course:

> *Alison:* I was doing Saturday mornings at the Royal College of
>   Music . . . a couple of instruments, and we did theory . . .
> *J.W.:* Which instruments did you do?
> *Alison:* Flute and harp most of the time. And I took my O level there
>   as well.

In one area several home educators have made use of a centre which operates
on a sessional rather than termly basis, so enabling children to try pottery,
drama, making things, once and see if they enjoy it. The need not to commit
themselves encourages people to have a go and perhaps develop new interests.

Outside Opportunities for Informal Learning

Outside facilities for less formal approaches to learning, and for supplementary formal courses, are numerous, as the quotation from Richard North at the
beginning of this section suggests. The range of resources available can be
illustrated by reference to the theme of scientific interests discussed above:
many have applications in other areas, which will be examined alongside their
use in science.

Urban versus rural

A first point to be made in connection with the use of outside facilities is that
urban- and rural-living home educators may find very different resources at
their disposal unless they have easy transport enabling them to make use of
what both environments offer.

Those in pursuit of branches of science such as geology, biology and
astronomy found that the natural world in its various forms provided an
excellent resource in terms of material for observation in context, which could
be studied further at home. One contributor to *Free Way to Learning* described how taking advantage of what the countryside has to offer in this way
can actually be made easier by the lack of a structured school day to adhere to,
so that resources which would be unavailable in school become a possibility:

> Not long ago we got up at four o'clock in the morning to go out to
> Ashridge. We stayed out four hours, and saw eight deer, three foxes,
> and four rabbits. If I had been at school this would have been
> impossible. (Head, 1974, p. 138)

Local branches of societies such as WATCH, the young conservationists'
group, and the Young Ornithologists' Club, run activities throughout the year
which some home educators take advantage of to set a growing awareness of
the natural world in a seasonal context. Mary Parsons used the field trips of the

local natural history society as a starting-off point for work on the geology of the area:

> We used to do a lot of geology, quite liked doing that. I went to classes, you see, for geology and he got quite interested because we went on field courses and so on. But I've not been to the classes for a while. We still go on field trips on our own from time to time . . . it's a good place for geology. Well, it's a good place for lots of things. It's a good place for natural history, you know, people think, 'Oh, it's an industrial city, iron and steel and so on, terrible', but in fact the countryside is very near; there are lots of natural history things to go and do even near the city boundaries.

Urban and rural resources are clearly equally available to the Parsons family, but Malcolm Gold, living in the Scottish islands, felt that lack of access to the facilities of a large town was a definite disadvantage, particularly in the area of access to books:

> Once a month there's a van comes round . . . you can borrow as many books until the next time it comes round which is in a month if it's all right but if the driver's ill or the van breaks down it's two months or three months before it turns up. It's something I certainly miss: before, I had the third biggest public library in the country plus all the university libraries. You could want a book and nine times out of ten it was there. Whereas here everything has to be ordered.

Lack of access to large museums is also a feature of life in very remote areas, and these are much used by families either pursuing specific interests in science, such as the various physical principles which are demonstrated by the 'hands-on' experiments at the Science Museum in London, or just browsing. Alison Head and Corinne Dey, both living in London, described regular visits to the capital's museums. The other area of interest well served by museums is that of history, whether local and usually comprehensive from prehistoric times to the present, or national, in which case the various museums devoted to specific themes such as war or toys or art may be useful. Many of the local museums run special interest clubs or classes for children, particularly in the school holidays.

Workplaces
A resource whose use is being developed in schools a little through work experience schemes for older pupils is that of workplaces, where informal visiting by home educated children is sometimes arranged. In America particularly, the 'sitting next to Nellie' aspect of learning by working alongside adult employees, whether these are parents or not, is one that forms a reward-

ing part of some families' home education programmes. (There is further discussion of this in Chapter 8.) In some cases it's an ad hoc experience, happening as part of the family's daily life:

> I had a forty-eight hour experiment going which had to be checked in the middle of the night. J. went in with me the first night and we had trouble with one of the machines, a fraction collector which moves test tubes along under the end of a length of fine tubing which slowly spits out the stuff to be collected. We stayed there until 5 a.m. and J. occupied himself almost the whole time with a stopwatch checking the rates of drips from the tubing, the rate of movement of the tubes, and the rate of a monitoring pen on another machine — all work that was necessary for getting the job done — and he revelled in it. . . . J. wanted to stay with it right till the end and did. He learned all sorts of things in that short span of time about units of volume and time, about multiplying and dividing, about fractions, about light absorption, magnets, solutions and probably other things. The same boy had been completely turned off school maths. and was regarded by some as 'slow' and 'lazy'. (Mother quoted in Holt, 1981, pp. 261–2)

Other families incorporate a system of workplace visits into their programmes. A mother writing in *Growing Without Schooling* 26 describes one of her children's planned experiences, this one not only of work but of a completely different way of life:

> The boys (eleven and nine) had three days prior to Christmas on their own with an Indian family that lives totally off the land (no water, electricity, heat etc., they eat only what they hunt, grow and raise) in a mountainous, very remote wilderness area north of Nashville. The boys milked goats, chopped firewood, drew water from a stream, played home-made hockey on a frozen pond, climbed mountains, learned about nature, the Indians' strong beliefs about the value of non-waste, water, land etc. They ate unusual food, slept on the floor of the hand-made dwelling. It was three degrees. The boys loved it and came home full of things to tell us. *Next* month, with an architect . . .

Considerable ingenuity may be needed, however, in gaining access to appropriate resources, as the Head family found when they attempted to visit places linked to the focus of their current project, the commonest way in which workplace trips were used by those interviewed for this study:

> The sugar project (which included natural science, international trade relations, diet and health, agriculture, the policy of the EEC, and a host of other things some of us had grown up with as 'subjects') took

three members of the family on a visit to Lincolnshire. We wandered in sugar-beet fields and talked with the workers and the farmer; the factory would not admit anyone under fourteen. The project also turned our thoughts to dockland. We found great difficulties in getting any docks to welcome us to see a sugar ship unloading. A number said they used to welcome parties, but it interrupted the work and was unsafe. This is just one example of how much of the 'real-life' about us is closed to those who want to learn at first-hand. We eventually found one private dock in Dagenham willing to give way to our persistence. (The car broke down on the way and we never made it.) (Head, 1974, p. 134)

As Richard North hints in the quotation which opened this section, the use of workplaces as learning environments for children is rather more potential than actual, in Britain at least, though places concerned with children, particularly informal places such as playgroups, seem to take a more enlightened attitude towards the idea. I know of three cases in which eleven-or twelve-year-old girls were taken on the staff of playgroups or nurseries to the satisfaction of all concerned. Alison Head described how this worked for her, emphasizing the doubts about her status expressed by her colleagues:

Alison: I started helping at a day nursery which shocked them all, they didn't know how to treat an eleven-year-old.

J.W.: How did you get involved with that?

Alison: Well, in the first place I went to the CAB in the local public library where we knew someone who got me in. They were never quite sure whether to treat me as a child who'd come to play with the kids or — but I got a lot of useful experience there.

J.W.: What was their reaction to you being out of school?

Alison: Pretty dubious, I should think. There was quite a nice play-group I went to in Notting Hill area where we were living after a while, and I think they probably accepted it more than the other organizers.

Illich's larger view of the development of access to work places for learning, in the context of a generally deschooled society, indicates what could be achieved, were a radical change possible in attitudes towards the public:

Much of the world's knowhow and most of its productive processes and equipment are locked within the walls of business firms, away from their customers, employees and stockholders, as well as from the general public, whose laws and facilities allow them to function. Money now spent on advertising in capitalist countries could be redirected towards education in and by General Electric, NBC-TV or Budweiser beer. That is, the plants and offices should be reorganized so that their daily operations could be more accessible to the public in ways that would make learning possible; and indeed, ways might be found to pay the companies for the learning people acquired from them. (Illich, 1971, p. 88)

Learning exchanges

The quotation above is taken from Illich's chapter entitled 'Learning webs', which discusses his vision of skill exchanges and peer-matching, ideas enthusiastically taken up in Britain by many alternative movements. The exchange run by EO, a highly detailed list of possessors of skills and resources varying from Esperanto to folk fiddle to silversmithing, which they are willing to share, appears not to have been used by any of those interviewed, perhaps because it was not very extensive at that time. There appear to be few data on its use by EO members, but a glance down the science classification shows that there are people willing to share expertise at some level in the following fields: agriculture, biology, chemistry, engineering, mechanics, general science, economics, electronics, microscopy, natural history, ornithology, physics, sociology, astronomy, environmental science, psychology, zoology and veterinary science.

Two drawbacks strike one which perhaps explain why the exchange is not as much used as it might be. The first is simply the geographical distance between teacher and taught. The second relates to the lack of a subject index, which would save one the trouble of going through the list of names page by page looking for appropriate subject code letters. Other reasons why this and other exchanges may not be successful are described by Dorothy Wise in her article about the Hackney Learning Exchange located at Centerprise:

> It appeared to me that once the name of a learner had been given to a teacher and vice versa all kinds of obstructions could arise to any learning taking place. . . . If neither owned a car and there was no connecting bus, transport might present a problem. They might not like each other when they met, as was the case with a pair of Russian speakers. These were the minor difficulties.
>
> The biggest difficulty was in maintaining a contact when in isolation from other learners and teachers, and where no curriculum was set. If one or other missed an appointment, the contact was often broken. By far the majority of people I put in contact with each other never met or, if they did, met no more than three or four times. I began to think that, on the whole, this informal teaching in each others' homes, at each others' convenience, was an inefficient, ineffectual, way to learn or teach. (Wise, no date, p. 11)

These comments have to be seen in the context of predominantly adult education in an area where alternative kinds of learning were unfamiliar to the people the exchange hoped to attract. In this way, and in the bringing together by a third person of two matched people as opposed to one taking the positive step of contacting another via a distributed list, it differs from the EO exchange. The remarks about possible transport difficulties, personality clash and isolation may, however, be pertinent, though the latter is perhaps a more familiar, and probably less problematic, difficulty for home educators than for those used to conventional methods of learning such as in schools or evening classes. The importance of a curriculum of some sort, so that a framework is established around which the learning can be based, is another point which applies more in the Centreprise type of situation, where specific appointments and lesson times need to be maintained, than in an informal family situation where learning may follow a less structured course.

There appears to be little evidence in Britain that learning exchanges play, or have played, a major part in solving resource problems or that they have been used with sufficient regularity to be able to provide a model for a form of education based on the learning exchange idea. Further investigation of the situation in other countries, and research into the use of the EO skills register, might suggest ways in which exchanges could be made to work as part of alternative education programmes such as home-based education and flexischooling.

Learning in the Home: Formal

The concept of the learning exchange bridges the gap between resources available outside the home and those employed within it. It introduces the use of teachers from other sources: the LEA home tuition service and private tutors in, for example, music.

Tutors

LEA home tutors had not been widely used by those interviewed. The explanation for this lies partly in some families' growing disillusionment with all aspects of the state education system, but mainly in the role which LEAs assign to their tutors, which makes them unavailable to families who make a positive decision to educate their children at home. A careers officer for one of the new cities explained the circumstances in which his authority would authorize home tuition and the form it would be likely to take:

> Home tuition is only done, because it's very expensive, when there's absolutely nowhere the kid will attend . . . you're saying to the kid,

'Well, look you're not allowed to work because you're not of school-leaving age, you haven't passed such-and-such a school-leaving date. By law you are required to be in education, we can prosecute you, there are some arm-twisters, right? So if you're not going to attend anywhere, OK, you don't like attending school, if you're prepared to have a home tutor we won't prosecute and we'll let you study at your own pace, right?' And a lot of people accept that, as an absolute last resort. They don't like the class situation because there's a lot of kids, you see, and this is where home tuition can benefit a kid, I think, probably the main uses I would say is for the kid really that doesn't like being seen to fail in front of his peers. . . . It's often part-time you know, two to three days a week, they set work and so on . . . English and maths. basically is the main two subjects, they hardly ever offer anything else, and they very rarely bring them up to exam standard.

These remarks make it clear that, in this authority at any rate, home tuition is not just there for the asking. The status of the child as a 'non-attender' is crucial here, and attendance somewhere (anywhere) rather than satisfactory home education is the goal. The experiences of those interviewed who had made use of the home tuition service differed in many respects from the perhaps typically contemporary form outlined above, in which home tutors are evidently in short supply due presumably to cuts in the relevant education budget. Four families had used home tutors, on the initiative of the LEA in three cases and under the direction of a lawyer in the fourth, that of Ian McGill. Two children, Daniel and Glenn, received home tuition on the grounds of illness preventing them from going to school, and two, Ian and Paul, on the basis of non-attendance at school, but without attempts to compel attendance elsewhere — alternative provision was not as highly developed in the days when Paul, at least, was of compulsory education age. What they received from the home tutors varied considerably. Paul Simmons appears to have had a fairly full and appropriate education programme, which the tutor shared with Paul's father:

> *Paul Simmons:* I did with her English and spelling and bits of history and geography I suppose. And the mathematics side my father taught me. . . . And that lasted until I was almost fifteen, which was the leaving age then . . .
> *J.W.:* She was tailoring that specifically to your own progress and not comparing it with any standards in school, or not?
> *Paul:* Yes, she was. She was just working solely with me.
> *Lynne:* His spelling was weak so she concentrated on that.

Ian McGill had a home tutor for two years, five hours a week, but this was stopped when he reached sixteen, due to LEA policy of not providing home tuition beyond the end of compulsory education. Ian's interest in science was catered for by his tutor alongside the basics:

> His own tutor did quite a bit of that (microscopy and dissecting) with him because he was a science teacher as well, specialized in science, and when he realized Ian had got this interest he elaborated on it a bit with him.

In both these cases, the families had good relationships with the tutor and felt that their children's needs were being met. Daniel Scheaffer, on the other hand, had an unconstructive encounter with the home tuition service at the age of five. It seemed that provision related to standard practice in the schools rather than the requirements of a particular individual, whose parents were allowed no say in the type of education offered:

> We did all sorts of things, nursery things, at home, all of us, and when they were painting or making raffia, or whatever they were doing, he did the same. So I said, 'Well, he is well ahead, so he doesn't require anything like, you know, the usual stuff and he gets very upset if things are presented to him which are very much his junior.' And she opened this large case she'd brought, and she brought out building bricks and so forth — and he nearly went berserk. Also, her manner of dealing with him was extremely condescending and extremely noisy, so we tried two days of this and by the second day, it was the singular time ever, that Graham had to come home from the office . . . because his autistic state suddenly slipped so badly that something had to be done very quickly. So I rang up the education authority and I said, 'I'm terribly sorry, but this will have to stop.' They were extremely abusive, very difficult. (Penelope Scheaffer)

After this experience of the home tuition service, the Scheaffer family, in consultation with their medical advisers, decided that it was a resource they could manage better without and had nothing more to do with it. Glenn Banks' experience with the home tutor, assigned to him on the basis of his illness and withdrawn quickly when the school doctor would not confirm that he was ill, was very brief. The local authority concerned (the one that employed the careers officer quoted above) was clearly unwilling to provide home tuition if there was any way in which it could be avoided, since it was such an expensive way of carrying out their duty to see that education was provided.

Several of those interviewed had found private tutors for areas in which they felt family expertise was inadequate to their children's needs, mostly in the creative arts. Finding suitable teachers when necessary does not appear to have been a problem:

J.W.: How have you found your music teachers?

Marie Gordon: There was a flute teacher in Desborough who lived a few doors down the road, and she started off piano with the flute teacher's husband. Then they moved about a year before we moved here, by which time we knew we were moving here. We managed to get some temporary people, it ended up being three, because one became ill. We found one from an advert in the paper and the other one was the music school she went to, you know, same as they have here, where they go for orchestras. . . . For dancing we wrote to the RAD and asked for a list of dancing schools.

Some teachers were used on a more informal basis; they were perhaps relatives or friends with a particular skill, very much the people learning exchanges sought to connect with eager learners, but found in this case through neighbourhood or family networks. Penelope Scheaffer recounts the follow-up to Daniel's experiences with the LEA home tutor:

Thereafter I sent Daniel over the road to a super girl who had a daughter about the same age as Daniel, and she said she would do something for Daniel . . . and he was with her for about two years and they did everything under the sun, nothing conventional but at the end of it he knew an awful lot.

Payment for private teaching varied from standard rates for lessons such as music to bartering of various kinds or completely free lessons, as Caroline Parker described:

I go on my bike to a lady who teaches me to do watercolour painting. And I also go on my bike horse-riding, it's here at the moment, we're looking after it as the owner's on holiday. . . . The horse-riding's free because I'm helping to exercise the horse and grooming and things like that. And the painting's free because Molly, who teaches me, says because she's not a qualified teacher she can't charge anything. She's quite happy to do that. It's about once a month usually.

None of the families interviewed had paid for private teachers of science, so that those who were not using the facilities of a local college or various elements of the environment outside devised strategies for copying with its demands at home. Children who wanted to follow formal science courses had two options: textbooks or correspondence courses. The provision of practical experience in the home will be discussed later: suffice it to say here that families often picked examination boards which did not require practicals at O level (as do some schools):

For the boards that require practicals you have to make your own arrangements to do practicals, which would be tricky. Obviously for mature students they (Wolsey Hall) suggest liaising with the local technical college which I guess would have been a possibility had I been a mature student with some sort of influence. But as a minor that wouldn't have worked and so we chose the non-practical boards for that reason. And I've got nothing against that educationally because the idea of the practical element being assessed at O level is ridiculous. (Jim Merriman)

Textbooks

Use of textbooks for formal science was widespread at the O level stage, sometimes in conjunction with a correspondence course, sometimes with a syllabus and past examination papers only. Jim Merriman suggests that knowing which books to use is crucial. He recommends the *Made Simple* series and then enthuses about a textbook he would recommend for physics O level (the ubiquitous Abbott):

It's fantastic, it's something I could read not for physics O level, just for interest . . . it's gone through about twenty editions. There are the good textbooks around and it's a life-saver for home education. But it is important to pick out the right things again and to be able to realize that you've got a dud.

Corinne Dey used books for science at a less advanced stage, and received advice from a friend about which books would be appropriate (local authority advisers can be another source of this kind of help). Generally, families had collections of books across a wide range of interests at home which they added to when money allowed or when prompted by a specific need. A couple, for example, had found it worthwhile to invest in reference books such as sets of encyclopaedias (particularly useful for those without easy access to the reference facilities of a library):

J.W.: Did you find it cost you anything financially, for books for the English and maths. for instance?

Malcolm Gold: I suppose most of them we had to a large extent, because Margaret was doing a lot of remedial work when she was teaching. And in fact the remedial workbooks for remedial adults are just as good for — it's written at a fairly elementary level, anyway. I think the only thing we bought specifically was kids' *Encyclopaedia Britannica* . . . and that's sixty quid.

Further discussion with the Golds indicated that those living like them in some degree of rural isolation, remote from convenient shops, had to make alternative arrangements for the purchase of books and other learning equipment:

> *Malcolm:* I think most people live out of catalogues, that's how most of the stuff we've bought has come. I should think books — it's not a bad little bookshop in Skeffton, that's quite nice. And not bad for kids. But I think every toy effectively we've bought for him since moving has come through the post, from Early Learning or whatever.

This points to another difficulty for rural dwellers in the provision of resources: the restriction of choice and the problems involved in buying things which might have to be returned if found to be unsuitable.

In most cases, where access to towns was easier, families made extensive and appreciative use of libraries to supplement buying with borrowing: 'I use the maths book from the library, it's practically mine by now, I take it out so much' (Tiffany McGill); 'Most of my education I consider to have been reading by myself, from the library. I do have a very wide general knowledge purely from reading' (Daniel Scheaffer). Families had evidently found out how to make the best use of libraries:

> They're very good here: if you want a book they'll phone up the main library and say, 'Have you got such and such a book?' and they'll say 'Yes, certainly' and they'll keep it back for you. Which I think's very good. (Phil Minchin)

Special facilities were sometimes made available to home educators, along the lines of lending to schools: 'I've always had a big collection of books anyway . . . and I also had an arrangement with the library that I could take books out on long-term loan so that was a help' (Sally Banks).

Correspondence courses

The other approach to the systematic learning of science and other subjects was that provided by various types of correspondence course. Those used by families in the study were the products of four organizations: Wolsey Hall, National Extension College (NEC), the American-based Calvert School and the Parents' National Educational Union (PNEU). The first two were straightforward examination-based courses in specific subjects which could be obtained individually as such, whereas the latter two form complete schemes of education for children from four or five years on, and rely on the parents' participation as teacher for their effectiveness, in contrast to the self-directed learning approach of the more adult-orientated examination courses. Wolsey Hall and NEC courses were used successfully by several of those interviewed, Alison Head, Jim Merriman and Grace Gordon among them. Advantages were seen as five-fold: they were geared to the taking of a specific exam; could be taken at the child's own pace; involved no face-to-face interaction with a teacher, which some, like Jim, appreciated after bad school experiences in this area; allowed for constructive feedback from tutors; and some, like the Wolsey Hall O level mathematics, physics and geography courses, assumed no previous knowledge of the subject. Apart from the cost involved, a factor applying to Calvert and PNEU too, two families had reservations about the appropriateness of the level of study expected and the extent to which the course designers were in touch with the demands of the exam:

> *Amy Dey:* We're using them for geography . . . I don't know much about geography and I find it rather old-fashioned.
> *Corinne:* Before I took it up I didn't know much about it and I find it difficult because it's not very clear. It's mostly written for adults you see and so it's rather — it's not very well set out. . . . The mapwork is extremely difficult.

Christine Merriman's experience of the same problem in Jim's case led her to advise others to adopt an alternative solution:

> With the experience of hindsight I would now advise parents to take correspondence courses only for those subjects which the child is likely to follow up at A level. The courses we did are mostly too advanced for O level work and for that reason are off-putting. The many study aids available in bookshops appear to be quite adequate (and much cheaper) for O level purposes. (*EO News* 20)

The Examiner Plan courses, not available in 1982 when the interviews were carried out, provide another route to GCE/GCSE, based on model answers rather than tutorial feedback.

One of the families who wrote to me about their experiences, the Badbys, had used the American Calvert School materials, which they apparently chose partly because of the Christian orientation of the course. Like the exam-orientated correspondence courses and the PNEU's scheme, it has the advantage that it can be embarked on at any time during the year, moves at the child's own pace, and feedback from tutors is available, in this case in the form of an optional Advisory Teaching Service. Heather Badby described her impressions of the Calvert courses in a letter:

> The study schemes are useful for any English-speaking child. The day-by-day instructions are complete, books carefully chosen, and if desired, a child can take monthly tests which monitor progress. It is a complete service — when purchased you receive all the books necessary for the year, your teacher's book, plus paper, pencils and crayons. A

friend recently used the Grade 1 for her five-year-old, although in America this beginning-to-read year is 'done' at age six. A child has to be mature to start so early — but of course one works at the child's own speed — going faster and slower as desired.

Interestingly, another reason why she chose to use this course with her dyslexic son was because she had used the material herself when not at school as a young teenager.

The other complete scheme of work, supplied by the PNEU, is more widely used in this country than the Calvert materials, though intended mainly for British families overseas. The stress is on helping the parent to teach rather than enabling children to study autonomously from the materials provided, and back-up is available from a tutor who meets the child from time to time and sees work done. The aim of the courses is to enable children to fit in to school again at any point, so that the curriculum parallels that of the school. Based, however, on the philosophy of Charlotte Mason, it is also broader in its concept than a basic primary school curriculum generally is (the materials cater only for children up to thirteen), and includes picture and music appreciation, science and the reading of a very wide range of good quality children's literature as part of the package. Hugh Boulter, director of WES/PNEU at the time of interviewing, illustrated the approach of both the majority of the parents involved and of the scheme, using the example of one area of science:

> The idea is to build upon the environment in which the children find themselves. The difficulty is, parents find options quite hard to cope with, because they really don't have the professional expertise or the confidence to make the decisions. On the whole they seem to prefer to be told what to do. But we have a book on environmental science called *Starting from a Walk*, for example, which has seventy-eight themes or topics which parents and children can do on environmental science pretty well anywhere in the world. It's not suggested you start at the beginning and work through it. It's suggested you pick out the ones that are of interest. And actually what I think is interesting is that parents not only pick out the ones from the folder, but it gives them ideas of other things that they can do which they wouldn't have thought of otherwise.

Daniel Scheaffer was the main user of PNEU among those in the study. His mother was more appreciative of the help given by them than was Daniel himself:

> Their attitude was very much 'How can we educate the person you wish to educate to best advantage, taking into account whatever it is

you're trying to overcome?' And they were perfectly willing to be academically organized.

Daniel had very specific criticisms of the content of some of the courses as they were then, particularly those for the upper age range. He added, 'this, I think, is one of the problems with home education, is finding a structured education which is reasonably useful'.

Resources for Learning in the Home: Informal

Practical science

For those who want a less structured approach to education at home, it is perfectly possible to make use of nothing but books and ordinary domestic equipment to study at least up to O level standard; and in science as much as other areas of interest. It may, as we have seen, be possible to borrow equipment from institutions for use at home but there are other more informal sources, such as local scientific societies, which can be utilized in this way: Jim Merriman borrowed a telescope to study astronomy, in which he was already interested, and the Parsons family borrowed a microscope to look at pond-water, an interest which developed out of attendance at the Natural History Society's meetings:

Household items were pressed into the service of many branches of science, often with considerable ingenuity. Christine Merriman described how she set about the practical side of biology O level with Jim:

> Biology is a gift because there are so many simple but nevertheless interesting experiments to be done, many of which are described in the textbook. Of course, some of them use the dreaded sophisticated equipment but many need only simple improvisations to get the same results. Wine-making equipment fulfils many of the requirements and for others just simple jam-jars; blotting paper; funnels; cotton wool; iodine; glucose; vinegar; chalk; plants; potatoes; seeds; leaves; dead flies; live pets . . . need I go on? With these you can test for starch, fat, protein, complex and simple sugars, show that roots take up water, demonstrate osmosis, respiration, geotropism, phototropism and hydrotropism. If you're not squeamish, or morally opposed, butchers can supply offal such as brains, ox eyes and kidneys for dissection. A good way to obtain bones for study is to have a rabbit stew. Keep all the bones, rinse them, then fit them together again. Owl pellets supply smaller vertebrate bones. And these examples are only a fraction of the practicals to be enjoyed. (*EO News* 28)

She goes on to extol the virtues of the garden pond. Daniel Scheaffer found that he needed no special knowledge at all for biology O level: through reading and the general life of the household he had absorbed all that was necessary. Similarly, he found that an understanding of physics at O level standard came about through watching household equipment being repaired and helping, himself, to repair it:

> The physics book . . . I read through it twice, just straight reading through it, and I got a B in it, which is just straight reading. Now that was an awful lot of seeing the stuff that I'd seen Dad do, electromagnets, all this sort of stuff, I'd talked about it, it was really a question of seeing what was required at O level . . . I wasn't able to do virtually any experiments, but on the other hand I knew what all this stuff like Ohm's Law, I knew it already before I got to it, so it wouldn't be necessary.

He was doubtful, though, whether chemistry O level, of the kind involving practical work, would be possible at home, and this does seem to have presented families with more of a problem. As we have seen, Corinne Dey learnt chemistry at first from her scientist father, with no equipment, and then, when the teaching relationship between them foundered, from books:

> *Amy:* I suppose we covered what they cover in about the first two years without the sort of basic experiments which are quite unnecessary really. But when she did go to school and joined the chemistry class she found she was quite well up with the other girls.
> *Corinne:* When I went to school I could take it quite easily because of the chemistry we'd been doing at home. . . . The chemistry were old textbooks. But usually, see, the older ones, they're not so much geared to experiments and things so it made it better really and I think you learnt just as much from them.

This quotation illustrates how closely resources are tied to the aims of education and the means to achieve those aims: clearly, proponents of the 'hands-on' method of science teaching would take a dim view of the Deys' approach and maintain that lack of resources was a handicap, while a more cynical attitude, seeing chemistry as an examination hurdle to be got over in whatever fashion, might regard scientific equipment as an unnecessary frill. Basic chemistry was often tackled using commercial chemistry sets, as were some branches of basic physics such as electricity, electronics and camera optics: Caroline Parker, Paul Simmons and Phil Minchin all used these with apparent satisfaction and enjoyment. A mother discussed the value of one particular kit for home educators, and an alternative approach to the study of chemistry, in *EO News* 31:

The mystery of test tubes and strange chemicals makes it as attractive to many children as any toy. The manual is very comprehensive and has a large amount of basic chemical information. . . . Whether you try to work through it step by step or let your child dip into it will depend on you and your child. Some members may object that it is an expensive way of buying the equipment, although compared to the costs of other toys I think it is very reasonable and in fact unless you are very knowledgable it is very difficult to construct your own kit which is easily accessible for a child to use. Also important, Thomas Salter spares, both chemicals and equipment, are available from larger toy shops so the basic kit can be built up.

PNEU/WES have also made available to EO members their previously mentioned *Starting from a Walk* project, and a kit containing high quality laboratory equipment for use in the home. People enrolling for Open University courses also receive the appropriate scientific equipment, and EO members have found this another way of obtaining what they regard as necessary resources, along with an interesting presentation of course material, which is often suitable for children without much adult interpretation. The general availability of science kits, and the opportunities they present for dipping into a subject, introduce the question of home resources which actually engender an interest, as opposed to satisfying a need which has already arisen. The direction of Paul Simmons' educational career was influenced by the early present of a Junior Electronic Engineer kit. Books are probably the most common source of the serendipitous encounter with future enthusiasms but visitors to the home, programmes on television and newspapers may be others.

An as yet undiscussed source of learning at home, as structured or unstructured as families want to make it, is the computer. Only one person (apart from Paul Simmons' semi-professional use) had used one, Caroline Parker. Most of her work on it was directed towards learning to program, a useful activity in itself, but using the computer as an end rather than a means.

Local authority expectations regarding curriculum are very varied, so that their influence, where parents take them into account at all, cannot be categorized. The constraints suggested by lack of suitable resources can often be overcome by ingenuity in the home or exploration of community facilities (which could be made more widely available). Chance discovery of particular resources can often lead the way to new practical or academic interests. It was not evident that lack of resources had had a constraining effect on choice of curriculum: an open mind appears to be the most important facilitator of a fulfilling home-based education.

Chapter 8

The 'How' of Home-based Education

This chapter considers what governs children's and parents' choice of processes appropriate to achieving their particular educational goals, how and why these processes change their characteristics, and how the type of learning/ teaching relationship adopted affects the direction of education, for instance, in terms of the development of self-discipline and independence in study on the part of the child or of further education on the part of the adult. I shall examine why a formally structured framework is often chosen initially and of what this structure consists, and discuss exceptions to the common rule in the shape of families who deliberately chose an informal approach to home education, introducing the question of development into informality and the exceptions to this: children who went back to the very structured and formal methods of school, or of FE teaching, from informal home education. The final section of the chapter deals with types of assessment used by the families.

Formally Structured Beginnings

As discussed in Chapters 6 and 7 (particularly Chapter 6), moving from a school career to one based on home education involved relinquishing a prescribed curriculum and resources, and, most relevant to this chapter, prescribed ways of working, to which there are several aspects.

Structuring of Time

The first is that of time: school time is usually heavily structured on a daily basis and timetabled on a weekly one, and the school year has marked terms implying 'education ends here'. Children just out of school may feel at a loss when faced with an amorphous day: so may their parents. They may need to divide the time up arbitrarily at first and then perhaps find that a more natural and flexible routine eventually asserts itself, based possibly on features such as meals, story times, walking the dog, school and other TV programmes, times of clubs and times when in-school friends are around (these formed the basis of my own son's daily pattern of home-based education). Penelope Scheaffer described the way in which Daniel's home education was structured on a daily basis which remained unchanged for many years:

> He did what I would call a rather social aspect of teaching in the morning and in the afternoon we did set work. But always in the morning there were conversations about either what we'd done yesterday or what was going to be done tomorrow or the day after or what. And always one tried to introduce into this life the things you knew, because you knew what you were going to teach in the afternoon, you knew what he hadn't got hold of yesterday by whichever method you happened to be using so tomorrow morning was the time when you were going to clear this up. . . . And whether he was helping me or whether he was doing something totally different, painting or craft or whatever, this was the talking time, and the time when he would do prep or whatever it was.

The benefit of this system was that advantage could be taken of a night's break before returning to something not understood, but still have it cleared up in time to move on to the next area.

In other families interviewed, for example, the Minchins, academic work tended to be done in the mornings, presumably on the rationale that children were fresher then and better able to concentrate, also that it left the rest of the day free for outings or lengthy practical activities:

> We used to do these things that I felt were more important in the morning, so that we had the afternoons free for whatever they wanted to do. . . . They used to do their diaries first from the previous day, and then for a long time we started with a story. (Marie Gordon)

This sort of system, influenced perhaps by the primary school day as it is often structured, is very common among families other than those in the study, for instance, the Wilkins family, in *Living* magazine:

> A typical education-at-home day begins with a few domestic chores. These done, Seth and Esther settle down at the table in their cosy, jumbled kitchen. . . . After a couple of hours it's time for refreshments and a story. The afternoons, when Victor is sometimes free to join them, are usually spent out of doors — gardening or enjoying an

outing or nature walk. During the evenings and at weekends the
children often attend local clubs. (Lantin, 1983, p. 52)

In the examples quoted so far, a clear distinction is being made between
academic work for which specific time is laid aside every day, and the less
definite activities of the afternoons. There is no sign of any blurring of academic work limits and those of daily life and we shall have to wait until the
section on development of ways of working to see whether this does in fact
become a reality for some families.

Structuring the week on a school-like basis, that is, with a timetable
allocating chunks of particular days to particular learning activities, was less
common among those interviewed and appears to be so among EO families in
general, perhaps because this kind of rigidity does not sit well with the
demands of domestic life, nor does it necessarily enable subjects to be studied
to the full while interest is fresh. Two families, however, had attempted to put
a weekly timetable into practice, based in the first case on the 'academic work
in the mornings' system described above:

We were quite ambitious at the beginning and we spent a long time
drawing up timetables . . . when we were working quite well at home
we could get through an awful lot in the mornings and very often the
afternoons were free. (Amy Dey)

Sally Banks' approach was more closely akin to that of the secondary school
her son would have attended, and developed out of her feeling that it was the
best way to ensure that he received the very academic education which she felt
he needed.

Another form of time-structuring relates to yearly patterns. To what
extent did families adopt a school-like system of terms and holidays? Did this
reflect a sense of education as a thing apart from daily life or was it a practical
measure, determined for instance by the availability of in-school friends to
play with? There was in fact only one example of adherence to a term pattern
and, though it was not explicitly stated, I had a feeling that the Scheaffers' ob-
servance of school terms and holidays was due to neither of the causes suggested above but to the fact that his elder siblings were in school and his
mother wanted to minimize the differences between them as far as possible.
The fact that they were using PNEU courses may also have been influential,
since PNEU recommends devoting a specific amount of time each day to the
work, and each course is based on a year's age range:

It does demand a degree of self-discipline by the parent. You've got to
be prepared to give up two or three hours every morning, come hell
or high water, and stick to it. It's no good giving up because you've got
to go to a coffee morning or your friends are going to come or

whatever it may be. I think larger things, larger scale, often one of our families will have a visit from Granny for three or four weeks. I don't think that matters, you take a chunk out and that's their holiday. (Hugh Boulter, ex-director of PNEU)

It would be hard, obviously, for any family using this sort of structure to relax into a more integrated form of day, with no separation between 'learning' and 'playing', and there is no evidence that this happened in Daniel's case, though this is not to say, as we have seen elsewhere, that a lot of informal learning did not go on through participation in the ordinary life of the household.

Structuring of Learning Activities

The other elements of structure through which education at home evolves are connected with the way in which the chosen learning activities are pursued in practice. They relate partly to the character of the work considered desirable: is the aim some kind of 'product' in the form of written work or a drawing, for example? At what depth is the activity to be pursued and how is this determined (for example, by parental expectation, the demands of a particular course, or by the child's own interest which would result perhaps in the more informal approach to be discussed later)? How are the activities approached: as discrete subjects or in more integrated fashion? Finally, how does the learning itself take place? Does the child study alone, does the parent adopt a traditional teaching role or is there some kind of mixture of these approaches? Are resources used as they would be in school?

> *The Outcome'* Why does there always have to be an 'outcome'? When I go to see something that interests me, I don't have to do a dance afterwards or make a six-foot papier mache map and hoist it to the ceiling. I can decide for myself what sort of outcome, if any, I want to have for my experience. More important, I can wait until the outcome reveals itself to me. This takes time, sometimes years. (Holt, 1977, p. 123)

There is considerable debate in the pages of the *EO Newsletter* about the value of tangible products of learning processes. One discussion concerned responses to this query from the mother of nine-year-old, home educated Cassandra:

> Cassandra has a head bursting with enthusiasms for investigations — but when it comes to getting some kind of end product — then I have difficulty — and this is proving a strain for all of us. Does an end product matter? At school Cassie was labelled a butterfly. (*EO News* 44)

A school teacher replied:

> Yes, I believe that an end product matters — though not every time. I agree with you that harnessing experience into say a story/picture/model/told story/letter is very important for creativity — and education.

Two parents wrote to *EO News* 45 to disagree with this approach:

> I would like to suggest that the child knows best when she has achieved the end product she needs and desires. The parent only requires reassurance that his/her child's enthusiasm is guidance enough. Often adults and children see the direction and the end product of a task very differently, but that is not to say that the child is wrong. I will give an example from my own experience. My son and I agree to make a cake together. We start by looking at recipe books and find one that looks good and for which we have all the ingredients. Invariably my inclination then is to move into the kitchen and start work on the cake. My son, however, insists we should continue to look at all the recipes in all the books for a while longer. Who is the butterfly?

The other mother, writing in the same newsletter from experience with her own daughter of similar age to Cassandra, made a different point:

> Only when the child stops feeling imposed upon from without, stops having to do things which are ultimately meaningless to her, will she find herself and how she wishes to spend her day. It demands a great deal of faith . . . by insisting on end products you will only delay her natural development. Most of us start things that never get finished. Does it matter and more important to whom does it matter? Not the child. Perhaps the neighbours, the parents, the LEA?

This correspondence encapsulates the arguments most often come across concerning end products: do these give children genuine satisfaction, are they in some way integral to learning or are they merely a focus for parents' worries about having something concrete to show the LEA advisers? Only a few of the families interviewed appeared to have questioned the school orientation towards production: most saw it as essential to a full education. The McGills were a case in point, expressing many of the traditional concerns of school teachers about presentation: tidiness and cleanliness in written work, for example. Corinne Dey's work was also based on exercise books in which she recorded most of her learning activities, some related to textbooks and some to other materials. For example, she showed me her RE and cookery notebooks which were used in conjunction with imaginative worksheets prepared by her mother. Those children using correspondence or similarly structured courses, or addressing examinations via some other route (for example, the use of syllabi and relevant textbooks), were also using written work as a way of processing their learning, either for purposes of assessment or as preparation for examinations based on written answers. The importance which some families gave this ability to write for examinations is illustrated by the immense amount of effort put in to allow Daniel to arrive at the point where he could do this. The argument that having to set your thoughts down on paper encourages their logical ordering and greater critical analysis was not explicitly put forward by anyone, but may well have been the rationale behind the writing of the children whose work was interest- and project-based. The argument for the value of products of other kinds, such as drawings or models, might be related to their potential for developing a child's powers of observation or various craft techniques.

Depth of study

The final aspect of the product approach (touched on briefly in the correspondence quoted earlier) concerns the next topic I shall discuss, the depth to which a subject is studied and who decides when investigation has gone far enough. A teacher writing in *EO News* 31, with, perhaps, an element of rationalization after the event, elaborates on the previously mentioned point of view of the child whose conception of the end of a learning activity relates to its intrinsic interest rather than to an extrinsically determined product:

> My own childhood was a time of powerful enthusiasms. I experimented with everything in sight, I tested the physical and emotional constitution of every object and relationship which became available to me. I was unable or unwilling to 'finish' every 'task' because, as far as I was concerned, I had 'finished' whenever the activity no longer gave me any satisfaction.

The question of how far into a particular subject a child is expected, or is free, to go relates partly to the way in which the learning process is tackled. For those pursuing formal courses, depth of study is controlled through the structure of the course (and this may not always be appropriate to its expressed aim, as we have seen in the case of some correspondence courses). Where parents lead the syllabus, as in Amy Dey's case, it seems that depth is more flexible, with the parent able to adjust the level of work to the child's interest. Children embarked on projects which they themselves originated appear to be able to investigate the topic concerned to the level at which they feel no further interest in pursuing it, rather than having to conform to an arbitrary standard such as time spent on it or amount of information gathered. This will be discussed further in the section on families which adopted informal ways of working from the start. It is worth noting that even those families with heavily structured timetables appear to recognize the value of flexibility in enabling a particular subject to be explored in greater depth.

Breadth of study and integration of subjects
Related to this question of depth of study is that of breadth: how far were the families interviewed touched by the debate about integration of subjects? John Holt, in *How Children Fail*, expressed a view held by one current faction of EO regarding the artificial splitting up and re-uniting of subjects practised in many British as well as American schools:

> In many ways, we break down children's convictions that things make sense. We do it, first of all, by breaking up life into arbitrary and disconnected hunks of subject matter, which we then try to 'integrate' by such artificial and irrelevant devices as having children sing Swiss folk songs while they are studying the geography of Switzerland, or do arithmetic problems about rail-splitting while they are studying the boyhood of Lincoln. (Holt, 1984, p. 275)

Art Harris, a parent of two home educated sons, quoted in *Teach Your Own*, elaborates on this approach:

> The narrow structuring of the school courses has always appalled us. Who are these schools to decide that architecture, archaeology, anthropology, astrology or astronomy (to take only the As) don't belong in the elementary grades? We believe that all subjects fuse and interlock and the mere definition of a subject is the first step in taking away some of its mystique. (Holt, 1981, p. 125)

A minority of the families interviewed took this view, and these were all families with younger children (as the advocates of this approach within EO tend to be). All came eventually to face the imposition of traditional subject division in the GCE system (a reversal of the trend from formality to informality), but were able to work, at least partly, along the lines of topics suggested by the children, as seen in the case of the Gordons, Maureen Cotton and Alison Head. Development of each topic was a natural progression of interest rather than an attempt by the parent/teacher to incorporate various 'subjects' such as geography, history or arithmetic which they considered desirable.

The majority of families adopted a traditional approach to subject divisions from the start, powerfully influenced perhaps by the modes of thinking instilled in them by their own schooling, and perhaps also by the previously mentioned need for a familiar confidence-building base. Those following examination courses, whether by correspondence or some other method such as FE college, had narrow limits to each subject defined for them by the examination boards, whose interpretation was accepted absolutely by preparers of course material intended to manoeuvre children through the obstacles of the examination, rather than to broaden their appreciation of the subject's scope and its relationship to other subjects. Those families following subject divisions untramelled by the demands of examinations appear to have accepted traditional limits in their formal work, but explored various overlapping areas in practical or otherwise informal activities, as Catherine Kiddle shows in her description of the activities of Ben Haward and the others, away from the limitations of the formally divided curriculum they followed in the mornings:

> On one occasion the children walked along a stretch of Roman road. Their imagination fired and a whole range of work resulted, mosaics, Roman numerals, plans of villas, cardboard armour. They held a Roman exhibition of all their work, and charged 2p for admission. Somehow a woolly knitted hat and an iron poker that the children had made found their way into the exhibition too. (Kiddle, 1981, p. 43)

(This shows that the connections between areas may be even more extensive than is apparent to observing adults!)

These activities were often inspired by the particular interest or expertise of adult members of 'The State' or of their frequent visiting artists: this introduces the question of how the role of the adults involved in children's learning affects the way that learning takes place, for example, in terms of the development of self-discipline in study.

Parents' Roles

Parents in some of the families interviewed, for example, the McGills and the Deys, had adopted a traditional transmissive type of teaching, based again perhaps on the familiar school situation for lack of any alternative model. (Provision of such models is less likely to be a problem nowadays, since better contact between home educating families ensures support and information of this sort for those who want it.) The most extreme example of the transmissive parent-teacher among those interviewed was probably Alison Hartfield's father:

> He sat us down and gave us lessons from a textbook. He expounded the textbook himself. He was very conscientious over this: he went over it all the night before . . . he used to spend a lot of the summer holidays in the evenings, you know, working away and getting ready for the next term's work.

Alison Hartfield's later description of the effort her father put into learning Latin reminded me that many of the parents, whether adopting wholly or only partly transmissive roles had had to re-learn some of what they taught their children themselves, sometimes working things out for the first time from basic principles, as I did myself when helping my son with mathematics which I had previously learnt by rote and never understood. This aspect of learning alongside or one jump ahead of the child is not only very rewarding for the adult on the level of personal enrichment but also, according to one point of view, contributes to a healthy teaching relationship in which the child knows the adult is not the source of all wisdom and is encouraged to a more questioning attitude.

Another role which some parents adopted was that of provider of opportunities and resources for learning, perhaps with guidance when asked for. This was mixed in some cases with a transmissive or learning-alongside approach, depending on the area under study or on family circumstances: 'when what I was studying you didn't have any knowledge of yourself, then I used books. And of course, when you were ill I taught myself' (Glenn Banks).

Another interesting aspect of the parent-as-teacher relationship, which goes some way to offset criticism that to be with only one teacher is a bad thing (though common practice in Steiner schools) is the extent to which both parents are involved in the children's education and how responsibility for particular areas is shared between them:

> In some respects we are fortunate in that my husband is a Chartered Engineer and, as such, is able to cover science and technical subjects with our sons . . . whilst I explore all other subjects and interests with them. (Mother, in *EO News* 23)

One might expect that one-parent families would find the burden of home education greater because unshared. Maureen Cotton lent this suggestion some credence: 'it was difficult for Dad to run a home, and make sure that I got all the attention that I needed for my school work'. Other single parents, mainly mothers who were perhaps more used to full-time responsibility for their children, found that it was not impossible to encompass the range of resources their children required, bringing in outside resources when necessary.

The Hidden Curriculum of Formal Materials

A final element of the 'how' of formal learning is the use of structured resources such as those described in Chapter 7: are these employed as they would be in school or is an effort made at home to counter any hidden curriculum aspects of the material the family becomes aware of? An example of this is the textbook course in history or religious studies reflecting the particular bias of its author. Instead of swallowing the presentation hook, line and sinker, families could use the perspective as a stimulus for discussion leading to a more questioning attitude towards the reporting and analysis of historical events, and sidestepping the indoctrination sometimes implicit in a school's adoption of the text. However, there was little evidence of this sort of approach among the families interviewed: where school textbook courses were chosen, this tended to be because parents sympathized with their authors' treatments, and they were used very much as they would have been in school, though often with more supplementary material (for example, Glenn Banks' use of Open University course units).

Informal Beginnings

Most aspects of informality in home education have inevitably been referred to as corollaries in the course of the section on a structured initial approach and will be developed further here, noting that a mixture of both formal and informal home education is probably typical of the way a majority of families start out on their home education careers, as it is of those interviewed. This section is not primarily about these families, whose approach has already been discussed: it concerns a minority who deliberately adopted a way of learning that was radically different from the school pattern in terms of time structure and, most importantly, aims and methods of learning. David Baker, Alison Head and Simon Parsons all experienced to a great extent an informal start to their home-based education in these terms, influenced explicitly by their parents' theoretical positions as discussed in Chapter 4.

Aims

The aims of informal learning are, as we have seen, less likely to be product orientated, that is, focused on a concrete piece of work, whether written, modelled or whatever. That is not to say that work of this kind was not produced, but that it was generally a by-product of other types of learning activity. The goal in the case of the three families mentioned in this context above was primarily the satisfaction of the child's interest in a particular self-chosen topic. For example, as I reported earlier, Simon Parsons decided to learn German because he became very interested in the Second World War, but examinations or other written evidence of his knowledge were seen by him and his mother as irrelevant to his purpose. Joy Baker, the first modern exponent of informal child-selected learning, described in the course of one of her appearances before Norfolk magistrates how her children pursued some of their interests:

I believe geography to be a necessary part of a child's education, but I don't believe you can make a class of children sit down and be told, 'Now this term we are going to do Africa' or whatever it may be. David had, in response to his own request, a globe of the world two years ago as a Christmas present, and has treasured it ever since. He has studied it in detail in a general way and asked questions about everything that interested him — which means that he asked a great many questions. As any country or area comes into the news he finds it on the globe and looks it up in his atlas. His interest draws the attention of the younger children and they all therefore absorb all the information we can collect about it. (Baker, 1964)

The achievement of understanding, and perhaps a better relationship between parent and child, reached through simply talking together, is often one of the aims of informal learning, and constitutes an element of informality even in more structured family situations, as Penelope Scheaffer has described. Veronica Budd emphasized the importance of this kind of communication in working towards independence in study:

I think really we've always been a family that talked a lot, and talking about why it was important, the reasons it might be important and what gates it would open up for her, and what she'd be barred from . . . we just sat chatting and in fact talked about things that they don't seem to have much time for in schools: what are the problems? ,why do you find it so difficult to sit there?

David Head explained how some other aims of informal learning had been fulfilled, referring incidentally to the 'product' argument discussed earlier:

In terms of books and paper filled, their year's work looks meagre compared with the contents of a school desk. But their work is in a special way their own. . . . Much more important is that they are learning how to learn, how to use reference books, where to get information, and how to discipline themselves to carry out a piece of work. (Head, 1974, p. 143)

Time

The planning of how time should be spent is another area in which notable differences exist between more and less formally orientated families. Those who from the start adopted an informal learning approach tended to allow a pattern of activities to develop naturally rather than to allocate time on a more or less arbitrary basis, and they ensured that a generous amount of flexibility was built in to whatever loose structure evolved. From *Free Way to Learning* again, Jean Head's notes before Operation Otherwise began: 'no detailed daily/weekly timetable — though someone will know at any time of day what everyone is doing and where. Self-regulating diet of work for each child within say a month' (Head, 1974, p. 135), and after the first year:

> We all appreciate the freedom which allows a lunchtime mid-week outing to hear Sir Bernard Miles read from John Donne's sermons on the steps of St.Paul's, followed by a wander in the City — including climbing the Monument. Martin has been able to go to a weekly series of lectures on The Compassionate Camera, which resulted in reading *The Grapes of Wrath* and our watching the film together. . . . While this flexibility has been one of the greatest of assets, there has been structure too. Certain things have been done each day, others every week. Music practice is unhurried at the beginning of the day — not crowded in (or out) before school, or when tired in the evenings. As we look ahead, there are several things we want to include — which will mean a more structured day. But always the chance is there to change plans — to lie in the garden and read when the weather is suddenly too hot for anything else, or to have an extended lunch-hour when there is an interesting visitor from another country or field of work. (Head, 1974, p. 142)

The Parsons and the Bakers used their time in an even less structured way than the Heads. As Joy Baker told the Dereham magistrates: 'I believe in education by natural development, and instruction given "on demand" and not by the calendar and clock. And it works' (Baker, 1964).

J.L. Carr, writing in *Where* about a period contemporary with some of those interviewed, pointed out the advantages of untimetabled learning in relationship to the arbitrary splitting up of subjects referred to earlier in the chapter:

> Since there was no need of a timetable to fit with other people's convenience, the artificial separation of 'subjects' mostly could be avoided. Who can tell where Egyptian geography/history/architecture/ art/religion/natural history/geology begin and end? (Carr, no date, p. 13)

The impression one receives from reading *EO News, Growing Without Schooling* and relevant articles elsewhere in the media is that this informal initial approach to the use of time is much more common than it was in the period in which those interviewed were educated, and that it is particularly common among families with young children (not surprisingly, since the pressures of formal examination requirements are further off for these families).

'Learning Through Life'

As previously discussed, choosing how to use time may involve a decision on whether to have learning times set aside from the general business of the day, with consequent demarcation of what constitutes education. As one might expect, families beginning home education along informal lines are much less inclined to see the curriculum as a thing apart from daily life and much more inclined to stress the value of continuity of experience implicit in this approach, sometimes referred to by educational writers as 'learning through life'.

Caroline Parker and Ben Haward in particular experienced the benefits of learning through the life of a rural commune in the one case and a travelling theatre company in the other, but this was in addition to an initial programme of formal learning of the basics (though this later developed into informality, as we shall see, in Caroline's case). Of those who adopted informality to begin with, the Bakers exemplify most clearly the learning from life approach, introducing also John Holt's vision of 'useful work' (illustrated in Holt, 1981, p. 268). This idea incorporates a feeling that children want and need to be a genuinely useful part of the adult world, and that through participation in it they can begin to grasp what useful work they might do in it as adults themselves. David Baker's experience illustrates both elements of this suggestion; from Joy Baker's testimony to the Divisional Courts:

> My eldest son David, who is now fourteen and a half, wants to be a farmer, and has worked on several different types of farm in our area during the past two years, gaining practical experience of farm work, during the time that, if he had been at school, he would have been playing games. (Baker, 1964)

Part of Alison Head's informal education was, as explained previously, regular work at a local day nursery. In *Free Way to Learning* she describes in detail her experiences there and what they meant to her, and her mother writes about the way in which they have acted as pointers towards possible future useful work:

> For Martin photography is to be used to illuminate how people live in their families and neighbourhoods, and to highlight the social evils and help eliminate them. The young children Alison works with are those who have been denied many good things in life through poor houses and surroundings, broken homes, lack of love and physical handicaps; and she tries to share with them her love of the natural world. (Head, 1974, pp. 143–4)

Use of Resources

Though the use of resources in informal types of learning has been discussed in Chapter 7, it may be useful to point out that, self-evidently, part of what characterizes the initially informal approach is the general lack of formal courses, textbooks and other structured materials, with a correspondingly greater need to look to the outside world for resources (see the quotation from Richard North in Chapter 7). This theme of contact with the wider community will be discussed further in Chapter 9 — for the moment, the following extract from the article in *Where* by J.L. Carr illustrates one of the kinds of opportunity that already exist:

> The Curator of Scarborough Museum had converted a vicarage on the edge of the moors and was running courses for young teenagers — seashore studies, wildlife, and the one Tom opted for — archaeological techniques. This was admirably conducted by a village schoolmaster . . . he succeeded in inspriring a desire to keep on learning. Tom is now reading archaeology at university. (Carr, no date, p. 13)

Change

I discussed in the earlier part of the chapter how most of the parents in the study adopted formal ways of working in academic subjects when they began home educating, usually combined with informal learning in areas such as those involving practical activities — the nature of a practical activity itself necessitating this, perhaps. A very few families planned to facilitate informal learning in all or most areas right from the start. We shall see now how events affected or effected change in the processes of education.

Development from Formality to Informality

It has often been observed in the literature on home education that development frequently takes place in the direction of greater informality in those families who make a more formal beginning.

The development of self-discipline in learning

Development of this sort was observed in some, but not all of the families interviewed (not, for example, the Banks family, where self-discipline appears to have been present from the beginning), and it varied in degree and substance. One interesting direction of change involved the child's increasing ability to organize his or her own learning. Some parents, among them the Minchins and the Deys, adopted a transmissive approach at first, hoping to allow this role to atrophy as habits of autonomous study developed: 'they teach me things. . . . They check my work, they do a lot more with the girls naturally, because I'm fifteen, just over fifteen, so I should be able to get on and do it myself' (Phil Minchin).

One mother explained, in *EO News* 39, how her children began to develop independence in learning outside their formal curriculum:

> One thing really strikes me. After nearly three years away from school (for Barry; Harriet has been out for two years) I can see the children quietly educating themselves in all sorts of ways that seem more valuable than the 'lesson'. They read a lot, play games, explore, help other people in work (including helping this working Mum run a house). They meet a variety of people, care for the dogs, and other people's babies. They 'take on' new activities: knitting, electrical repairs, baking. They were even able to pick grapes for a week, and thereby earned about eighty pounds each for ski equipment.

In some cases this independence in learning never developed (perhaps because the parent was unable to give up the transmissive role sufficiently, though there is no evidence for this):

> If I'm doing it with her, she's OK. But that's one thing that didn't develop as I'd rather hoped it would, that she'd get to the age of about fourteen, that she'd strike out on her own — work hard on her own — but she didn't do that. . . . You know, you hear about these marvellous kids in Education Otherwise who set up all kinds of projects. I'm afraid Corinne wasn't really like that. (Amy Dey)

Those who used correspondence courses, Jim Merriman and Daniel Scheaffer, for example, became accustomed in their early teens to working entirely on their own, though with a great effort of will in Jim's case:

> It was about five months and then, come September, I started working. I must admit it was a bit of an effort, the first time I sat down on the first course, because I'd been psyched out of it so much that nobody thought I could even begin these courses, because I was the youngest ever to do that, so I must admit I was bit worried but I got going with things quite quickly.

Some children developed such conscientious self-discipline in their study at home that they found FE college standards of work rather relaxed:

> J.W.: Having worked informally for so long, the outside pressures didn't bother you?

George: A lack of pressure, a distinct lack. I used to push myself a lot, lot more.

Were there other ways in which parents' parts in their children's learning changed? One might expect that alongside a diminution of the transmissive role would go an increase in the time parents spent learning with their children or searching out interesting resources and opportunities. There is little evidence of this in the interviewed families except in the case of the Gordons, quoted previously. However, Nancy Wallace, writing in the 'Afterword' of her book *Better Than School*, explains how her son's new-found understanding of mathematics is enabling him to help her learn, where previously she had helped him:

> He finally seems to be competent with numbers, and he definitely picks up on new mathematical ideas more quickly than I do. Now it's me struggling to make sense of decimals and per cents, not him, and I love it. (Wallace, 1983, p. 248)

The development of informality in learning methods
Changes in the direction of informality in the methods by which learning was tackled were more evident in families than changes in the parents' role and this is another theme common in the pages of *EO News*. One mother writes about the increasing confidence which enabled her to take a step towards greater informality even within the confines of working for examinations:

> Now we know the ropes we're going to manage without correspondence courses. There are good textbooks covering the O level syllabuses and it's not difficult to work out the practicalities of obtaining exam regulations, syllabuses and past papers. . . . The correspondence courses were useful first time round in boosting our confidence that all the necessary work had been covered to the right standard. . . . Parents who lack confidence about being able to help with O level work are probably worrying needlessly if they have taken O levels themselves. (*EO News* 44)

Relaxation in the structuring of time was even more apparent:

J.W.:   So did you change your approach or —?
Marie: More relaxed, I think, and they certainly choose exactly what they're doing and when they're doing it.

The Gold parents tried gradually to wean their daughter Karen off the daily timetabled subject approach she had been used to in school and onto unscheduled projects which related to her own interests:

Initially she suffered very much from, she wanted home to be a reflection of school. And I began like that, set a timetable down, but that very quickly went as a strict timetable. The only rule we had in terms of what she did was that she had to do a bit of something that we would call English and something that we would call maths every day. And the rest of the day her activities had to be 'School' as such but she was pretty free to choose whether it was art, cookery, whether she watched the studies programmes on TV or —. It was just up to her to choose. And it worked very well, after a bit. It took a lot of time for her to get used to the freedom of that. Once she'd actually got into it, it worked wonders.

Time limits frequently became natural rather than arbitrary, sometimes after several attempts at finding a way of organizing things sensibly:

We tried several different methods — first of all they tried the schooling method, 9 till 1 and have the afternoon off but work Saturdays and Sundays as well. But we found it was a bit silly, specially when we got to here, because of the fact of the land, so now they said, right, you've got to do an hour of maths, an hour of English and some other subject for as long as you want. (Phil Minchin)

Sarah Guthrie, quoted in *The Times*, had the same experience of adapting the use of time to fit in with daily domestic life:

Sarah Guthrie, in common with many parents embarking upon teaching their own children, began in a very structured way 'feeling we had to do certain things every day'. Soon she realized that 'Learning is so much a part of living that it is much better to be relaxed and do things as they occur'. (Brompton, 1985, p. 9)

School terms tended to be ignored after a while: 'I don't have any holidays. I don't have six weeks' summer holiday. I don't break up until Christmas Eve, and then I have two days off and that's it' (Phil Minchin).

Sometimes changes towards informality in the use of time result from changes in family circumstances, much as the planning and progress of careers in the job sense can be affected by the demands of family life:

J.W.: You said you kept up that restricting it to the mornings and doing it at set times for a couple of years. What happened after that?

Amy: We moved didn't we . . . the house was in great disorder.

Corinne: Yes. This house was in a terrible state, we were living in one room and it was very difficult . . . for one thing it stopped at about 3.30 because that's when the children came home.

Changes of this kind can result in informal arrangements which are regarded by the families as rather unsatisfactory:

> My parents' marriage broke up a year after we began, so six months after B. joined us she had to go back to school because my Mum wasn't here. My brother got sent back to school, and I ended up doing a kind of commuting in between here and where my aunt lived. I used to go up there for ten days so she could supervise my maths. (Maureen Cotton)

Home-based education is obviously highly vulnerable to upsets caused by family disruption of various sorts, but, as we have seen, single-parenthood is not necessarily a barrier to carrying it out to everyone's satisfaction.

Another development towards informality which contrasts especially with school scheduling of time for particular tasks is the advantage, noted by Daniel Scheaffer and Gerry Budd, of getting used to leaving work that's not going well and picking it up again when the mind is refreshed (though some might regard this as a way of escaping from a job which would be better stuck to in preparation for adult life):

> She is someone who tends to get rather bored with things quickly. If in fact she just couldn't sit down I'd say, 'Well, go and make a cake, or why don't you go and feed the cat,' or something — you know, I used to think of something else to do and say have a break and come back to it later. This was the thing she expressed most — I think she would now: 'If I get interested, Mum, I can sit and do it for four hours and if I'm not interested I can go away and come back when I feel like it,' and the self-discipline — it came to her far more naturally, she could accept it far more readily. (Veronica Budd)

A mother writes on the same theme in *Growing Without Schooling* 58, but discusses the benefits she has begun to find from even longer breaks:

> I have come to understand that most learning cannot be measured, and is even invisible. Ideas and concepts will gestate for many months in my kids and then reappear in, somehow, a more mature form than when first introduced.

The development of informality in the curriculum

In the earlier part of this chapter I referred briefly to the blurring of academic work and the activities of daily life, which is one of the ideals of some home educators, and was partly exemplified by the 'learning through life' approach of those who adopted informal learning from the start. Some of the other families interviewed were becoming aware of small opportunities for this sort of thing:

> This is practical work picking strawberries, not only just picking them and taking them up to the shop but knowing what kind of strawberries they're picking . . . so that they can recognize these in the fields, you see, where one row changes from Cambridge Favourite to the Red Gauntlet and this morning they were up there and they were pruning raspberry plants, so this was practical horticulture you know, a little bit of an insight into that. (Andrew McGill)

The activities of 'The State' touring company began to involve the children in using elements of their morning formal curriculum in an informal context:

> They'd help us with our maths with working out things like how much fuel we'd need, to go a certain distance. That was helpful. . . . And learning about maps, helping to navigate the way, when you get there helping to put up all the tents. (Ben Haward)

These two cases, though they demonstrate instances of specific areas of the curriculum being encouraged to overlap with everyday life, do not exemplify the sort of general merging of life and learning which is the subject of this paragraph. Developments in the type and direction of learning at Trunkles Top, referred to earlier, were really the only examples of this in the study. Nancy Wallace, *Growing Without Schooling* 58, writes about her family's experience of the gradual merging of curriculum and daily life: 'the longer we homeschooled the more interrelated all of our activities seemed, and the more disconcerting it was when our friends acted as if there was some kind of distinction between schoolwork and pleasure' (Wallace, 1987, p. 24).

Changes from Informality to Formality

Changes of this sort fell into two categories: families who began informally in the children's early years and became more formal as examinations loomed larger, and those who learnt informally at home but encountered formality at FE college.

Examples of early informality are the Gordon and Scheaffer families. We have already seen that Daniel's education for two years with the 'girl over the road' was unconventional, unstructured and did not involve the three Rs, but that, on joining PNEU, he began to work in a more tightly scheduled way, following their pre-planned courses. The Gordons continued for longer with informal ways of learning:

> *Marie:* We didn't think very much in subjects till they were much older . . . you didn't start on formal maths books till you were about ten, eleven, did you?. . . . We just kind of got to an end of doing just

anything that was practical that came up and so he decided he'd have to see the books, and he whipped through those.

In both these families there was a feeling that informality was only appropriate up to a certain level of study. For the Heads and Parsons formality was considered only a necessity of *institutional* learning and was not encountered until attendance at college, for a catering course in Simon's case, and O levels in Alison's, made it inevitable. Another reason for abandoning informality for a more structured approach can be pressure from a local education authority, as this report in *EO News* 44 makes clear:

> We had a small trauma in the autumn when the LEA, after a short visit, wrote to say that they were not satisfied with the education being given. . . . This challenge to our whole way of life was shattering but it did concentrate our minds and we've had a productive time since. We've adopted a much more definite structure with approximate school days and hours, doing regular maths, French and projects and Petra working hard on her O level correspondence courses, as well as a lot of music and crafts.

Assessment

One issue integral to a discussion of the process of home education, but so far touched on only implicitly, is that of assessment. It may affect directly the degree of formality chosen by home educators and the direction which this takes over time; for example, the recognition of a need for qualifications in the form of externally assessed examinations may result in more highly structured learning, as shown earlier. The interrelated questions of why assessment is done and what is being assessed, who does it, and how it is done, constitute the important aspects of an examination of its place in home education, which continues to follow the theme of development from one level of formality and structure to another.

The most often expressed need for assessment among those studied, as in a school population, relates to the goal of examination qualifications, for which preparation at home, assessed on lines dictated by examination conditions and specimen answers, may be regarded as necessary. The Hartfield and Gordon families both employed this kind of home testing of the children's adequacy in terms of both coverage of the curriculum and examination techniques. In what was anyway a rather formal situation, learning with the structure of a test in mind would lead in the direction of even greater formality (self-imposed in the Gordons' case but imposed by their father on the Hartfield girls):

> About the last year, a lot of our work consisted in fact of working through old matric papers in the different subjects, you know, working to time, and as nearly under exam conditions as possible. (Alison Hartfield)

In the Gordons' case this was seen as essential to the children's future educational careers, though the whole family disagreed very much with the philosophy of academic competition, feeling rather that progress in academic subjects should be measured only by a child's own previous standards. Another feature of school assessment, comparison with other members of the peer-group, was found only rarely among those studied, and in the context either of possible eventual return to school (for example, Corinne's case, where an effort was made to achieve the standard reflected in the appropriate textbooks for her age), or in terms of needing to know the standard of those who would be taking the same examinations.

These reasons for assessment took second place among families in the study to the need to keep track of personal improvement. Formal and detailed assessment of progress along these lines was supplied for correspondence course students (if required) by their tutors. Jim Merriman did not find this particularly helpful:

> The tutorial system wasn't really much, it wasn't a large part of the course. Each course was divided into lessons and at the end was your test which you sent off, which was quite a good idea but it wasn't really an important part.

Another problem of this distance learning approach was, he discovered, that the time lapse between sending off a piece of work or specific problem and receiving a response to it occasionally held learning up.

Among those working either more informally or very informally, some form of assessment of personal progress was always present. Sometimes formal assessment was requested of reluctant parents by their children: 'all that "What's me mark?", that kind of thing. That took a long time to get over. . . . And "Will you write 'good' on the bottom?" And I'd write "good" on the bottom' (Margaret Gold).

The need for this kind of formal assessment diminished predictably as the Golds moved further away from school-like ways of learning, but it is interesting to note that formal testing was also requested by children who were much younger and much less 'schooled', perhaps indicating a universal desire to see occasionally how one measures up against absolute standards:

> The children will sometimes ask if they can do a spelling test or something like that, sometimes a grown-up'll be looking through a

book of tests and someone'll come up and say, 'You give us a test' or something like that. They quite like that. (Caroline Parker)

The Gordons have already been mentioned as examples of children who themselves felt a need for personal assessment. This may have originated partly in their daily diary-keeping. This provided a useful summary of activities and progress for the whole family, and was popular with some other families in the study, such as the Heads. Many parents, including myself, have found diary-keeping a helpful way of assessing progress, and also of ensuring that activities over a long period of time reflect some sort of balance in the curriculum, where this is considered desirable. It also appears to be common for this form of assessment to dwindle away as confidence in informal learning grows (and, perhaps, parents become busier). Other parents kept a watch on their children's progress without writing anything down:

J.W.: You didn't do any kind of systematic assessment?
Sally Banks: No, no. I was just interested in him being happy and getting a good education.

It must be borne in mind that the fairly formal methods this family was using probably made very informal assessment of this sort easier.

One possible need for assessment not yet dealt with relates to demands from the LEA or a feeling that they will expect to see proof of activities carried out. The LEAs' concerns about educational content and the way in which they approach and assess families will be discussed in Chapter 10. For now, I want to establish how (if at all) their assessment procedures affected the families' own, and whether the doing of home-based education was in turn affected by this as far as formality in its various aspects goes.

The LEAs' assessment requirements can be divided into the same three categories as those perceived by families themselves: those concerned with examinations, those related to peer-group comparison and those which measure personal progress. (There may in time be a fourth category of concern: measurement against the standards of the National Curriculum, though private educators are not legally bound to take it into account.)

Where children were undertaking exam-orientated correspondence courses, the evidence of these appeared to be adequate as far as assessment went: 'they said they were satisfied. It was partly because I did it in a structured way. We simply had a correspondence course which he used for O levels' (Pat Maxwell). This was also the case with Jim Merriman. In neither family did the education authority's method of assessing affect in any way the formality of the home education provided.

Assessments related to peer-group comparison appeared more problematic because the requirements were less explicitly stated. The McGill girls, for instance, who were using a fairly formal traditional curriculum, were very briefly assessed by the LEA and pronounced unsatisfactory but no guidance was ever given as to where they fell short of the required peer-group stand-ards, which meant that the McGills could do nothing to change the method and content of their learning.

Like the majority of families, LEAs appeared to be more concerned with personal progress than with peer group standards, but they varied widely in the way in which they liked to see this assessed. Some required parents and/ or children to keep records, among them Trunkles Top and the Minchins. The difference in these advisers' attitudes, though they both came from the same LEA, makes interesting reading (note that the parents in the first case are mainly trained teachers, whereas the Minchins are not):

> This lady from the education authority used to come, she was a very nice lady, she used to ask us to keep records of things we'd done but she hasn't been since and she hasn't asked us to keep any records again, so I think they must have forgotten about us or something. I think they're quite satisfied. (Caroline Parker)

> I'm not very academic, I'm more practical, but the education adviser doesn't like that. He's all 'Write this, write that, write the other'. He said to Mum and Dad, 'Don't you write down everything that he does?' I mean, you try writing down everything that a person does in his life or does in his few years of education you'd end up with a room full of papers . . . Mum knows what I'm doing, she knows what book I'm working on and how far I've got in the book, she might go and tell me to do something. (Phil Minchin)

It is sad to reflect that this sort of recording might have resulted in a greater understanding by the advisers of the Minchins' education and improved what was always a very difficult relationship.

Other LEA assessments of personal progress relied entirely on talking to the children and looking at their work:

> She heard the two eldest read and looked at their books and said she was more than satisfied. She was very helpful and encouraging. We even confessed that we did not stick to the plan of work or the timetable, she said it didn't matter, the children were being educated and were happy and self-confident. (*EO News* 38)

A formal start to working at home, to give confidence and a familiar structure to both parents and children, often developed into a less formal use of time and materials as confidence and children's independence grew. The parents' role would sometimes then change from that of traditionally transmissive teacher to provider of opportunities and help when asked for. Some children, whose parents were qualified teachers, began informally and encountered formality and structure at the examination stage. They found themselves well able to organize themselves to do the work involved here but tended to resent the manner in which it was presented to them by the authorities.

Chapter 9

Activities With Others

This chapter is concerned with the ways in which home educated children come into contact with other people, either in the home education movement or in the wider community. The effects of this contact on the process of home educating are discussed, and some attempt made to characterize the range of reactions to home educating families' activities in the outside world.

The Development of Sociability

A major theme of this chapter is that of 'socialization', the term used by educationists to describe the process by which children learn, in varying degrees, to cooperate with others, to respect others' rights and feelings, and to enjoy their company. One of the most frequently voiced objections to home education concerns this area of development, and the expected social isolation of the home educated child.

I imagine few would dispute that sustained relationships with a wide variety of people are necessary to the building up of a picture of what people are like, and to the ability to make the kinds of judgments and predictions a successful adult social life depends on. Andy Sluckin quotes the following research:

> In some communities children grow up with very few opportunities to meet and play with their contemporaries. What little evidence there is about these children's development comes from a study by Hollos and Cowan comparing seven to nine year olds from three Norwegian settings. Some of them came from a town, others from a village and others from a dispersed farming community in the Arctic tundra. These last ones rarely left their own homesteads before school age (eight years), except for important holidays and family occasions.

Their interactions were confined to the family and mainly to one or two siblings.

The only difference in the farm children's mental development was in terms of their ability to put themselves in someone else's shoes. The tasks measured the extent to which they could report what another person would see, how well they could repeat a story to another person who hadn't heard it before, and whether they could take the role of storyteller in a cartoon picture sequence. The farm children scored lowest on all these tasks.

The researchers concluded that a minimum level of interaction with peers and adults is necessary for the adequate development of roletaking and that the children in the farming community were below it. (Sluckin, 1981, p. 116)

(It would be interesting to repeat this research with groups of unschooled and schooled eight-year-olds in Britain.)

Three of the home educated children interviewed made the point under discussion: 'this probably sounds surprising, but if you haven't met very many people from the start it's very, very difficult to get to know what to say' (Daniel Scheaffer).

One wonders whether, in this case, things were actually very different for his independently schooled brother and sister, and we must note as well that the circumstances of his home education were exceptional in that they made it hard for him to participate in outside activities. However, when he went to FE college and later university, he apparently had no trouble in establishing a busy and enjoyable social life, so that it seems that any early disadvantages of this sort can be compensated for in some cases. Ben Haward, who made the same point about not knowing how to react at first, also made friends and settled down socially at school. The third person to make this point was Paul Simmons and he, alone of all those interviewed, continued to find social life difficult (he was twenty-nine at the time of the interview): 'I can get on well with people on a superficial level but I can't make relationships with people. I've got very few friends. I've felt pretty isolated. I haven't mixed with people my own age very much at all'. His mother added that he had no relatives living close by and was an only child, and there are hints throughout the interview that he was something of a loner by nature:

Lynne: He really was a misfit.
Paul: The thing I've missed out on is the social skills . . . where I would have got it, how I would have acquired it I don't know or whether I could have acquired it I don't know.

Given that everyone interviewed, and most lay and professional people outside the home education movement, would agree with these views on the importance of a wide variety of relationships, what are the arguments for and against school as an agent of socialization? C.W. Valentine, after pointing out that four of his own five children went to school late, and that the later they went, the easier they found it to adjust, nevertheless comes to the following conclusion after summarizing the evidence for and against school as the best milieu for social development:

> We have no conclusive evidence that social development is permanently injured by absence of schooling before 5:0 or 6:0 or probably even a somewhat older age, but that so much is gained from association with others, that it seems very probable that social development will be hindered in the great majority if schooling be delayed much longer. (Valentine, 1956, p. 173)

It becomes clear that he bases this statement on a lack of awareness of the possibilities for 'association with others' which may be available out of school and which will be the subject of the rest of this chapter. Fletcher sheds further light on the possible role of school in social development:

> Children grow used to mixing together, singing together, eating together, dancing and sharing games etc. . . . . Such occasions acquaint them, too, with the manners, politenesses, courtesies, associated with them, and, in this, can be liberating — giving children a greater social confidence, setting them more at ease, enabling them to establish social relationships more readily, effectively, securely; overcoming their anxieties and diffidence. (Fletcher, 1984, p. 235)

Valentine's and Fletcher's discussions cover a very wide range of traits related to sociability in a general way. Sluckin concentrates on very specific areas in which school playtime may contribute to social development, though he does not consider that a child without this experience will necessarily be unable to learn the needed social skills later:

> Just as the rituals of the playground may be introducing children to the idea that many everyday problems can be solved by verbal formulae, so their games may serve as an introduction to the attitudes, values and sex-roles appropriate for adult society. (Sluckin, 1981, p. 110)

As well as the play element of school socialization, there are to be considered the possible advantages of working in groups (learning to cooperate, to be patient and tolerant, and to recognize the contributions of others). This extract from my verbatim notes on a conversation with an LEA adviser makes clear how strongly some school professionals feel about this:

He knew a family with two otherwise lovely children who couldn't share in a learning situation because they didn't go to school until seven, and these were children of knowledgable and concerned parents. Learning in schools, he said, is shifting more and more towards working in groups, particularly in science and, with the influence of Cockcroft, in maths. In a group situation at school challenges from a wide variety of people are involved, but at home the only challenge is from parents or siblings and this limits the quality of the challenge.

(He seems to be talking here about social *and* intellectual development — the intellectual challenge could presumably be equally well catered for by books and/or teachers.)

These arguments for socialization in school are for the most part powerful ones. How does it come about then that, with the exception of Paul Simmons, on his own admission, all the home educated people I spoke to were remarkably outgoing, articulate, self-confident and friendly and had evidently had no problems adjusting to peer-group, and adult, social life? Part of the reason could lie in the counterarguments to those above, put forward by deschoolers such as John Holt. An educational psychologist I interviewed gave the less common professional view (he worked for the same LEA as the adviser quoted above):

He didn't see peer group contact as a significant issue except where a family was *very* isolated. Plenty of clubs and out of school activities available to most people. Some children were perfectly well-adjusted with minimal social contact and others were without a friend in a whole playground full of children. There was no real evidence either way as to the importance of social contact in school. In the future however, with many more families doing it with the growth of computer-aided learning, there might be a general effect on social competence and then clubs etc. wouldn't be adequate.

(The latter is an interesting point I have not seen made anywhere in the literature on home education.) Maire Mullarney goes into further detail on the question of the value of constant participation in groups raised by the educational psychologist:

How much group consciousness do we need? In later life, unless we join the army or a large religious community, we hardly ever need to think of ourselves as one of a group of thirty. It is, on the other hand, extremely valuable to be able to do things by yourself, even to be comfortable alone, without company. It is possible that too much group consciousness too soon may result in adults who cannot be alone. (Mullarney, 1983, p. 14)

The point about children being without friends at school was made by some of the home educating families as well, who had had experience of this. In the previously discussed cases of Martin Maxwell and Emma Williams, school organization prevented them from being with friends they had already made. In Jim Merriman's case, being smaller and brighter was one of the isolating factors, leading in turn to bullying. Alison Head found that conflict between her background and that of most of the others in her class was the cause of social problems:

> I was very anti-social at school, I never really got on with people very well. . . . You can be as alone amongst twenty-five of your peers as sitting in a room on your own . . . particularly at the second one because it was such a culture shock I suppose . . . working class kids had lived there all their lives and someone who's newly come from Hampstead Garden Suburb is not really the accepted person.

This illustrates what some home educators would consider a drawback of school as an agent of socialization: that it restricts children's social interaction, for a large part of their time, to a particular, rather narrow, age group and often to social class or intellectual ability cliques, and that this, apart from being a limiting thing in itself, makes conformity seem very important. There are frequent echoes of this point of view in *EO Newsletter*:

> The nature of the 'socializing' permitted and encouraged in schools — more especially secondary schools — is as limited and artificial as that in many prisons. Yet social skills are supposed to be learned to enable the individual to cope with life. And in the great big world outside the authoritarian institutions social intercourse is certainly not restricted to 'playtimes' and with people of like age (or sentence) who happen to be defined by some authority as 'peers'. Looked at in this way, the social interaction within schools can be positively harmful. (*EO News* 34)

Another view often expressed by home educators concerns the quality of school social life, rather than, or as well as, its range. They regard it as unacceptably shallow and attribute this partly to the institutional situation. Another point, made very forcefully by John Holt, is that the social life of school is frequently preparing children to function anti-socially, to 'look after number one', because of the need to defend oneself against hostility and because of the high prestige accorded to the materially better off. Teachers may wittingly or unwittingly reinforce these attitudes by their own responses, as may the parents Holt quotes:

> When I point out to people that the social life of most schools and classrooms is mean-spirited, status-oriented, competitive, and snobbish, I am always astonished by their responses. Not *one* person of the hundreds with whom I've discussed this has yet said to me that the social life at school is kindly, generous, supporting, democratic, friendly, loving, or good for children. No, without exception, when I condemn the social life of school, people say, 'But that's what the children are going to meet in Real Life.' (Holt, 1981, p. 49)

Leaving aside the point that if things do not change in schools, Real Life is unlikely to improve either, some home educators take the view that the sort of anxious, defensive or aggressive people who may emerge from school are not best prepared on a personal level to lead happy and fulfilled lives, and that social interaction outside school may be much healthier from this point of view. Though poor social atmosphere at school featured as a major concern of only five of those interviewed, it may be as well to remind ourselves that in the EO survey (Grant, 1983) quoted earlier, more than twice the number of parents in any other category gave as a reason for joining EO that they did not approve of the 'morals and social attitudes implanted by schools'. These excerpts from an article in *EO News* 32 are typical of the views one frequently sees expressed, and they summarize what are seen as the main problems of socialization in school:

> There are many things wrong with the social contact to which children are subjected in the school system. The main fault I believe, is the splitting up of children into two distinct groups — relying only on their genital sex, not upon their suitability as personalities — to be lumped together. . . . Another major fault is in the peer grouping. . . . People are people whatever their age, from the cradle to the grave, and schools should not enforce a doctrine of division based upon age. . . . The social environment in schools tends to extract all the major faults of society at large and condense them into a much more concentrated form. This appears to be an inevitable and apparently (?) acceptable part of the school system structure. There is therefore a great atmosphere of competition which pervades all aspects of social life, and is heightened within social contact.

So, since from one point of view school social life may not after all be a bad thing to miss out on, what provision for social development do home educators make in its place?

Relationships and Activities With Other Home Educating Families

Families Who Found Them Unnecessary

Before examining the reasons why families did seek out contact with other home educators, and the sorts of relationship which they hoped would develop, it is necessary to point out that in certain circumstances contact of this sort, and indeed of all sorts, was considered either not particularly important or downright undesirable. The most outstanding example of the isolationist point of view must be that of the Welsh family described by Michael Deakin in *The Children on the Hill*:

> Only in peace, away from every form of irrelevant stimulation or outside pressure, can the child develop harmoniously with all its evolutionary processes developing at the same rate, avoiding schizoid or unbalanced characteristics in later life. (Deakin, 1973, p. 43)

Other situations where contact with fellow home educators may not seem crucial are families with large numbers of siblings all out of school, and families living in communities where all the children are home educated. In the first case, it is useful to repeat the observation that where one child may be home educated for a reason specific to that child, its siblings may follow. One element in the taking of this decision may often be a social one: that the child at home may feel lonely and left out if its siblings are at school, as well as the already discussed rationale that school education is no longer seen as useful for any member of the family since the experiences of one have pointed out deficiencies of which the parents were not previously aware. Large families such as the Mullarneys and the Bakers had good conditions for providing companionship of various ages without needing to go outside the family, but did not deliberately exclude contact of this sort.

The other group, commune dwellers, are similarly placed except that more children and adults may be involved. 'May' is the important word here, as one member of the Signposts community explained in a letter:

> Unfortunately most of the communes choose to send their kids back into the system that most of their parents have decided to reject — a very strange attitude — probably reflecting fear and strong conditioning which is very difficult to overcome. There is also always the fear of social isolation which is less of a problem in deschooling in communities (as opposed to single-parent or nuclear families) but nevertheless still a problem.

Trunkles Top, where I interviewed Caroline Parker, was the only community with all its child members (four of school age, five under five) out of school. In an article in *EO News* 20 various writers put forward some of the social advantages of their situation: 'in the eighteen months that Minnie has been taught at home she has developed a very distinct personality — she has emerged as a second mother to our baby and toddler here,' and:

> I can observe a tremendous change both in Kiri and the other children over the past fifteen months. Kiri's drawing and colouring capabilities have progressed in leaps and bounds, her number knowledge is to me at times quite amazing. Her vocabulary is vast and her use of English very good. Much of this I do not think would have been achieved yet without the communal life in which we share and the older children being educated at home.

These comments must be balanced against Caroline Parker's observation that, as the oldest child, she missed having friends of her own age around: since communes tend to be in rural, often isolated, areas, the make-up of the commune itself can be crucial in this respect. However, moral support for parents, as well as relief for some from social isolation, can be another benefit of communal living. Indeed, though there were only two communities educating all their children at home at the time of the interviews, it seems from the constant articles and advertisements in *EO News*, that there are a large number of home educating nuclear families wanting to move into a community situation of some sort for social reasons, and those of moral support.

The Need for Relationships With Other Home Educators

The existence of these movements provides a strong indication of the need of many nuclear families to associate with other home educators — the support of like-minded individuals can be crucial to maintaining confidence and reducing any feelings of social isolation, particularly during school hours. Margaret Gold explains how this support (unavailable to them and many others during the period under discussion because home educating families were so thin on the ground) could have helped Karen:

> She suffered from this not really knowing whether she was just different from everybody else and in spite of us saying she was just being taught in another way, but again that wore off. It would have been nice to have had somebody we could have gone down the road to and spent, you know, going to the Baths or something.

The Head family originally had a vision of a learning community which would operate on an extended-family pattern, with all the social and educational advantages implicit in this:

> What we had in mind was a programme of education outside the state system, for which a group of persons of varying ages, and about twenty-four in number, would take communal responsibility. For the children of school age, this would be the full-time alternative to school. The group would consist of parents and children from the same families, and single persons. We should call upon all the personal resources available in such a group, and on the services of advisers and 'resource people'. . . . This programme would be the joint responsibility of the educational community. By 'community', we were not referring to people living in the same neighbourhood (though we would need to be accessible to one another) nor to a commune-type of experience. The sharing would be in the learning, and because the learning would be closely related to everyday living, this would require close relationships and a strong sense of mutual accountability. Regular meetings for consultation would be needed, though much scope would be left for family and personal initiatives. (Head, 1974, p. 127)

The Reality of Inter-family Relationships

As the reader might guess from the tone of this heading, the home educators interviewed were on the whole disappointed with the contacts they made, which varied from fleeting conversations with one or two individuals to attendance at large local meetings.

The Gold family managed only brief and rather unsatisfactory contact with other home educating families:

> *Malcolm:* We didn't actually meet anyone to discuss *our* problems.
> *Margaret:* It was just people ringing us up and talking. Again we were in the position that although there were people around in the area they were very widespread and getting people together was quite a difficult problem so it tended to be telephone conversations rather than face-to-face meetings.

Apart from a certain benefit to the parents in knowing that other families were undertaking home education and perhaps having similar problems, the social value of this sort of interaction, particularly to the children, is probably negligible. Large local meetings of the kind the Golds describe above as desirable proved useful as a forum for ideas to some, but, perhaps because of an

unfamiliar structure, or lack of one altogether, were a disillusioning experience
for others:

> *J.W.:* Have you had support from anyone else?
> *Caroline Parker:* Well, we go to Education Otherwise meetings and
>   things like that, we've been to a lot of meetings.
> *J.W.:* Local or national ones?
> *Caroline:* Mainly local ones. We can't really go to places that are
>   quite a way away because we can't afford the petrol.

and:

> *Phil Minchin:* We went to several things with the EO. We weren't
>   that impressed with it actually up there, it wasn't very good, they
>   were flitting from here to there and everything.
> *J.W.:* What sort of things were you expecting from it?
> *Phil:* Well, we used to have proper meetings but I don't think Mum
>   and Dad expected it to be like it was. It was very, go and join in
>   with everybody, you know, you ask them a question and you'd get
>   everybody answering. There wasn't anybody in charge, it was all,
>   everybody in.

Attempts to establish contact with individual families, perhaps to facilitate
group learning of some sort as well as for social purposes, were successful for
only a few families. The Gordons in particular had lots of one-off visits for
advice at the time when EO was being established, and the Cottons, Gordons
and Heads were in contact with each other and with another girl for a while,
mostly for sporadic swimming visits. This type of contact, though valuable
socially, obviously falls a long way short of the kind of association with other
families envisaged by the Heads in the passage quoted earlier. The Deys and
Minchins had regular contact with only one family each. Why was it that so few
families regularly met other home educators? Reasons of finance in connection with geographical spread have already been mentioned. In some cases, it
was because they felt they had little in common: 'I did once try to set up a
neighbourhood link, got some very odd people ringing me, with three-month
babies. Sometimes I thought these people shouldn't be keeping their children
at home' (Amy Dey).

The Heads, writing in *Free Way to Learning*, show how their experience
of trying to form a learning community changed their ideas of what might in
fact be possible:

> In our comparative freedom, and with a new home base, we are still
> looking for other families to work with. It appears that we are unlikely
> to find enough people accessible to us (especially with secondary-age

children) to set up the close-knit unit we dreamt of. It is more likely that we shall be able to join with others in sewing together a network of relationships, where there can be some shared activities, and some mutual support and consultation. (Head, 1974, p. 139)

It is important to point out that few families nowadays are in the position of those interviewed: since the huge increase in EO membership has come about, most areas have numerous regular social meetings, trips and activities organized by members themselves and the local coordinator. There are also national meetings with plenty of activities for children, but here, of course, financial strictures still apply.

Activities Elsewhere in the Community

Previous quotations have indicated the value of the community as an educational resource, and there has already been some discussion about this in Chapter 7. The emphasis in this section is on the social aspects of this use of resources: the ease with which an enormous variety of opportunities for meeting people and sharing common interests is available, in all but the most isolated places, when home educators get into the habit of looking out for them. This finding was simultaneously confirmed for me both by the families interviewed and by my own experience with my son's deschooling: we found far more interesting opportunities for all kinds of shared activities, both in and out of school hours, than we could possibly make time for. The idea of a network, mentioned by David Head in the previous section, helps here in showing how one contact almost inevitably leads to others, so that once a home educating family has taken the plunge and launched itself upon the local community, it will in most cases have little difficulty either in catering for interests already extant or finding, in a haphazard fashion, stimuli for new ones.

The sorts of activities families discovered through which they met other people fell into five broad categories. Perhaps the most traditionally educational relationships were those with people met through project work or a serious hobby, where the imparting of information played a large part. Phil Minchin, for example, did a project on the police service, in the course of which he became friendly with a local policeman. Jim Merriman made a good friend in the same way:

Roger: He was very friendly with the old man next door funnily enough, very friendly.

Jim: Yes. I used to go round a lot because he was interested in electronics and that was one of my passions so we used to do quite some amazing things for my age.

Simon Parson's snooker-playing neighbour and the more traditional tutors which Caroline had for horse-riding and painting, and Grace Gordon had for music, are other examples of this type of relationship. Shared classes were another way in which families met people from varied backgrounds. Maureen and Corinne, as already described, both attended adult education classes where their presence presumably served to reinforce the idea of learning as a process to which age is irrelevant. Clubs and groups of various kinds were very popular among home educating families as ways of both pursuing an interest and meeting people. Peace groups, youth clubs, church groups, science groups, amateur dramatic societies; the list of possibilities discovered and made use of is very long. Here is one example, that of Phil Minchin:

I belong to several organizations. I belong to Young Farmers, St. John's, I'm doing first aid make-up as well, and hopefully I'm going to belong to the Braunton CB club . . . I used to belong to the Scouts but I gave it up because it was too expensive to go.

In connection with this, trips and visits, attendance at, or hosting of, special interest events or festivals, were other ways in which families met like-minded others. Caroline Parker described how she'd been to Sidmouth Folk Festival (where among others she'd met teams of dancers from other countries), a mime workshop, Hood Fair, to stay at another community and had briefly enjoyed the company of numerous people through WWOOF (Working Weekends On Organic Farms) at Trunkles Top. Phil also made the sort of relationships which would prepare him for the adult employment world (doing gardening work for a retired army officer) as did Gerry Budd, the McGills and Martin and Alison Head (in widely varying occupations, as described earlier). The voluntary activities undertaken by Phil and Gerry with Cheshire Homes and Child Poverty Action Group, respectively, performed a similar function in easing the participants into Real Life, to use John Holt's term, and familiarizing them with some of its workings, as well as enabling them to form equal-status relationships with clients and other adults (Phil talked about a friend of his at the Cheshire Home who had a CB set attached to her wheelchair). Finally, it seems that some of the children met people who became friends completely by chance or because they happened to live in the neighbourhood and be around:

The chap I'm friendliest with now I actually met in Smith's. He was working and I was looking for a new book, and I asked him if it was coming out soon, I'm Dr. Who mad, and it took off from there. We're very close friends. (Glenn Banks)

It seems, then, from the evidence presented here, and from a reading of *EO News* and *Growing Without Schooling*, that there is no shortage of opportunities for meeting people. The very wide range of ages, levels of ability and backgrounds that is available to home educated children is likely to ensure that social development is fully adequate for the demands of the outside world. The popular picture of a sheltered, unprepared 'hot-house plant' was not generally confirmed.

Two other, mutually unconnected, points are interesting in the context of this section. One is that some children (the Golds) found they got on well, once out of school, with the very children they had not been friendly with in the school situation — an illustration perhaps of one aspect of institutional effects on relationships. The second point concerns the two-way social and educational relationship which can be noted in the activities of home educated children in the community: those they work, learn or play with are becoming familiar with a (probably) new idea: that children can be educated, and sociable, without going to school. The remainder of this chapter discusses in detail the reactions of those involved.

Reactions to Home-based Education

It would be artificially simplifying the range of reactions to divide them into wholly hostile versus wholly sympathetic, though examples of these extreme ends of the spectrum do exist. For instance, the phenomenon of 'fear of infection' sometimes produces, among the ultra-conventional, dogmatic condemnation of the course taken by the home educator: 'I think some people were scared that Corinne's rebellion might spill over onto their children' (Amy Dey).

A few families do seem to suffer from general extreme hostility to home education (and in their case support from other home educators must be crucial):

Our . . . encounter with the Education Board here has been a mere breeze, compared with the icy gales of disapproval from our families, all the harder to bear because they love the children too, and genuinely feel we are wrong.

Perhaps in large cities, or remote rural areas, neighbours are less of a problem than in villages, but surely we can't be the only ones who skulk at home until after 3.30 p.m. term time? It's not so much that I mind explaining, it's just that we are heartily sick of *having* to explain. (*EO News* 46)

At the other end of the range were those who had personal reasons for being completely sympathetic to the idea, for example, Maureen Cotton's tutor at FE college, who found it easy to approve because of previous familiarity with education out of school. Apart from these isolated expressions of vehement condemnation or support, most families experienced a mixture of reactions, as described by the following interviewees:

> People's reactions varied from total support to outright opposition; and it was often the opposite of what you would expect from a particular person. And there were many people, of course, who just didn't understand why we were doing what we were doing. (David Baker)

Marie Gordon ends her description of the mixture of comments she received on taking George out of school with a point about society in general:

> *J.W.:* What reaction did you get from other people when you first took him out?
>
> *Marie:* Absolutely everything: 'What a good idea', 'Lucky thing', 'Won't they miss other children?', 'Didn't know you could do that'. But whenever we used to go out when other children were at school people used to say, 'Oh, not at school today?' Usually the opening gambit whenever you go anywhere new is 'What school do you go to?' I didn't realize until we did it how much school-orientated everyone is.

It may be interesting to discuss the reactions to home education of various groups of individuals who are characterized by a particular relationship to the children being educated. Again, the various background experiences of the group's members may be important in determining the view they take.

The reactions of relatives, as illustrated earlier, can be vital from the point of view of providing support, particularly if they are emotionally and geographically close. Conversely, their disapproval can be very confidence-sapping. Each of these reactions was typical of the experience of some of the families interviewed, and this is a situation in which interested but non-committal reactions are less likely because of the close bonds involved. The Parsons family was one of those which suffered from unsympathetic relations: 'they're very puzzled, they don't understand it at all. And they're against it. My sister thinks it very peculiar, so do my parents. You know, she thinks the children are going to the dogs'.

In some cases, an initially hostile reaction to the idea mellowed under the influence of observation of the effects of home educating: 'Nan, I think, when we first started, thought it was a lot of work, it was too much for Mum and Dad but I think she's changed her mind now . . . we get on with what we've got to do' (Phil Minchin). Others had the support of sympathetic relatives from the beginning: 'none of them were against it. Everybody asked questions and were genuinely interested I think. Everybody was very nice' (Caroline Parker). Ironically, the Parker family was probably less in need of support from their relatives, educating in a commune, than were some of the nuclear families interviewed who were without it.

An important group as far as the children themselves are concerned, and for the peace of mind of parents worried about social life, is that which comprises other children (old schoolfriends and neighbours) and their parents. (Little was said by the parents interviewed about the reactions of their own friends, so it is not possible to discuss this in detail.) Predictably, jealousy played a big part in the reactions of most other children, usually following a period of disbelief and amazement that the sacred cow of school could be slaughtered — a very big political discovery for some older pupils, one would have thought, and one that may not have made their teachers' jobs any easier: 'they couldn't believe it at first, they said, "Really? Are you? You can't do that, can you"' (Caroline Parker).

> *Dickie Tansley:* At first, they didn't believe me before I left, or didn't wanna believe me. When I left they still didn't believe me, they just thought I was playing truant.
> *J.W.:* Your friends haven't said to their parents, 'Look what Richard's doing?'
> *Dickie:* They have, definitely, yes.

The problem of jealousy among other kids is more pronounced where younger children are involved and in situations where a child is attending school part-time and therefore visibly receiving less schooling than the other pupils: 'Etty's only reason for attendance was a social one, but we found it didn't really work very well, as other children were, I think, jealous of Etty's freedom from full-time schooling' (*EO News* 18). There is a problem here for parents as well, in that they have to explain why their children must go to school when so-and-so's do not. Less truthful, or perhaps less informed, parents have told their children that so-and-so's children won't learn to read and write because they don't go to school, and that so-and-so will be put in prison for keeping his children out. It is easy to see what harm these comments can do if passed on to the children concerned, as they have sometimes been.

Another result of this sort of questioning can be forbidding the two sets of children to play together, and this had happened to both the McGills and the Simmonses:

> *Lynne Simmons:* Their friendship came to a halt because they went to school and he didn't ... I think it was the parents' decision,

they'd had a comeback from the boys you see: 'He doesn't go to
school, why should we?'

Another large group of interested people, with very diverse views, is that of the
professionals involved, mainly teachers and psychologists. It is difficult here
not to present views as polarized for and against, and again there were examples of this, negative reactions being perhaps the result of seeing it as a
threat to professional status, as this description of Ben Haward's reception at
school after home-based education may indicate:

> The school was in a panic, bringing this child in who had never been
> to school, it was astonishing, they were in a flat panic as to what this
> child would be like. I really feel they thought he would swing from the
> chandeliers and eat his food with his hands, and they kept coming up
> to me for the first three weeks and saying, 'But he can read, but he
> can —'. I said, 'Of course he can read, you don't need school for that.'
> (Kate Haward)

The worry about professional status might well be less in a situation like that
of Corinne Dey where most of her siblings were in school and therefore the
family as a whole was not presenting a criticism of the system. However,
though the reaction of other teachers to children returning to school or FE
college was on the whole less startled and more helpful, as we have seen in the
case of Maureen Cotton's tutor, Corinne still experienced some pressure to
return to school on a full-time basis:

> Mostly they were interested and instead of badgering me about coming
> back to school they'd ask. I remember my maths teacher saying, she
> said, 'If I ever had any children and I could do that, I'd do it.' You
> know, if they were unhappy . . . but one or two teachers used to come
> up and say, 'Oh, you should be at school. Why aren't you at school? I
> don't know how your mother can let you be so rebellious' and all that
> kind of thing.

The presence of a part-time pupil obviously constitutes a threat to a school that
hopes to operate by enforcing spurious elements of compulsion, similar to the
threat presented by a child who leaves to be educated entirely at home. This
may be why, in at least one case, that of Dickie Tansley, rumours appear to
have been circulated that the child concerned had been expelled. The attitude
of Corinne's interested mathematics teacher was perhaps more typical of the
approach of teachers who found themselves involved with home educated
children. Pity, rather than a feeling of being threatened, featured in some of
these reactions, as this quotation, in which Veronica Budd describes her
teaching colleagues' responses, shows:

> *Veronica:* My teaching friends were sad. They thought it was a pity
> that there was any necessity to do it but they weren't particularly
> surprised . . . they'd got children a couple of years younger, there
> were three people with children and they could see these problems
> looming up for them.

The reaction of independent psychologists involved with the families interviewed appears to have been positive and enthusiastic. I have already quoted
the LEA psychologist who discussed the social aspect of home education. The
psychologist who tested the ten-year-old Daniel Scheaffer was interested in
what she saw as the intellectual advantages, having no previous awareness of
the possibility of home education:

> She had a great sense of humour, she's French, and she said at the end
> of it: 'This is ever so interesting, I really have enjoyed myself', and I
> said, 'Good', you know, and she said, 'Well it's very interesting to see
> a mind that is unpolluted.' And she said, 'He approaches things very
> logically and very clearly and he asks questions, and so often I get
> children in here who won't ask and they just sit there and it's terribly
> difficult because you don't know whether they're dumb, dim, daft or
> just terrified, and at the end of it I've got question marks all over
> everywhere', and she had no experience of it, she said, 'If this is home
> education I'm for this very much indeed.' (Penelope Scheaffer)

The reactions of LEA officers in general, which may include teachers and
psychologists as representatives of the authority rather than as individuals, will
be discussed in the next chapter, which is devoted to relationships between
home educating families and the LEAs.

Ample opportunities exist for the home educated child to meet and make
friends with people of all ages and interests through involvement in community activities. The social confidence of nearly all the teenagers spoken to was
remarkable, suggesting that self-esteem and understanding of a wide range of
people's feelings and attitudes are more important factors in sociability than
lengthy exposure to a large group of one's peers.

Chapter 10

Relationships Between Families and the LEA

The chapter opens with an examination of the LEA's approach to dealing with the responsibility which it feels itself to have for home educating families: does it have a formal policy to guide officers involved with home educators? Of what does its approach consist and in what terms does it see the role of its officers? What concerns does it have about the education provided? These questions are examined partly through the evidence of conversation with LEA officers and partly through examples given by the families interviewed. In the latter case particularly, it must be borne in mind that the LEA's view is being filtered through that of the family. The second part of the chapter deals with the reaction of families to their contact with the LEA, including the extent to which they become more politically aware, and how this affects the process of home educating.

The LEA's Approach

Does It Have a Formal Policy?

The vigorousness of their supervision seems to vary . . . LEAs which appeared to have more systematic procedures were — Berkshire, which carries out termly reviews and aims at 're-integration' into school; Cleveland; Derbyshire, which produces a termly report following inspection and is preparing guidance for parents; Gloucestershire, where the Area Education Officer and Chief Inspector visit initially and advice is given, books provided and progress examined; Gwent, where the Education Committee considers advisers' reports; Staffordshire, where parents must submit timetables etc.; Bradford, where details of teachers and education are required; St. Helens, which requires written reports from parents; Walsall, which requires curriculum details; Hillingdon, the most systematic, where details are required about teacher qualifications, the teaching venue, the hours and organization of teaching, learning materials, and subject content; Enfield. (ACE, 1983)

The variety exemplified by this collection of policies was also a feature of my study, evident more as individual approaches made to home educating families than as formal policy statements. Perhaps these formal policies did exist but families were unaware of them. Two of the authorities involved, the ILEA and a generally-forward thinking shire county, did have thoughts on the advisability of such a policy. The ILEA had taken steps to formulate one and promote its practical application: 'we got this form from the ILEA, when they said that I wasn't going to go on to secondary school, and we got this form, saying "Where will she be having PE training?"' (Alison Head).

It appears that this LEA had developed standardized and detailed requirements: how appropriate these were will be discussed in the sub-section on home educators. The shire county Chief Education Officer (CEO) interviewed expressed a contrasting attitude, already quoted: 'we're an authority without policies, really. We don't believe in policies. Our policy is not to have policies'. His Primary Education Officer expanded on the practical implications of such a flexible approach, which tended strongly towards the informal:

We obviously want to discuss this with them and usually either a secondary adviser or one of the primary advisers, on whose patch the family lives, will visit the family, talk to them about their aims and their reasons and how they think they'll go about it, because we do have a duty to see that parents do educate their children which we can't escape. Parents in an ideal world will always know what's best for their children and be able to do it; but we live in a practical world and so after that visit we have to decide 'Does this look as if this will be in the interests of the child, or is there a danger that the child will in any way suffer?' And nobody is perfect. We have to make a judgment but basically we lean towards not interfering with the parents unless we're really worried.

Officers in a neighbouring authority, who also had no guiding formal policy, showed a varied interpretation of the law on home education and its implications for LEA responsibility, starting with the previously mentioned careers officer who thought that parents were technically not supposed to teach, through the Education Welfare Officer (EWO) who thought the authority too lenient and would have insisted on the twin criteria of his previous LEA (written curriculum and qualified tutors) had it been his decision, and ending with a very liberal educational psychologist who would positively recommend home education where he thought it might be helpful. The adviser for this authority was aware of the law and stated that procedure for dealing with home educating families was 'pretty standard throughout the county, though not rigidly so'.

Variation in interpretation of the law and in the policies it gives rise to is less common today in terms of total ignorance of the right of parents to educate at home, though this was apparently still quite prevalent when some of those interviewed were out of school: 'we argued, you see, that a child doesn't have to go to school, he only has to be educated and they argued the other way, and it was a series of arguments' (Lynne Simmons).

This sort of experience was also found in the pages of *EO News* at the time of the interviews. It appears that some EWOs in particular are so used to dealing with truant pupils and unconcerned parents, that the law regarding home education is an irrelevance which they often don't take the trouble to investigate when confronted, unusually, with a caring family genuinely interested in a constructive alternative to school. However, it is not clear to what extent statements regarding the professed illegality of home education may have been bluff on the part of some LEAs, intent on frightening people into keeping their children at school:

> They sent this little man round, didn't they, who, I think he was the school Welfare officer, and he said, 'Why isn't Karen at school?' so we said, 'Well, we've asked for her to be deregistered.' 'Oh, you can't do that, it's against the law.' Well, he'd chosen the wrong people. I mean, we were very polite to him, we just sort of told him to go and look up his law . . . he really shouldn't go around telling people things like that. (Margaret Gold)

Other areas of the law on home-based education are couched in imprecise terms, as discussed in Chapter 1, which encourage variation in interpretation and therefore policy. This does, of course, mean that there is plenty of leeway for home educators to argue their point, and in cases of dispute the courts have to make the final judgment as to whether the LEA or the home educating family is interpreting the words of the Act more accurately. A major legal issue which has been contentious even among home educators is the question of whether the LEA has any right to demand to assess home educated children. The debate centred on the first paragraph of Section 37 (see Chapter 1), and one side of the argument, put forward initially in 1979 (*EO News* 9) and reinforced in 1982, ran thus:

> By demanding access the LEA are acting outside the law. Section 37 — 'If it *appears* to an authority that parents are failing, etc.' Not, you will note, the authority must *confirm* that parents are fulfilling their

obligations . . . when the parents have informed their LEA in writing that in order to fulfil the obligations imposed in Section 36 they are educating otherwise, we feel that Section 37 is no longer applicable. (*EO News* 23)

However, a case reported by David Deutsch and Kolya Wolf in their paper 'Home education and the law' seems to establish a legal precedent for the opposite point of view:

Mr. Phillips was a parent of a child who was not attending school. The LEA asked him for details of the child's education. Mr. Phillips refused to comply, saying only that he was fulfilling his Section 36 duties. He was then served with a notice under Section 37 (1) requiring him to 'satisfy the authority that the child is receiving efficient . . . education'. He again refused to comply, saying that the LEA was not entitled to serve the notice because Section 37 empowers them to do this only if 'it appears to them' that Section 36 was being violated, and, there being absolutely no evidence of such a violation, it could not have appeared that there had been one.

This totally uncompromising position, refusing to give any information whatsoever about the child's education, was eventually rejected both by the magistrate and, in effect, by the judicial Review of Judge Donaldson. (Deutsch and Wolf, 1986, p. 7)

In What Terms Does the LEA See the Roles of Its Officers?

The important issue regarding the role of advisers was that of whom they were supposed to be advising. There was a clear distinction between the two authorities interviewed on this matter. One regarded the adviser's job as to advise the CEO that the family was being satisfactorily educated, rather than to advise the family. The other authority interviewed saw the role as a dual one, with the emphasis on advising the family in a sympathetic way:

Secondary adviser: We have also a statutory duty presumably to satisfy ourselves that all is well. . . . But I mean I could do that in a fairly formal way but I've always taken it much further, in, as I say, seeing them as an institution that is one of mine and so offered the same sort of facility as I would to a headmaster.

Primary adviser: Well, that's where authorities vary again I suppose in that I have heard people say that the adviser's job is purely to advise the Chief Education Officer. That's certainly not the way we operate here.

There was a dichotomy evident also between the roles of educational psychologists and EWOs in various authorities, which concerned directly the interests of schools versus those of the family. In Piers Arthur's case there was an expectation at work that the psychologist would assist the headmaster in compelling Piers to return to school:

> He was obviously totally constrained by what he was meant to do: his brief was to get them back to school. His brief wasn't to look at what does this young person really need. It just wasn't, it was quite ludicrous. (Jenny Arthur)

Mary Parsons also felt that the achievement of orthodoxy was the LEA psychologist's goal:

> I wouldn't advise anyone to go and see any educational psychologist connected with the LEA. I wouldn't touch it with a barge-pole. All they're there for is to make sure that people conform. . . . You've got to be very careful with psychologists in general, I think. If they're no good they can do a lot of harm.

One of the advisers interviewed emphasized that she definitely did not seek to return children to school:

> I was a school welfare officer before, so I'm used to going into people's homes, and I'm used to the reaction of people to the office and the feelings that they build up about it, so that the first thing I do, very early on, is establish that I haven't come to try and persuade them to send their child to school. And that's ever so important.

The psychologist I interviewed appeared to be taking a similarly positive line, although his LEA was in general only rather warily neutral about home-based education (an example of the independent-mindedness apparent among some LEA officers). Having said that he would sometimes suggest it as a solution to a child's educational problems, he explained the circumstances in which he might do this (where there was a conflict between the values of home and school). He considered his main responsibility was to the child rather than the LEA and he would, therefore, be accountable to the family, not to the adviser.

What Concerns Does the LEA Have About the Education Provided?

The concerns voiced by LEA representatives centred around firstly, the content of the home education provided and secondly, the method by which it was carried out. One might expect that in more traditionally-minded LEAs (for instance, those which still have selective schooling) advisers' expectations might also be more traditional, perhaps relating achievements to peer-group standards of some sort or expecting to see a strictly three Rs-orientated curriculum. There was only limited evidence that this was the case: for example, the adviser for a traditional LEA whom I interviewed said he assessed a child's level to see 'whether it's roughly commensurate' though the same adviser was open-minded about the content of the work: he had 'no definite ideas about what parents should aim to have covered in general'.

The neighbouring authority, a rather progressive one generally, was positively in favour of an unschool-like approach to the content of home education:

> You've got to start from first principles you know, encouraging them to cope with their child on their own, and you don't try and do things that would be better done in large groups just because you think that that will please the authority. (Secondary adviser)

To examine specific areas of content of interest to LEA advisers, we have to turn to the evidence of the families interviewed. Leaving the choosing of the curriculum to the family as long as it included the basics and appeared fairly broad seemed to be a common attitude as far as one could tell: families were often not clear about what their advisers had expected, since, as described by Mary Parsons, many gave little away, so there is plenty of evidence as to what families did, but not much indication as to what parts of what they did were of direct concern to the LEA.

Basic mathematics and English appeared frequently among the subjects which advisers visiting older teenagers, for example, Dickie Tansley and Gerry Budd, expected to see studied: 'the man we had, who was a very nice man . . . said . . . she should do the basics, maths, a science and English language' (Veronica Budd). There seemed to be no uniformity at all about the other subjects advisers either expected to see or were interested in. The evidence from families shows a wide variety of concerns: 'religion, that was the first thing, about religion' (Tiffany McGill), (perhaps reflecting the subject's status at that time as the only compulsory feature of the curriculum). PE was a subject which only some authorities were interested in, as these contrasting experiences show:

> *J.W.:* the local authority weren't at all interested in . . . PE?
> *Pat Maxwell:* Oh yes, well that was one of the things of course. But we were extremely lucky because he had to be banned from doing PE because he had a knee problem,

and:

J.W.: Did they worry about things like you missing out on the...physical activity you would have had at school? Was there any discussion about that?

Paul: No, because the school sport at the Steiner school was voluntary anyway, there was no compulsory games or sport and I did very little of that although I used to go up on the Common and play cricket with my father.

Method of working appeared to be a concern of some authorities: the Minchins' adviser, who wanted to see more written work, has been cited earlier. One of the advisers I interviewed put a different point of view on this subject, perhaps surprisingly, since he came from a traditional, very academically orientated, LEA (from my notes):

> He expects to see some written work but has no preconceptions about the form it should take, and regards evidence that e.g. the child is gaining some understanding of sequencing ideas as more important than reams of laborious written work.

Development of self-discipline and the ability to work hard and systematically appeared to be a major concern of some other advisers:

> He actively encouraged and always wanted to know and I think she kept a diary, yes, she kept a diary of all the things she did. It was mainly to see when she studied and how she studied and was she getting any better at it, was she managing to sit there for a bit longer. (Veronica Budd)

(What appears to be concern about keeping noses to the grindstone could also be worry about keeping children off the streets and, as Veronica Budd pointed out, out of trouble with the law.)

There is a little more information about the authorities' approaches to children's social lives, since probing on this subject presumably indicates special concern about it, whereas general discussion about the range of the curriculum may often reveal what the LEA wants to know without special investigation. Martin Maxwell and Paul Simmons, both quite shy and withdrawn, experienced two opposite viewpoints on the social question: 'I think there was something said about his social life. I was prepared for them to and I can't remember how we got over that. He wasn't interested in the social life, it really didn't bother me' (Pat Maxwell), and:

J.W.: The Local Education Authority weren't worried about that, provided you were getting some sort of social mixing, they weren't worried that you were missing out on . . . being in a large group?

> *Lynne:* They didn't concentrate on that side of it at all, it was the academic side they seemed concerned about.

There was variation, too, in the attitudes of the LEA officers interviewed to the provision of social opportunities of various sorts: we have already seen, in the section on socialization, that a psychologist and adviser for the same LEA had conflicting views on the importance of being part of a large school group, and these opposing viewpoints were demonstrated elsewhere in the interview material. Advisers for the latter LEA's neighbouring authority put a point of view which emphasized the importance of good, not necessarily numerous, friendships and the ability to relate to people with a reasonable degree of self-confidence:

> *J.W.:* Is that one of your concerns, the social aspects of being out of school?
>
> *Secondary adviser:* Yes. It's one of the things I talk about, I mean, the particular girl, one of the things I asked her was how was she going to maintain her friendships?
>
> *J.W.:* What, the previous school friendships?
>
> *Secondary adviser:* Yes . . . but I was really very satisfied that . . . she'd got her riding school and that she wasn't on her own just with one person. Yes, I had to follow my nose on this.
>
> *Primary adviser:* I mean, basically I think we would air the subject with the parents, want to go along with the parents beyond that, unless it seemed to us by visits that the child really looked terribly socially withdrawn and shy and really giving great concern.

There remain two final points to make about what is of concern to LEAs. One is that parents usually know clearly and in detail what their children are currently doing but in some cases they seem unable to put this across convincingly to the LEA, who then demand time-consuming record-keeping (as in the cases of Caroline and Phil). This may be one reason why those families who opted for a structured scheme of work, such as a correspondence course, where progress was easier for LEA officers to assess in the short time available to them, found themselves looked upon favourably.

The other point relates to parents with teaching qualifications: except in the case of the McGills, where the qualification was a Scottish one, it appears that families where at least one parent was a teacher got less of a rough ride than families without. One could put forward several reasons for this: their home education, once examined, was in fact very satisfactory from the particular LEA's point of view; or, the LEA assumed teachers would know what they were doing and so left them alone (the Gordons, for example, had very few contacts with their LEA); or, teachers could talk to the LEA advisers in their own language and were in any case used to being articulate in a way to which the LEA would respond positively. The latter point recurs in the last section, where there is some discussion about possible disadvantages faced by parents who are not naturally very articulate.

Of What Does the LEA's Approach Consist?

It is not surprising that the controversy and vagueness surrounding most aspects of the law regarding home education are reflected in the lack of agreement among LEA policies and therefore in the approaches to dealing with home educating families which are the subject of this section. Approaches, in the past particularly, have often been ill-informed, rude, tactless and imperious and, as we shall see, this was indeed the experience of one of the families interviewed (the McGills). The effect of these rather hamfisted dealings has been to create a view, strongly held in some quarters, of the LEA as an enemy intent on depriving families of their rights, a persecuting (in some cases prosecuting) monster: 'when I think of an administrator I think of a mad dog' (quote from floor speaker at April 1982 Birmingham EO Conference). The damage done by an insensitive adviser can be as great as that done by an inappropriate school:

> I took to it well for a start and then after that there was one inspector came, and he was really anti-, and he started psyching me out and generally convinced me that I'd only get Cs . . . I guess I was ready for a bit of an NBD about it. (Jim Merriman)

But the occurrence of demoralizing incidents such as these seems, from the evidence of the approaches made to most of the families interviewed, to be exaggerated: situations where the LEA was hostile were in a minority of five to sixteen, as we shall see from the following examination of the ways in which LEAs tackled what they saw as their duty.

Where children have been in school, the LEA's first approach to contact with the family has sometimes been through the school authorities, usually the head. In Piers Arthur's case, the head appears to have taken the law, quite improperly, into his own hands, when the question of deregistering arose in order to enable Piers to go to FE college: 'despite the fact I said Piers was never, *never* going back there in his life, Piers also said he wouldn't, he refused point blank, the headmaster refused point blank to authorize him to go' (Jenny Arthur).

One common approach direct from the LEA is an initial request for written information of some kind, if this has not been submitted voluntarily. Formal timetables, curricula or work plans are frequently asked for, as a reading of *EO News* and the ACE survey (ACE, 1983) makes plain. This approach may represent the full requirements of the authority, or they may follow it up with a visit, either routinely or if there are parts of the written information that they want to discuss, or specifically for assessment after some time has elapsed since home education began. In one case the motive for visiting was related more to the education of the advisers than that of the child being visited: 'the adviser seemed quite keen and initially he said, "What I'll do, to give my people experience of home education I'll send a different discipline every time"' (Christine Merriman).

Most of the families had received visits from advisers or EWOs (the latter appeared to be responsible only until it was established that truancy was not involved). Where authorities were able to satisfy themselves quickly that the education being given was satisfactory in their terms, they seemed only too happy to forget about home educating families, or at least to visit very infrequently:

> I had no problem with the local authorities, they were ever so helpful. They were very helpful. They sent somebody round once to see what we were doing and they said they were satisfied. It was partly because I did it in a structured way. We simply had a correspondence course which he used for O levels. (Pat Maxwell)

In other cases, visits became depressingly frequent: 'they began arriving here again at the door, officials . . . there came, I think there came, about three or four different ones' (Andrew McGill). In this case, it appears that the primary purpose of these visits was the serving of an Attendance Order rather than assessment of the home education being undertaken by Ian.

This brings us to the question of the form taken by the visits, which seem generally to have been rather informal discussions with parents and children: 'she used to come and ask me questions about my work and things. She was quite helpful, she wasn't anti, she thought this was quite a good idea, deschooled children' (Caroline Parker). In cases where the LEA was less comfortable about the idea of home education, in either the abstract or the particular, more formal testing was sometimes used. Joy Baker reports a formal assessment of her two older sons in the book *Children in Chancery* (Baker, 1964). In this case, because the right to home educate was not an option often exercised in the 1950s, experience of appropriate forms of assessment did not exist and, in addition, the legal specialists involved in attempting to enforce Attendance Orders may have expected this type of formal evidence of progress.

The formation of relationships between LEAs and home educating families may affect the process of home education in various ways. In the very worst situation the LEA decides, either as a result of unsatisfactory visits for assessment or on other less well justified grounds, that the children concerned should be in school, and issues an Attendance Order. The EWO I interviewed told me that in only one instance since 1980 in his LEA had the chain of events begun in this way resulted in a court appearance, and this seems typical of the experience of the families I talked to who had received Attendance Orders: only the Bakers, at a time when home education was unfamiliar to almost everyone, actually ended up in court. This result would obviously be very traumatic for the children involved, necessarily disrupting their education from the point of view of emotional disturbance. Two of the other families interviewed had received Attendance Orders and both had ignored them. The fact that neither LEA had tried to force their compliance perhaps suggests an element of 'trying it on' as a substitute for constructive suggestion:

> We didn't hear anything, it went dead again . . . for about six months, and then it flared up, they came and checked us, checked me again, they said, 'Well, he hasn't done enough, I'm going to have to put in a bad report' and he put in a bad report and said that I ought to go to school. So we received a school order, well, we didn't reply to it, we threw it straight in the dustbin, and then we didn't hear anything, it went dead. (Phil Minchin)

Two other families received threats of a vague kind, either written or verbal, from representatives of the LEA; one of these was the Arthurs: 'we had letters from them, which were sometimes delivered in hand by one of the teachers . . . truant officers threatening me with fines of a hundred pounds' (Jenny Arthur).

The effects of these kinds of threats on the families in terms of the creation of insecurity were very evident:

> I noticed that even now, and it was dark weather, of course, January, winter weather, but he was leaving his coat down here, his raincoat. . . . And this had gone on for a few days, and then it came to me like a flash, just like that after four days it had gone on, in case 'They' came to collect him his coat was ready, not to go with them, but to get out through this back door, through these gardens and up the field to where we know the area at the top. That was his idea. (Andrew McGill)

Andrew felt that part of the LEA's intention was actually to engender insecurity, in order perhaps to pressurize the family into conforming with their wishes. Where the authority was less belligerent, but still unwilling to agree to home education in the shape the family proposed, it often attempted to strike some kind of bargain. As we have seen in Jim Merriman's case, this sometimes related to the content of the education. Offering labels such as 'maladjusted' or 'school phobic' are other ways in which the LEA seeks to define relationships with families who see the fault as lying with the system rather than the child, as is shown by the experience of the Arthurs, previously described. Two families cited earlier, the Budds and the Golds, were asked to agree to bargains which worked in favour of home education — either they would be home educated or the school would expel them: 'he just said, "All right, I'm sorry but, take him out or we have to expel him. He'll be out anyway but it gets classed as being expelled rather than withdrawn"' (Malcolm Gold).

Help From the LEA

The discussion so far has focused mainly on ways in which the home education process was adversely affected by contact with the LEA: time then to examine the ways in which it benefited.

Financial help as such was nowhere available and at least one LEA representative felt that this should remain the case:

> J.W.: Has anybody ever asked you to subsidize home education, perhaps on the basis of a grant?
>
> *Primary adviser:* No ... by analogy with the parent using a private school who says can he have a refund for a private school — well, I know what I'd say to that person.

Several families said they had not applied to the LEA for financial help, preferring to keep as low a profile as possible and get on quietly with the business of home education. There was some recognition, though, that parents, having automatically paid for state education, were entitled to claim something from it. Jean Mortimer, the headmistress, made this point earlier and put belief into practice by making her own school resources available to home educators:

> J.W.: I know you've helped the H. Family — did you offer them help with books?
>
> *Mrs. Mortimer:* Yes. I simply said the child was being educated but obviously she hasn't access to the same sort of books as we have. How can she? ... it seemed important that if she wished to stay outside the education system, which she did: the child is a child, and then fine, come and use these books.

Some LEAs allow parents to visit the various teachers' centres to look at and/ or borrow materials. Some will advise on suitable resources: 'he suggested one or two books, that one there, the red, blue and green books over there: *Modern Mathematics for Schools*' (Phil Minchin), an ironic choice, perhaps, for a home educating family.

Another way in which LEAs are able to help home educating families if they wish is in the provision of part-time formal education facilities, either at school or FE college (as described in Chapter 8). The factors which operate in a situation where this provision has been requested must include assessment of the ability of the child to cope with what is proposed, the willingness of the head or principal to cooperate, whether places are available, and the general attitude of the LEA towards flexibility and choice in education. Some of the children interviewed, as mentioned earlier, found that FE colleges were willing to admit them early:

> His birthday being at the end of August, they accepted him in the September, so he was only just fifteen when they accepted him, to do O levels, but in actual fact after a few weeks there he went straight to doing the A level Language. (Sally Banks)

In Piers Arthur's case, as already mentioned, the college agreed to let him start early on the headmaster's say-so, which was not forthcoming, but he had in fact attended for two weeks before this became clear and he was asked to leave and return when he was sixteen. Clearly, better coordination by the LEA of its various employees could have saved Piers uncertainty and a term's lost education (lost in every way since he became worried and depressed and so unable to study for a while). The role of FE colleges in providing an escape route for mature teenagers unhappy at school seems an important one, and one that depends on flexibility in the LEA — greater recognition of this might avoid some of the problems which teenagers like Piers encountered. There seems to be some way to go before all authorities become this flexible: one adviser told me 'waiving the lower age limit at FE college could not be contemplated because it is statutory'.

A final point regarding contact with the LEA: we have seen that previous experience of home education in the LEA can be important in the authority's approach to the family and that approaches can vary from adviser to adviser. In this connection, one family found that it was difficult to change an unsympathetic adviser: 'we asked for another adviser and they wouldn't send one' (Phil Minchin).

Families' Parts in Their Relationship With the LEA

The discussion so far has focused on the ways in which LEAs attempted to define the course of home education and the terms of their assessment of it. How did families prepare for these attempts and how did they respond to them?

The question of whether access to assess a child must be allowed the LEA has already been discussed, and in fact all those interviewed, except the Bakers, accepted that this would probably follow the receiving of the family's letter concerning deregistration and/or home education. Cynical advice is often given in *EO Newsletter* based on the premise that the LEA will never understand your philosophy or approve of what you believe to be worthwhile, so that it is advisable to humour them by playing their game. Another view-point, counselling constructive cooperation with the LEA, is put by this writer:

> My own feeling is that a good LEA will realize the potential of EO and do all they can to help. Don't be afraid to say to them: 'Why can't we work together on this? We can do with help and advice in this particular — are there any particular ways in which we can try things out for you? Is there any way by which we can make your job of monitoring what we are doing easier for you?' (*EO News* 19)

The cynical attitude was represented by implication in the views of some of those interviewed — the Merrimans and the Parsons, for example: 'from my point of view it's all a bit of a waste of time, I'd rather not bother. But I just have to put up with it though really, I feel (Mary Parsons).

Most families, in fact, appeared resigned rather than enthusiastic about the LEA's role in their home education, though the Gordons and Budds, particularly, found they got on very well with their advisers and liked them as people. Both sets of parents contained a teacher, which may go some way to explain why the relationship was a comfortable one. The families whose relationships with the LEA ran a smooth course seemed also to be those which to some extent conformed, even if reluctantly, with what the LEA appeared to require. Some families sought the help of outside bodies in their efforts to fulfil their side of one of the bargains discussed earlier; Amy Dey got some advice from within the system:

> I just tried to find out which books they were using, that was really preparatory to writing up this programme that I submitted to the Education Office. I was lucky because this man, he was the headmaster in the primary school.

Really conforming, or making a show of doing so, may in some cases put pressure on parents and children who feel a conflict between what the LEA wants them to do in a particular area and what they want to do. This has already been demonstrated in the case of the adviser who required Phil Minchin to do more written work. However, there were two families, the Gordons and the Heads, where the parents refused altogether to conform to the LEA's demands, for paperwork in this case, and this did not stand in the way of a future good relationship with them (the key to this may be, again, that both families contained qualified teachers): 'he asked for, I think it was just a loose curriculum, it wasn't a timetable. I didn't give him one and he didn't ask again' (Marie Gordon). In these cases, there was little pressure on the children to learn particular things in a particular way, since the families had not committed themselves to anything the LEA could expect to find done: the conditions for learning would therefore be more relaxed, encouraging, according to John Holt's point of view, for example, greater curiosity and confidence in the children than in situations where families felt they had predetermined goals to meet.

Apart from those who conformed for the sake of a quiet life and those who did not conform and got away with it, there was a third group, of families who went their own ways and had problems with their LEAs in consequence; the Bakers, the Arthurs, the Minchins and the McGills were the most notable in this connection and all showed determination and ingenuity in seeking out appropriate help from MPs, solicitors, friendly psychiatrists and even, in the McGills' case, the NSPCC (who must have found it unusual to be called in to protect a family against the Establishment). They also showed bravery, even if it did express itself as aggression at times, in pursuing a principle, but this must be weighed against the already discussed cost to the family in terms of disrupted education, insecurity, and court appearances in the Bakers' case. For the Arthurs, the problem revolved around Piers' projected attendance at FE college. Jenny Arthur was prepared to fight the fines she was threatened with, in court if necessary; she was really spoiling for a fight, in fact, since she wanted to expose what she saw as the LEA's maladministration to a wider public. Perhaps because of her dangerous articulacy and the fact that she was part of the educational system herself, the LEA did not pursue their threats.

It has been pointed out elsewhere (Meighan, 1984c) that less articulate, perhaps working-class, families are sometimes victimized because they lack the challenging articulacy, and perhaps friends in high places, of families such as the Arthurs. The McGills were a case in point: though Andrew McGill was certainly articulate, he lacked a knowledge of how the system worked which might have enabled him to communicate better with its officers. Though he clearly saw the LEA as a threat to the well-being and happiness of his family, he was anxious not to become involved in legal confrontation: 'we were a little bit frightened because we thought: "Well, we don't want to get taken to court for not having him at school".' This anxiety may have led the LEA to think it could browbeat him into sending the two girls back to school by repeatedly asking for assessments which were then found to be unsatisfactory. Support from outside bodies helped to overcome the LEA's persistence in this case. In other families such as the Minchins and the much-publicized Harrisons, dragging out assessment or legal procedures until the children reached the age of sixteen was a solution, though one which would appear to be likely to put almost intolerable pressure on the family.

Meighan mentions another aspect of the reactions of families who had some sort of serious trouble in their relationship with the LEA (Meighan, 1984b): the way in which members of these families became increasingly politically aware. Jenny Arthur and Andrew McGill were explicit about this:

> The Director of Education himself, he was absolutely appalling, he was so rude and so unobtainable. Certainly made me much more of a rebel — I mean I didn't realize I was much of a rebel before because I've tended to work with authorities before and I never found any problem there, but up here it just seemed to be that you're up against an absolute monolith and you don't realize how rigid and hidebound they are until you're up against them. And I was quite horrified. (Jenny Arthur)

> *Andrew:* I was a bit daft myself then at that stage because I was prepared to take people very much at face value then . . .
> *Tiffany:* And six years of them since then — we know what they're like.

A quite different, but equally interesting, case of increasing political awareness was that of Sally Banks:

> It all came about with having problems with Glenn and not getting cooperation with the teaching staff, particularly at his infants' school here. The headmistress felt that what went on in the school was no business of the parents. She was one of those felt that; and it was at that time I saw the advert, you know, wanting a school governor, so I thought, I'm going to get in on the inside and find out what should or shouldn't happen.

Earlier in the interview she had explained that she continued as governor of two schools for four years, including re-election, when Glenn was out of school: an interesting situation from both her and the schools' points of view.

In summary, it seems that the undoubtedly very bad experiences of some families, for example, the McGills and Bakers, may have blinded them to any good within the system elsewhere and forced them to take an egocentric view that does not recognize that most people for one reason or another are unwilling or unable to take the step that they have taken or, if they do, that they may prefer to compromise with the LEAs' demands. Since these families receive a great deal of publicity and are often vociferous in the media and in *EO News*, an impression that all LEAs are 'out to get' home educators has grown up, which is not justified by the evidence of many families who have established at least neutral, if not positively helpful, relationships with their authorities.

Perhaps local authorities are themselves partly responsible for the suspicion with which they are treated: if they were willing to publicize home-based education as an option which they would support in appropriate circumstances, more open relationships would perhaps develop which could benefit both sides.

Chapter 11

What Next?

Martin (now nineteen) is in his first year at the Polytechnic of Central London, starting a degree course in Media Studies. He did his necessary O and A levels at Kingsway Princeton College of Further Education. . . . During these three years, he also crewed in the Tall Ships Transatlantic Race, arriving in New York and Boston for the Bicentenary celebrations in July 1976. He has also worked backstage with the National Youth Theatre for the last two summers, so he is not a product of a hothouse academic atmosphere. (Head, 1977, p. 18)

I was on the Youth Training Scheme for a year, also passed phase 1 City and Guilds in Agriculture at day-release . . . the course I am taking at college is NCA (National Certificate in Agriculture) — I also took O level in maths last year at evening classes . . . I was a lot more prepared for the world than my friends at school. (Letter from Phil Minchin)

David worked on the dairy farm for four years, and then left to get a wider experience of work and people. He had developed an interest in journalism and broadcasting when we were all being continually interviewed for the press, radio and television; finally he went to America and got a job on the editorial staff of a weekly newspaper, while working part-time for a radio station; he is now a feature writer and full-time broadcaster in New York. Robin qualified as a plasterer and continued in the same trade; he now has his own firm. Felicity went to London and worked as an advertizing executive; she is now married with two small children, and works as a freelance photographer, specializing in portraits of children at home. (Baker, 1987, p. 8)

This chapter concerns the very interesting questions which, in part, motivated this study: what do home educated people do once their period of compulsory education is over? What sort of lives do they lead? Are they able to pursue happy social relationships? What parts do they play in their community? Are they able to get the sort of jobs or further education they want, or do they find their unorthodox education hampers them in this respect, perhaps due to employer prejudice or to their lack of formal qualifications? Some of these matters have been touched on briefly in previous chapters: the nature of children's social relationships, for example, and some opportunities for getting interesting jobs without academic qualifications. They will be discussed in greater detail here in the context of a general survey of home educated children's lives after the age of sixteen, bearing in mind that information about interviewees' further education and work is incomplete in some cases, because they did not reply to my follow-up letters (see Chapter 3).

Further Education

My interpretation of this heading includes not only conventional 'further' and 'higher' education but also the concept of 'lifelong learning', whether informal and/or spasmodic or more structured, as exemplified by the Open University and University of the Third Age, and by the initiative of some schools which have invited adult participation in school classes.

One might have expected that those of the interviewees who had had very bad school learning experiences would have rejected any further education. This was not the case, although sometimes, as I have noted before, a period of recovery was necessary before learning could begin again. Christine Merriman believed that caring parents could undo any damage done to the will to learn by the school: 'They can bounce back, given love and care and protection'. Brian Budd hoped that learning would continue in spite of school, but did not seem very optimistic:

> I think Gerry and our other children at the end of the day they'll still have got by, at the end of the day one hopes that they will have made up for some of the learning they lost at school by still being interested in it for the rest of their lives; maybe that's an act of faith.

All of those interviewed (except perhaps Karen Gold, who went on to become a wife and mother but, as far as I know, has not pursued any further studies as yet) retained an enthusiasm for learning which may be a characteristic product of less controlled educational programmes, as this quotation from an ex-pupil of Neill's Summerhill suggests: '"I always enjoyed learning, even if I didn't learn a tremendous amount," one man recalled. "I never got put off anything, because nobody made me feel it was boring by forcing it on me."' (Croall, 1983, p. 404).

This interest in further learning manifested itself in many different ways. Four teenagers took formal routes into higher education, taking GCEs at local FE colleges and then applying, successfully in all cases, for university entrance. George Gordon did forestry, Alison Head drama, Daniel Scheaffer geography and Jim Merriman mathematics. It appears that they encountered no prejudice against home education among the interviewers. It is unclear whether this was because of previous attendance at FE college (part of the system) or because they impressed the interviewers with their personality and motivation — perhaps a mixture of both.

As well as these four teenagers, Phil Minchin, Gerry Budd, Simon Parsons and Glenn Banks all decided to pursue their post-sixteen education at FE college. There seem to have been few problems involved in being accepted by the authorities, even where the required academic criteria could not be conventionally satisfied (as we have seen in Simon Parson's case):

> She was saying she wanted to be a vet . . . and so she went to Oxford to convince them that that was what she wanted to do and that she was quite capable of being a vet . . . she managed to persuade them that she was capable of getting A level physics . . . and then she confronted the local education authority, who were very, very good, and said in fact they really ought to let her go to Oxford FE because that was the only place she could do her physics. (Veronica Budd)

Personality and articulacy appear to have been two of the factors important here, since Gerry had no formal qualifications at all. She managed to get herself enrolled in the same way on an A level art course a year later, still without O levels, and this led eventually to Art School.

The desire of FE college principals to fill their courses perhaps needs to be taken into account as an influence on the ease with which home educated children were accepted for them, or even, for Jim Merriman and Glenn Banks, the ease with which they could manipulate them to their own advantage (it was obvious that some of the teenagers not only retained or recovered their enthusiasm for learning, but also developed a powerful determination to do it the way they thought was most useful, whatever the received wisdom from college authorities).

Social acceptance at college appears also to have been uncomplicated for those interviewed — they appear to have been able to relate sociably to other students, and there does not seem to have been prejudice against them because of their home education, perhaps because students from many different schools were thrown together, or because there was no occasion for it to be known about:

> To my own surprise I had no difficulty fitting in and made friends without bother . . . I am doing all the really stupid stuff students do —

and am part of the rag committee so have a license to commit mayhem. I play squash quite a lot and am currently using the college multi-gym every day. (Letter from Daniel Scheaffer)

A comment of Jim's indicates that perhaps the home educated teenagers were actually more socially mature than their conventionally educated peers at college, in that he at any rate was aware that the social scene was perhaps rather limited and limiting but was able to accept this for the sake of sociability:

> At that place the social environment is very tight and if you don't conform you are very much on the outside. I think at university perhaps it is a bit more expansive so I don't know how I'll react, have to wait and see. Because for me at the moment I'm quite happy to conform to their social values and not feel like I'm stuck with it permanently.

An exception to this general observation must be Alison Hartfield who felt, on going to teacher training college in the forties, that she was very immature and socially inept, perhaps because she had until then led an oddly isolated and sheltered family life:

> I know I am a bit conformist, and I think this was one other product of my peculiar education, because we felt so different from other children. . . . For instance, I remember I was very ill-equipped to deal with the opposite sex, in fact I was not exactly terrified of them but I just had a feeling they were better left alone . . . that sort of social lack of expertise, I don't know that I've ever completely outgrown it.

Others of those interviewed pursued rather less institutionalized further education, some aspects of which will be discussed in the section on lifestyles at the end of the chapter. Paul Simmons provides an illustration of possibilities in the area of sport, personal growth, vocational training and practical electronics:

> I can't remember how it happened now, I got interested in electronics. I did a correspondence course . . . British National Radio School they were called, they were in the Channel Islands . . . somehow, slowly, I got into computers. I did an evening class on programming, machine-code programming . . . I've done badminton for two years. In 1975 I did a year's Open University post-experience course on environmental control and public health . . . I did an evening class run by a local person in transactional analysis, which is a sort of humanistic psychology, which was quite useful actually, I enjoyed that because that helped with the meeting people because you were in a small group and you talked about yourself, got to know each other as a group.

Maureen Cotton followed up, informally, two of her academic interests: 'I got interested in sociology for a while . . . That was just mostly reading . . . It was just something to do because it was interesting and philosophy I did the same'.

Work Experience Courses

Like its predecessor, YOP, the Youth Training Scheme is claimed by its organizers to act as a transition between Secondary education and work in the outside world, including both practical and further educational elements. Because these programmes do not demand formal qualifications, they are available to every home educated sixteen or seventeen year old but, as is widely known, their quality in terms of level of interest and the prospect of jobs at the end is very variable. This was demonstrated by the experiences of those in the study. Two teenagers were fortunate in finding schemes which gave them experience in the areas in which they were interested and which eventually led to jobs, Phil in agriculture and Martin in kennel work, where the scheme was set up specifically for him. Tim and Karen Gold, however, were less fortunate or, perhaps, less motivated, in that neither had definite ideas about the work they wanted to do and therefore did not take their time on the schemes seriously:

> He decided to live in a bedsit with another lad, and after a few months of bedsitting and bad company, eventually was thrown off the scheme — after six months rather than a year: bad timekeeping, untidy, etc. He's still looking for something to do, and wasting his artistic talents. . . . She left school in May, started a YTS in June, doing community care, which she enjoyed. Like her brother, she decided to live with a girl in a bedsit and with spending days enjoying life instead of going to work, was thrown off her YTS. She was accepted onto another — I still don't know how she fiddled it. (Letter from Malcolm Gold)

Perhaps the fact that both these schemes took place in the north of England affected their enthusiasm for them, since the prospect of jobs afterwards would be much slighter than in the south, where Phil and Martin did theirs.

Jim Merriman applied for pre-university work experience, in the form of a year's industrial electronics training. Living away from home and mixing with the other trainees, whom he found academically bright but unselfconfident and impractical, were perhaps more important experiences than the work itself which, on the whole, he found uninspiring (one school of thought would say that this in itself was a valuable thing to learn, since adult work often is boring).

Employment

The majority of those interviewed appeared to accept the conventional view of the importance of regular paid work (whether as a source of income, self-esteem, interest or all three, I didn't think to find out) and planned their education accordingly. About half of these were still in some form of further education at the time of the interviews. Alison Head, Piers Arthur and Glenn Banks saw their lives differently, and the ways in which they occupied their time will therefore be discussed in the next section, under the heading 'Lifestyles.'

Finding Work with No Qualifications

It became clear that although many employers said they wanted a certain number of qualifications, this was often just a vague guideline, and that if an applicant exhibited desirable personal characteristics, the demand for qualifications could be reduced or waived entirely. ... Employers, particularly those recruiting below the Higher grade level, may simply have been using qualifications because they are there: youngsters offer them and the education system is geared to provide them. (Hunt and Small, 1981)

At the time of Hunt and Small's report and the two years afterwards (the years in which the interviews for this study took place), article after article appeared in *Times Educational Supplement* (*TES*) giving details of surveys which suggested that employers were placing much less emphasis on examination results as criteria for selection of prospective employees:

Only half of the employers who responded to a survey on recruitment of school-leavers said that they considered examinations essential to selection.

Just under half were dissatisfied with the information about young people's attainment and potential as conveyed by the present examination results. ... Two thirds of the respondents thought that schools and colleges should provide a profile of non-academic information covering such aspects as assessment of character, interests, potential, timekeeping, leadership, attitudes to discipline, family background, community involvement, sickness and absenteeism and honesty. (Heron, 1982; see also *TES* 26.6.81 'Swotting for exams a waste of time, say firms' and *TES* 7.1.83 'Pitons a help on career ladder')

A dissenting voice sounded in 1984 in a Schools Council survey which asked whether the more drastic step of totally replacing academic exams at sixteen by profiles would be welcomed by employers:

> The proportion rejecting the idea of a profile in place of O level exams was never less than three quarters of the respondents in all types of institution. But seven out of ten school teachers favoured a profile to supplement the O level certificate. (Lodge, 1984)

However, in 1986, Industry Year, another article in the *TES*, by Chris Marsden of British Petroleum, suggested that the emphasis among industrialists should not be on examination qualifications (though it often was):

> Industry is often unable to see any inconsistency between wanting youngsters to be flexible, technologically capable, economically literate, team-working problem solvers and yet refusing to interview them unless they have at least five O levels. (Marsden, 1986, p. 21)

The balance of opinion in these articles is clearly that factors such as personality are becoming more important to employers, and examination qualifications less so. Might home educated job seekers, who have not chosen to pursue formal qualifications but who may have developed mature and interesting personalities through their other activities and their independence from the relentless peer group pressure of school, find this trend to their advantage? There is a little evidence in favour of this theory from those interviewed in the study, although most had some kind of further or higher education qualification when they applied for jobs: Gerry Budd and Paul Simmons, however, appear to have found all sorts of work without them. Like David Baker, quoted at the beginning of the chapter, they appear to have got this work by going along and talking people into giving them the jobs they wanted:

> *Paul:* I started a paper round again then . . . and I did odd jobs, gardening . . . in 1973 we moved back down here and I got a job with, well it was the local council then, at the sewage works, which was advertized in the paper and from there, I moved about a year later up to the Water Works so I've been working there for the water authority ever since
> *J.W.:* And what about the authority, when they came to employ you, they didn't ask you for any kind of qualifications?
> *Paul:* It wasn't necessary, it was a manual job.

Self-employment

This is an area in which lack of qualifications is very unlikely to be a disadvantage to the home educated teenager who has acquired a marketable skill or interest. Work on smallholdings, such as that practised by Piers Arthur and the Harrisons, is a good example of this, since it can involve the selling of excess produce or skills developed in the course of the work, such as building and plumbing, as Dickie Tansley's remark quoted previously suggested. Corinne Dey was employed in another family concern, as a letter from her mother explained (she had actually acquired five O levels and two A levels, but these were quite irrelevant to her job):

> I had started a small shop catering for the horse riding community. She now works there for most of the week . . . She enjoys working in the shop on her own. I go in one and a half days a week to give her a break. If I could afford to make it over to her entirely I think she would be quite happy.

It is perhaps likely that proportionately more possibilities for earning a living in this way will exist among home educating families than among the population in general, since self-employment of various kinds, with its flexibility and autonomy, probably appeals to the kind of independent-minded parent who would consider home education, and might make the education easier to carry out and more fulfilling. One of those interviewed, Piers Arthur, had used a government-sponsored scheme for those starting out in self-employment, hoping to set up a personal business to supplement his work on the family smallholding. His mother described, in a letter, how he spent his time:

> He has done almost all the electrical work at the Mill, completing wiring four old stone barns, also works with the goats, etc. Throughout the past three years he has spent most of his time with his (self-made) computer — designing programmes, etc. He started an MSC Enterprise Scheme last year trying to sell programmes, but at the end of the twelve months hadn't made enough money to keep going so is now on the dole again.

Employment With Qualifications

Those who had completed a further or higher education course of some kind all got jobs at the end of it, if they wanted them. We have seen that Alison Hartfield became a teacher, researcher and finally teacher trainer. It is perhaps not surprising that none of the others interviewed had opted for a career in teaching. Exceedingly little information is available in the literature (on either side of the Atlantic, but particularly in Britain) about the further educational and employment careers of home educated people, presumably because the modern home educating movement has only come about in the last ten years, so it is not possible to discover whether there are home educated teenagers considering it as a way of changing the educational system from the inside. The whole area of employment of the home educated is one which would prove interesting to research in another ten years' time. At the moment there appears to be no particular pattern or characteristic type of employment being taken up by home educated children, and one might perhaps expect that in a decade or so types of jobs will be spread very widely, because of the emphasis on developing individual talents.

The experiences of those who had qualifications when they looked for work suggest that employers, as well as college academics, were unprejudiced against those who had not had a conventional education. Maureen, with some O levels and her Private Secretary's Certificate, found satisfying work quite easily in a travel agency. Martin Maxwell, as already mentioned, was able to work in a kennels exactly as he had wanted. It would be interesting to know whether he achieved his ambition to become an RSPCA Inspector (he had the requisite English language O level). Simon Parsons got a job as a second commis chef in charge of afternoon tea at a hotel, after completing his catering City and Guilds courses. None appears to have had difficulty in doing the things they were interested in, having presumably demonstrated their enthusiasm and competence to their prospective employers.

Another important point is that these teenagers, and those who are still on their further education courses, had sufficient self-knowledge to be able to assess not only what they would enjoy doing but whether it was an appropriate goal to attempt. The only exception to this general observation was Gerry Budd, whose mother remarked:

> She might still do something interesting . . . but she can't see the need to concentrate on any one of her talents for a period of time to get some real accomplishment. She rather veers from one ambition to another and never really gives herself any sense of real achievement in the eyes of the world.

Lifestyles

Two features in particular originally intrigued me about the home education movement: one was its emphasis on living life fully and enthusiastically, and the other was its stress on taking control over aspects of life generally organized for us (education, finding a job), and on questioning the decisions made by others on our behalf. This is not to say that such elements are found exclusively in alternative education, to deny that they are not also present in parts of the formal schooling system, but they appear to be obvious characteristics of such groups as EO and Growing Without Schooling, almost as part of the definition of these groups' reasons for existence. I expected that these would be noticeable elements of the lifestyles of those who had been educated at home, and found my expectations very much confirmed by the families I talked to and the follow-up letters I received from them later.

Firstly, the confidence and self-esteem necessary to positive direction of one's own life were clearly present in all but one or two of those interviewed, and particularly marked in the Gordons and Daniel Scheaffer. Interestingly these children had been almost entirely educated at home and had therefore been relatively free of school influences. The main influence on the home educated child's self-esteem is the parent, and one aspect of the lifestyle of the families involved appears often (not in all cases) to be a continuing friendship between parents and children through the teenage years and into adulthood, seeming to a large extent to avoid the often cited generation gap (which may sometimes be exaggerated by age banding in school):

> We went on holiday to France for three weeks last summer and it could have been absolutely disastrous, she hadn't got any friends with her, just us two, and, really, we got on like a house on fire. So that's something . . . not that we haven't fallen out but on the whole we get on pretty well. (Veronica Budd)

Corinne Dey is explicit about the ways in which home education made her close to her mother:

> *Corinne:* We've always got on particularly well in our school lessons. . . . It's fun to, sort of, learn with her, to do things together. I think a lot of people don't know their parents because, you think about it, most of their life is spent with people entirely strangers to them. . . . When they go home they don't really talk to their parents.
>
> *Amy:* This is how people are put into age groups, and very often my friends who have various young teenage children: they're incredibly tongue-tied, they don't know what to do with their leisure time and if they think of having parties they must get their parents out of the way, it isn't even as if they want to do anything terrible, it's just because they feel awkward.

The enjoyment of a close relationship between parent and child, (while obviously not the sole prerogative of home educating families) and, more particularly, appreciation of the benefits of home education, might be expected to lead to home educated children in the next generation of these families, as Jim Merriman suggested would be so in his case. None of those interviewed had yet reached this stage in their lives so we must rely on documentary evidence to give the possibility some credence. This comes from the Mullarneys, who were educated at home only until the age of eight or so. Two of her eleven children, Maire Claire and Aidan, are educating their own children:

> She married Morgan when she was twenty-two; they now have three children, Michael, Hanna and Katy, and live in a little house in the woods in County Wicklow. We are constantly in touch, and she tells me 'lessons' in the mornings are going fine, especially Colour Factor . . . Aidan continues to be his own master, living in one of the most beautiful parts of County Wicklow with a wife and two children to match . . . the two children, Jasper and Martha, are learning at home as a matter of course. (Mullarney, 1983, pp. 74 and 76)

This will undoubtedly be another interesting area for research in ten or fifteen years' time. A.S. Neill suggested that 'Summerhill good does not appear until the second generation' (Neill, 1972, p. 160). Perhaps the same may be true of home education to the extent that freedom from worry about doing the unconventional thing and about whether home education can equip you properly for a fulfilling life will be much stronger in a person who has him- or herself been home educated.

One might expect that questioning of the accepted system of education, especially where this was originally, or developed into, a matter of principle rather than expedience, might encourage questioning in other areas of life normally taken for granted and that there might be among the home educated, people who had adopted alternative lifestyles of other sorts. This was generally not the case, (as the preceding discussion of jobs and training, in the context of conventional home backgrounds, confirms), although it must be noted that only a small number of children had reached the stage of deciding how to live. Alison Head, and to a lesser extent Piers Arthur and Glenn Banks, were the only representatives, for example, of an ethos which rejected regular paid employment and relied on dole money for survival. In Alison's case, voluntary work in the community and self-expression through writing and music took the place of employment, and house sharing took the place of life in a conventional nuclear family:

> A lot of the last year has been spent setting up Hull's first Housing Cooperative and buying a house in which six of us hope to live communally. . . . We hope to be as self-sufficient as it is possible to be in the city (chickens and vegetables to start with), and have shared

resources such as a music room (hopefully eventually with sound-recording potential) for ourselves and others to use . . .

From a later letter:

I am trying to find more time to write, not always successfully. I sent the first draft of my novel to the Harvester Press and they wrote back saying they were interested. However I have not been getting on very well with the second draft. I am developing my music . . . and a few of us are experimenting once a week in a theatre workshop. The group for young unemployed didn't last long . . . I have done various bits and pieces since then, including a drama workshop at a local Peace Festival. My main involvement at the moment is with the local Women's Centre, also with various peace and 'green' groups. My priorities shift from time to time but are basically to do with finding alternatives to the institutionalized, paranoiac and suicidal society around me. I have not been applying for jobs, because I treasure my freedom of choice and movement too much and because I reject the 'work ethic' that says you are only of value if you are in paid employment.

Alison's was the only example of a radically alternative lifestyle among those interviewed. Piers Arthur and Glenn Banks, while rejecting paid employment as a necessary of life, carried out their other activities, animal husbandry and electronics in Piers' case, and writing in Glenn's, while living in a conventional way in their family homes.

The area of hobbies and other involvements also needs to be discussed. Most of those interviewed had several of these. They were widely varied: from collecting sugar lump wrappers, through dressing up as a Victorian, to membership of Friends of the Earth. There seemed to be no discernible emphasis on particular sorts of hobby: as with jobs, the stress laid on bringing out individual talents and interests through home education is reflected in the highly individual ways in which home educated teenagers and adults spend their leisure (if that is an appropriate expression). Perhaps there was a lack of interest in team games: no-one belonged to a football or cricket team, though several participated in sports such as running or squash. Several played musical instruments, some to a very high standard, and two of the girls danced. Membership of clubs and groups was common too: among those mentioned were Guides, Pax Christi, Men of the Trees (George's forestry interest) and those already referred to in Chapter 7.

The variety of jobs, training and lifestyle chosen by those interviewed echoes the earlier suggestion of diversity in approach to home-based education, and raises the question of whether the families concerned share any features which could be said to be characteristic of home educators. Since the individual circumstances introducing it, and personalities undertaking it, vary so much it would not be sensible to generalize other than to say that it appears, from all the evidence above, that home education is not, as some have suggested, a barrier to leading a full life in the ordinary world and that it may equip people to make the most of their opportunities very well in fact, particularly in the areas where self-confidence, sociability and articulacy are important. Further research in ten years' time, in conjunction with the documentary information which may by then be available in publications such as *Growing Without Schooling* and *EO Newsletter*, would give a more complete and interesting picture.

Chapter 12

The Relationship Between Home-based Education and Society in General

This study took seven years to complete, during which time the educational climate changed fairly dramatically. My original intention, to explore the results of home education for those who undertook it and to describe and analyze the ways in which these results were achieved, appears to be increasingly relevant to a society in which important educational decisions are becoming more and more centralized, with less choice in the areas which matter (for example, the curriculum) being available to pupils, parents and teachers. As I shall discuss later, this has created a revival of the activity of the 1970s which produced so many Free Schools (most of which have since closed) and has presumably contributed greatly to the growth of Education Otherwise. The main thrust of this thesis — that home-based education can be a fulfilling substitute for school in all the important areas of a child's development: psychological, academic and social — is of greater significance now that the option to home educate is more widely known about and the need for viable alternatives to school so much greater.

Its lessons for those involved in educational policymaking and, more specifically, for heads of schools, are, I think, as important as Holt (Holt, 1983) predicted they could be. From the point of view of the curriculum designers, it indicates ways in which modular approaches could be effective (most home educators operating an informal system of this sort with rather greater choice than is available in school), if linked to the ideas of self-directed study in a flexischooling situation where resources outside the school could be used to extent the range of choice. (See Roland Meighan's book *Flexischooling* (Meighan, 1988) for a detailed study of these possibilities.)

One of the things indicated by the study which is appropriate to the problems of heads is the extent to which families can be a resource for school in particular and the community in general, confirming the suggestions made by Meighan (Meighan, 1981a). The ability of the non-teacher parents in the study to teach their own children, with various sorts of guidance where they felt the need for it, has many implications for the greater involvement of parents as teachers (rather than auxiliary cheese-scone makers) in schools and in the positive support of schoolwork at home, possibly on a flexischooling basis. The fact that the involvement of parents, particularly at secondary level, does not appear to have changed much since Meighan's article is probably a reflection of the threat to their professionalism which many teachers would feel such a move to represent.

Home educating families can also provide resources for the rest of the community to use. An obvious example is 'The State' touring company, who tried, and failed, to swap their skills and expertise for the use of LEA facilities. Those in the study had been available to the community in many different ways, mostly those in the 'socially useful' category but also through involvement in art and drama projects. They also provide an educational resource through local meetings which are open to anyone interested in alternatives to the system and which can be very valuable to individual members of the community, since one of the hypotheses which could be tentatively put forward on the basis of this study is that the few cases of desperate need for alternatives to the orthodox educational system which I investigated are representative of many more which do not find constructive help.

These might include families unable to take on home-based education for various reasons, but who still need something different for their children. One implication of this is that the schools concerned should seriously consider whether they could be more flexible, less regimented or could allow the child to pursue a more relevant curriculum (on the basis perhaps of part-time schooling) — that they should consider, in other words, whether they, rather than the child, are at fault and whether some changes in ethos or practicalities might not be of benefit to all pupils. Where heads are unwilling to do this, families must look outside the child's current school for suitable education. For some, the present government's scheme for assisted places might provide the way in to a more appropriate education, and for others an alternative school of the 'Free' sort would be attractive in its size and in its encouragement of self-confidence in an unregimented and democratic atmosphere. There are some signs of a renewed interest in the provision of schools of this kind through the establishment recently of the Small School at Hartland in Devon (North, 1987) under the aegis of the Schumacher Society's Campaign for Human-Scale Education, and Dame Catherine's in Derbyshire (Gibbons, 1989). It seemed at one time that the government's provision for state schools to apply for grant-maintained status (opting out) might enable many small schools to survive and perhaps become alternative or that funding might be made available under these provisions for new small schools. However, the wording of the Act does not take the second of these possibilities into consideration and makes the first seem difficult, since the Secretary of State is in a position to decide whether schools with under 300 pupils may become grant-maintained. Until alternative schools become generally accessible to those who want them (the Greens are the only political party to propose the establishment of alternative schools in their manifesto, and the only party to recognize, and attach importance to, the right of parents to educate at home) — until then, the only option where the system is seen to be failing or likely to fail the child is still, for those who cannot afford one of the progressive independent schools, home-based education. Its future under the 1988 Education Act will probably be one of further rapid growth as far as numbers of active participants are concerned, since the combined effect of teaching to the test encouraged by the seven, eleven and fourteen tests already mentioned, and the limitations of a centrally prescribed National Curriculum, may undo most of the good done by the Plowden Report and more recently the GCSE proposals, and make school learning too restrictive and pressure-ridden for many of those families who find it tolerable at present.

Now to a more optimistic view of education, contrasting curiously with the direction of the orthodox state system. Christine Brown suggested in 1978 that EO provided an indication that open learning was becoming an option for people at every stage of their educational career (Brown, 1978). Since she wrote this, referring to the Open University as the example of adult open learning, we have the Open College, Open Tech and Open College of the Arts, as well as numerous flexistudy schemes attached to AE and FE centres. The growth in numbers of families practising home-based education, taken in conjunction with these, would seem to confirm the trend she remarked. This excerpt from an article in the *TES* (18.3.88) concerning the possibility of home-based education becoming a realistic option for everyone who wants or needs it, provides a constructive note on which to end:

'Open school' scheme could help GCSE pupils to opt out

A radical alternative to school which would allow children to study for the GCSE without setting foot in a classroom has been proposed.

Backers of the idea, due to be discussed by members of the Dartington Hall Trust, say than an 'open school' offering distance-learning materials and support would appeal to parents who are dissatisfied with the school system and who want to educate their children at home . . .

Sources involved in the project believe that an open school would attract thousands of enquiries. They suggest that Education Otherwise, which encourages parents who teach their children at home, could be the tip of the iceberg.

It is envisaged that such a 'school' would start on a small scale, possibly catering for GCSE and perhaps also for mainstream subjects for the 11 to 14 age range . . .

If all went to plan, it would also provide for youngsters who wanted to supplement their school studies. Other ideas that have been floated include a consultancy service, short-term residential crash courses and inservice training for parents in tutoring skills. (Surkes, 1988)

References

ADVISORY CENTRE FOR EDUCATION (ACE) (1983) *Survey: dealing with non-attendance*, 18 Victoria Park Square, London.

BAKER, C. (1983) 'Alternative education', *Living*, November.

BAKER, J. (1964) *Children in Chancery*, London, Hutchinson.

BAKER, J. (1987) 'Home-based education from birth to adulthood', *EO News*, **52**.

BENDELL, J. (1987) *School's Out: Educating Your Child at Home*, Bath, Ashgrove Press.

BERG, I. (1981) 'School refusal in early adolescence', in HERSOV, L. and BERG, I. *et al. Out of School*, New York, Wiley.

BERG, L. (1984) 'Reading and living (and loving)', *EO News*, **38**.

BLACK, D. (1984) 'The unorthodox alternative', *Sunday Times*, 18 March.

BLACKER, S. (1981) 'Case Studies in Home Education', unpublished MEd thesis, University of Sussex.

BLAT-GIMENO, J. (1972) 'Should we abolish the schooling of children?', *Prospects*, **2**, 4, pp. 442–4.

BLINSTON, K. (1982) 'Home Education', unpublished BEd dissertation, Leicester University.

BLISHEN, E. (1969) *The School That I'd Like*, Harmondsworth, Penguin.

BROMPTON, S. (1985) 'The children in a class of their own', *The Times*, 25 March.

BROWN, C. (1978) 'Education Otherwise: A Sociological Case-study of One Alternative to State Schooling', unpublished MEd thesis, University of Birmingham.

BROWN, C. (1982) 'Education Otherwise: Some emerging questions', *Wolverhampton Polytechnic Faculty of Education Journal*, Spring.

CARR, J.L. (no date) 'How I educated my son for a term', *Where*, pp. 12–13.

CHITTY, S. (1971) *The Woman Who Wrote 'Black Beauty'*, London, Hodder and Stoughton.

COBBETT, W. (1825) *Rural Rides*, quoted in *Growing Without Schooling*, **24**, 1977.

CROALL, J. (1983) *Neill of Summerhill — The Permanent Rebel*, London, Routledge and Kegan Paul.

CROWLEY, T. (no date) *Ideas for Self-employment and Part-time Work*, as quoted in *EO News* **47**.

DEAKIN, M. (1973) *The Children on the Hill*, London, Quartet.

DEUTSCH, D. and WOLF, K. (1986) 'Home education and the law', unpublished paper available from Education Otherwise.

References

DURRELL, G. (1976) *My Family and Other Animals*, Harmondsworth, Penguin.
EDUCATION OTHERWISE (1980) *Early Years*, Hemmingford Abbots.
EDUCATION OTHERWISE (1985) *School Is Not Compulsory*, Hemmingford Abbots.
EDUCATIONAL REVIEW (1989) 'Parents and education', *Special Issue (21)*, **41**, 2.
EDUCATION OTHERWISE (1986) *Later Years*, Hemmingford Abbots.
FARJEON, E. (1960) *A Nursery in the Nineties*, London, Gollancz.
FLETCHER, R. (1984) *Education in Society: The Promethean Fire*, Harmondsworth, Penguin.
FREIRE, P. (1972) *Pedagogy of the Oppressed*, Harmondsworth, Penguin.
GABRIEL, J. (1984) *Unqualified Success: A Comprehensive Guide for School Leavers*, Harmondsworth, Penguin.
GALLOWAY, D. (1985) *Schools and Persistent Absenteeism*, Oxford, Pergamon.
GIBBONS, J. (1989) 'Craft works', *Times Educational Supplement*, 3 March.
GLASER, B.G. and STRAUSS, A.L. (1967) *The Discovery of Grounded Theory: Strategies for Qualitative Research*, London, Weidenfeld and Nicolson.
GOFFMAN, E. (1961) *Asylums*, Harmondsworth, Penguin.
GOODMAN, P. (1964) *Compulsory Mis-education*, New York, Horizon.
√ GRANT, C. (1983) 'What is EO made of?', *EO News*, **27**.
The Guardian (1983) 'Turban test case proves Sikhs are ethnic group', 25 March.
HANSEN, S. and JENSEN, J. (1971) *The Little Red School Book*, London, Stage 1.
HEAD, D. (Ed.) (1974) *Free Way to Learning: Educational Alternatives in Action*, Harmondsworth, Penguin.   *LC 189.5 H4*
HEAD, D. and J. (1977) *EO News Digest*, 1–4.
HERON, L. (1982) 'Employers split over exams' importance', *Times Educational Supplement*, 17 September.
HERSOV, L. and BERG, I. *et al.* (1981) *Out of School*, New York, Wiley.
HOLT, J. (1971) *The Underachieving School*, Harmondsworth, Penguin.
HOLT, J. (1974) 'Reformulations: A letter written after two weeks in Cuernavaca', in LISTER, I. (Ed.) *Deschooling*, Cambridge, Cambridge University Press.
HOLT, J. (1977) *Instead of Education: Ways to Help People Do Things Better*, Harmondsworth, Penguin.
HOLT, J. (1981) *Teach Your Own — A Hopeful Path for Education*, Brightlingsea, Lighthouse.
HOLT, J. (1983) 'Schools and home schoolers: a fruitful partnership', *Phi Delta Kappan*, February, p. 393.
HOLT, J. (1984) *How Children Fail*, revised edition, Harmondsworth, Penguin.
HOYLES, M. (1979) *Changing Childhood*, London, Writers and Readers. *LB 1115 H6*
HUNT, J. and SMALL, P. (1981) *Employing Young People: A Study of Employers' Attitudes, Policies and Practice*, Scottish Council for Research in Education.
ILLICH, I. (1971) *Deschooling Society*, Harmondsworth, Penguin.
ILLICH, I. (1975) *Tools for Conviviality*, London, Harper and Row.
ILLICH, I. (1976) *After Deschooling What?*, London, Writers and Readers.
KAHN, J. and NURSTEN, J. (1975) 'School phobia or school refusal — a medico-social problem', in KAHN, J., NURSTEN, J. and CAROL, H. (Eds) *Unwillingly to School*, Oxford, Pergamon.
KIDDLE, C. (1981) *What Shall We Do With the Children?*, Barnstaple, Spindlewood.
KITTO, D. (1981) 'Doing it their way', *Times Educational Supplement*, 10 July, p. 113.
KITTO, D. (1984) 'The deschooling alternative', in HARBER, C. *et al. Alternative Educational Futures*, London, Holt Rinehart and Winston.

LC4581.K6

KNOX, P. (1988) *Troubled Children: A Fresh Look at School Phobia*, Holyhead, Knox.

LANTIN, B. (1983) 'Is school the best place for your child's education?', *Woman's World*, pp. 52–5.

LISTER, I. (1974) *Deschooling*, Cambridge, Cambridge University Press.

LISTER, I. (1976) 'Deschooling revisited', in ILLICH, I. *After Deschooling What?*, London, Writers and Readers.

LODGE, B. (1984) 'Employers prefer exams to profiles', *Times Educational Supplement*, 8 June.

MAIDEN, J. (1982) 'Without Schools: An Investigation of Otherwise Education', unpublished MA thesis, University of East Anglia.

MARSDEN, C. (1986) 'Industry expects . . .', *Times Educational Supplement*, 10 January.

MEIGHAN, R. (1981a) 'A new teaching force? Some implications raised by seeing parents as educators and the implications for teacher education', *Educational Review*, **33**, 2, pp. 133–42.

MEIGHAN, R. (1981b) *A Sociology of Educating*, London, Holt Rinehart and Winston.

MEIGHAN, R. (1984a) 'Flexischooling', in HARBER, C. *et al. Alternative Educational Futures*, London, Holt Rinehart and Winston.

MEIGHAN, R. (1984b) 'Political consciousness and home-based education', *Educational Review*, **36**, 2, pp. 165–73.

MEIGHAN, R. (1984c) 'Home-based educators and education authorities: The attempt to maintain a mythology', *Educational Studies*, **10**, 3, pp. 273–86.

MEIGHAN, R. (1988) *Flexischooling — Education for Tomorrow; Starting Yesterday*, Ticknall, Education Now.

MEIGHAN, R. and BROWN, C. (1980) 'Locations of learning and ideologies of education: Some issues raised by a study of Education Otherwise', in BARTON, L. *et al. Schooling, Ideology and the Curriculum* Lewes, Falmer Press.

MENUHIN, Y. (1977) *Unfinished Journey*, London, Macdonald and Janes.

MILL, J.S. (1964) *Autobigraphy*, Signet.

MULLARNEY, M. (1983) *Anything School Can Do You Can Do Better*, Dublin, Arlen House.

NASSIF, R. (1975) 'The theory of "de-schooling" between paradox and utopianism', *Prospects*, **5**, 3, pp. 329–40.

NEILL, A.S. (1972) *Neill, Neill, Orange Peel*, Harmondsworth, Penguin.

NEWSON, J. (1984) 'When school is out: Why are hundreds of teachers refusing to send their own children to school?', *Times Educational Supplement*, 17 February, p. 20.

NORTH, R. (1982) 'All the world's a school', *Times Educational Supplement*, 9 April, p. 15.

NORTH, R. (1987) *Schools of Tomorrow: Education As If People Matter*, Hartland, Green Books.

POSTMAN, N. and WEINGARTNER, C. (1971) *Teaching as a Subversive Activity*, Harmondsworth, Penguin.

REID, K. (1985) *Truancy and School Absenteeism*, London, Hodder and Stoughton.

REIMER, E. (1971) *School Is Dead: Alternatives in Education*, New York, Doubleday.

REYNOLDS, D. *et al.* (1980) 'School factors and truancy', in HERSOV, I. and BERG, L. *et al. Out of School*, New York, Wiley.

ROUSSEAU, J-J. (1911) *Emile: Or, Education*, London, Dent.

References

Rousseau, J-J. (1972, orig. 1893) *The Social Contract*, Oxford, Oxford University Press.

Russell, B. (1967) *The Autobiography of Bertrand Russell Volume I*, London, Allen and Unwin.

Russell, B. (1968) *The Autobiography of Bertrand Russell Volume II*, London, Allen and Unwin.

Sluckin, A. (1981) *Growing Up in the Playground: The Social Development of Children*, London, Routledge and Kegan Paul. LB 1137·55

Steele, J. (1978) 'Educated at home', *New Society*, 18 October.   LC225·S

Stone, J. and Taylor, F. (1976) *The Parents' Schoolbook*, Harmondsworth, Penguin.

Surkes, S. (1988) ' "Open school" scheme could help GCSE pupils to opt out', *Times Educational Supplement*, 18 March.

Thompson, F. (1973) *Lark Rise to Candleford*, Harmondsworth, Penguin.

Tyerman, M.J. (1968) *Truancy*, London, University of London Press. LB 3081.T9

Valentine, C.W. (1956) *The Normal Child and Some of his Abnormalities*, Harmondsworth, Penguin.

Wallace, N. (1983) *Better Than School: One Family's Declaration of Independence*, New York, Larson.

Wallace, N. (1987) 'Breaking ties with school', *Growing Without Schooling*, 58.

West Glamorgan Humanist Group (1977) 'The alternative society', *New Humanist*, August.

White, R. (1980) *Absent With Cause: Lessons of Truancy*, London, Routledge and Kegan Paul.

Wise, D. (no date) 'The Learning Exchange', paper, London, Centerprise.

Woods, P. (1977) *The Pupil's Experience*, Milton Keynes, The Open University.

Author Index

Baker, J. 11, 28, 42, 133–134, 136, 174, 182
Bendell, J. 11
Berg, L. 90
Blacker, S. 20, 25, 94
Blat-Gimeno, J. 4
Blinston, K. 20
Blishen, E. 50
Brown, C. 19, 20, 25, 197

Chitty, S. 8
Cobbett, W. 10
Croall, J. 183

Deakin, M. 2, 6, 11, 154
Deutsch, D. 13, 168
Durrell, G. 1

Edgeworth, M. and R. 8

Farjeon, E. 9
Fletcher, R. 150
Freire, P. 3, 6, 39–40

Gabriel, J. 82
Gibbons, J. 196
Glaser, B. 22
Goffman, I. 20
Goodman, P. 5
Grant, C. 35, 153

Head family 5, 93, 110–111, 136, 156–158
Heron, L. 187

Holt, J. 3, 4–6, 18, 39, 40–41, 59, 88, 90, 94, 130, 136, 152–153, 195
Hoyles, M. 7
Hunt, J. 187

Illich, I. 2, 3, 5, 6, 39–40, 59, 111–112

Kiddle, C. 11, 131
Kitto, D. 11, 40
Knox, P. 21

Lister, I. 4, 97–98
Lodge, B. 188

Maiden, J. 21, 25
Marsden, C. 188
Meighan, R. 11, 19–20, 31, 58, 103–104, 179, 180, 195–196
Menuhin, Y. 10
Mill, J.S. 7–8
Moore, P. 28
Mullarney, M. 11, 151–152, 192

Nassif, R. 4
Neill, A.S. 192
North, R. 33, 102, 196

Postman, N. 3

Reimer, E. 2, 3, 5, 6
Rousseau, J.-J. 2, 5, 6, 8
Russell, B. 9

Sluckin, A. 148–149, 150
Small, P. 187

Author Index

Steele, J. 1–2
Stone, J. 50
Strauss, A.L. 22
Surkes, S. 198

Taylor, F. 50
Thompson, F. 9–10

Valentine, C.W. 150

Wallace, N. 11
Weingartner, C. 3
West Glamorgan Humanist Group 14
Wolf, K. 13, 168
Woods, P. 44

Subject Index

activities with others 15, 151–160
age, of interviewees 26
'Alternative Society' 14
aristocracy 10
art 12, 96, 116
articulacy 26
Art School entrance 184
assessment
　by families 143–145
　by LEAs 20, 145–146, 167–168, 174
autism 51
autonomy
　in alternative schools 57
　in home education (see learning,
　　home-based)

Baker family 11, 12, 14, 28, 42, 63–64,
　65, 133–134, 136, 154, 174, 179, 182
'banking' 40
Boulter, H. 120, 126–127
breadth of study 130–131
bullying (see reasons for home
　education)

'Campaign for Human-Scale Education'
　57
'Campaign for State-Supported
　Alternative Schools' 57
careers (see jobs)
Center for Intercultural Documentation
　(CIDOC) 3, 4
Certificate of Secondary Education
　(CSE) 79

child benefit 13
children
　legal rights 13
　with special needs 10, 12, 13,
　　101–102
　views of, on own education 35, 64–67
'Children on the Hill' 2, 6, 28, 154
class prejudice 47
clubs 159, 193
'co-intentional education' 3
colour prejudice 47
communes/communities (see learning,
　home-based, in groups)
community centres 107–108
compulsory education 6, 9
computers
　as a resource 123
　as a subject of study 87, 88, 123
'conviviality' 4
correspondence courses 116–117,
　118–121
cross-dominance 46, 51, 52
Cuernavaca 3, 4
curriculum (see also individual subject
　areas)
　anti-sexist 87
　balance in 91–93
　child-led 77–78 (see also learning,
　　home-based)
　effect of aims of home education
　　77–84
　hidden, of home education 96–98
　hidden, of resources 132–133
　influence of LEA 99–102

influence of resources 103–123
parent-led 85–86, 89

Dame Catherine's School, Ticknall 196
dance 116
Dartington Hall 55, 57, 197
decision-making 61–67
Denmark 57
depth of study 129–130
deregistration 13, 74
deregistratin 13, 74
deschooling theory 2–6
   educative substitutes for school 5
   influence on home educators 34,
     38–40
   origins in South America 3
   origins in Western World 3
   practical uses in Third World 4
   relationship to political power 3
   relationship to social change 3
disability (see children, with special
   needs)
discussion 8
drama 81–82, 96
dyslexia 51, 87, 90, 101

Education Acts
   Elementary Education Act 1870 6, 10
   Elementary Education Act
     1876–1880 6
   Education Act 1944 12
   Education Act 1981 12
   interpretation of 1944/1981 Acts 12,
     13, 59, 166–169
'Educational Review' 21
Education Otherwise (EO) 14–16, 20,
   21, 57–58, 59, 61, 63, 98, 191, 197
   legal group 16
   meetings 157–158
   publications 16
   questionnaire returns 58, 61
   special needs group 16
'efficiency' 12
employers 78, 187–188

fear 7, 38, 39
finance 63, 176
flexischooling 103–105, 195
formality (see learning, home-based)

Free Schools 196–197
Further Education (FE) colleges 38,
   105–106, 177, 184

General Certificate of Education (GCE)
   79–81, 83, 130
General Certificate of Secondary
   Education (GCSE) 79, 197
geographical isolation (see reasons for
   home education)
governesses (see tutors)
Green Party 197
grounded theory 22, 24
Growing Without Schooling (GWS) 191
gypsies (see travellers)

handicap (see children, with special
   needs)
Harrison family 11, 12, 14, 19, 59,
   87–88, 95, 101, 179
Head family 5, 63–64, 91, 93, 110–111,
   133, 136, 156–166, 192–193
hobbies 193
humanities 110–111
hypothermia 50–51

illness (see also children, with special
   needs) school-induced 73–75
integration of subjects 130–131, 135
International Baccalaureate (IB) 79

jobs
   as aims of home education 79–81,
     82–84
   of interviewees 182, 187–190
   self-employment 71, 189

Kilquhanity 56
Kirkdale 57
Kitto, D. 11, 14, 20, 40

'labelling' 100, 114, 175–176
   as maladjusted 44–45
   as school phobic 21
   as school refuser 74
languages 81, 93
law (see Education Acts)
Lawrence family 7, 28
learning, home-based (see also reasons
   for home education and curriculum)

aims of 77–84, 133–134
autonomous 5, 11, 64, 87–88
exchanges 5, 6, 15, 112–113
flexibility 77
formality 10, 103–143
groups 11, 27, 45, 64, 97, 155
'learning through life' 136–137
lifelong 6, 183–186
methods 124–147
relevance to school education 18, 195–196
'Lib Ed' 57
lifestyles
  families 87–88, 191–192
  interviewees as adults 182, 185, 190–194
literacy 10, 12, 89–91, 95
Local Education Authorities (LEAs) 21, 27, 42, 50
  concerns about home curriculum 99–102, 143, 169–172
  co-operation 60, 107, 169, 174, 176–177
  home tutors 113–115
  hostility 11, 14, 173, 174–175
  ignorance 11, 14, 58
  interpretation of law 12, 166–169
  responsibilities 13, 165–173
location of interviewees 26

maladjustment (see 'labelling')
matriculation 79
media 58
Montessori 11
moving house 74
Mullarney family 11, 12, 151–152, 154, 192
museums 109
music 12, 108, 116

'natural education' 5, 6
Neill, A.S. 40, 42, 88, 192
numeracy 10, 12, 89–91, 95

Open College 197
Open College of the Arts 197
'Open Door' 58
Open School 197–198
Open Tech 197

Open University, The 17, 20, 42, 93, 197
'Operation Otherwise' (see also Head family) 14, 93

parents as educators
  background 20, 42, 59–60, 62, 93–98
  expectations 8
  ideals (see reasons for home education)
  legal rights of 10, 12
  relationship with children 7, 19, 20, 93, 96, 131–132
  relationship with LEAs 19, 178–181
  self-confidence 19, 61–62, 85
  single 27, 62, 132, 141
Parents' National Education Union (PNEU) 52
Parkway Program 5
part-time schooling (see school)
political power (see deschooling theory)
practical skills training 82–83, 84, 87–88, 95, 182, 186
product as evidence of learning 127–129
'Programme for Political Education' 4
'Project on Alternatives in low-income countries' 4
psychosomatic illness (see illness, school-induced)

Quaker schools 55, 56, 57
qualifications
  academic 79–81
  ad hoc tests 81
  profiles 78
  skills training 81–84
qualified teachers, home educating 20, 31, 36–38, 94, 178

racial prejudice 47
reactions to home education 61, 160–164
reading (see literacy)
reasons for home education 11, 19, 35
  furthering of social change (including alternative lifestyle) 27, 33–34, 35, 43, 45
  geographical isolation 11

home/school value conflict 34, 43–46
regimentation of school 34, 37, 42, 44, 48
religion 35, 97
school-induced illness 34
social aspects of school (including bullying) 33, 34, 35, 36, 38, 42, 43, 46–48
special needs 10, 34, 50–51
teaching methods and curriculum of school 11, 33–34, 35, 36–38, 41, 43, 48, 51–52
travel 34, 52–53
religious education
at home (see reasons for home education)
in school 45
research
methods 18, 22–32
origins 17
others' 19–21
resources
community 5, 103–113
hidden curriculum 132–133
home 114–123
home educating families as 195–196
rural 108–109
urban 109

school 6, 9 (see also flexischooling)
alternatives considered 55–57
Attendance Officer 9
Attendance Order 13, 175
experience of interviewees 65–66
influence on home curriculum 85–88
leaving 67–76
objections to (see reasons for home education)
part-time 12, 19, 104–105, 162, 163
phobia (see 'labelling' and illness, school-induced)
recovery from 75
refusal (see 'labelling')
role of parents 20, 195–196
uniform 49–50
Schools Council 188
sciences 96
resources 104–105, 107, 108–109, 112, 116–117, 121–123

self-confidence
interviewees 26, 191, 194
school children 37, 38
parents (see parents as educators)
self-discipline
development of 137–139
Sewell, Anna, Mary and Philip 8
sexism in school curriculum 43, 48, 87
sex of interviewees 26
Small School, Hartland 196
social change (see deschooling theory and reasons for home education)
socialization 12, 148–160
home educated children 151, 153, 154–160, 184–185, 188
Norwegian study 148–149
school 150–153
South America 3, 4
special needs (see children and reasons for home education)
sport 107, 116
Statement of Special Educational Needs 13, 101–102
Steele family 1–2
Steiner, R. 41
Steiner schools 55, 57, 132

teachers (see qualified teachers and parents as educators)
teaching methods (see learning, home-based)
technology
domination of, in society 3
role in the home 19
textbooks 117–118
'The State' 53, 131, 196
time 124–127, 134–135, 139–140
travellers 53
truanting
in 1800s 9
of interviewees 34, 48, 68–73
tutors
LEA 113–115
private 6, 9, 115–116

unauthorized absence (see truanting and illness, school-induced)
uniform 49–50

United States of America 11, 18, 109–110
university entrance 80–81, 184

volunteering 159, 196

Wallace family 11, 12
Wilkins family 125
Windass, S. 14
work experience (see workplaces and practical skills training)
workplaces 109–112, 159, 186
World-Wide Education Service (WES) 52
writing (see literacy)

Youth Opportunity Scheme (YOP) 83–84
Youth Training Scheme (YTS) 84